KU-493-984

Leeds Metropolitan University

17 0132110 4

*Reading the Book
of Himself*

Reading the Book of Himself

NARRATIVE STRATEGIES
IN THE WORKS OF
JAMES JOYCE

Michael Patrick Gillespie

OHIO STATE UNIVERSITY PRESS
Columbus

LEEDS METROPOLITAN
UNIVERSITY LIBRARY

170132110年

B SIC ✓

386346 57.96

19 . 8 . 96

823.9 JOY

Copyright © 1989 by the Ohio State University Press.
All rights reserved.

Library of Congress Cataloging-in-Publication Data

Gillespie, Michael Patrick.
     Reading the book of himself : narrative strategies in the works of James Joyce /
Michael Patrick Gillespie.
          p. cm.
     Bibliography: p.
     Includes index.
     ISBN 0-8142-0488-0 (alk. paper)
     1. Joyce, James, 1882–1941—Technique.   2. Narration (Rhetoric)   3. Self in
literature.   I. Title.
PR6019.O9Z53358   1989
823'.912—dc 19   89-3143
                                                                                        CIP

The paper in this book meets the guidelines for permanence and durability of the
Committee on Production Guidelines for Book Longevity of the Council on Library
Resources.

Printed in the U.S.A.

9 8 7 6 5 4 3 2 1

for Paula
who sees more clearly

Contents

Acknowledgments

The kindness and interest of many people at various stages of this project greatly contributed to whatever coherence it finally achieved.

I would especially like to thank the following individuals for their encouragement and suggestions: Morris Beja, Rev. Robert Boyle, S.J., Susan Brienza, Edward Duffy, Melvin Friedman, David Hayman, Phillip F. Herring, Claudia Johnson, David Krause, Christine Krueger, A. Walton Litz, Patrick McCarthy, Cate McClenahan, Albert Rivero, and Florence Walzl.

Alex Holzman provided generous editorial support and patient assistance throughout the long process of preparing the manuscript for publication.

My deepest debts are to my colleague John Boly and to my wife, Paula Gillespie. Both saw more merit in this project than I was able to perceive, and each made me aware of strengths that I needed to exploit and of weaknesses that I needed to correct.

I am very grateful for financial support provided by a Marquette University Faculty Fellowship and by several Faculty Development Awards, by a research grant from the American Philosophical Society, and by a National Endowment for the Humanities Independent Research Fellowship.

An earlier version of Chapter 2 appeared in *Language and Style* and an earlier version of Chapter 10 appeared in *James Joyce Quarterly.* Both are reprinted with the kind permission of the editors.

Abbreviations

To reduce the cumbersome number of notes that would otherwise be necessary, I have used the following abbreviations throughout, with page numbers cited parenthetically, when referring to works by Joyce. Most of these conform to the usage established by the *James Joyce Quarterly* (*JJQ*). For publication details, see the bibliography.

CW	*The Critical Writings of James Joyce*
D	*Dubliners*
E	*Exiles*
FW	*Finnegans Wake*
JJA	*The James Joyce Archive*
Letters I, II, III	*Letters of James Joyce*
P	*A Portrait of the Artist as a Young Man*
SH	*Stephen Hero*
U	*Ulysses* (1984)

I | Introduction

(Stoop) if you are abcedminded, to this claybook, what curios of
signs (please stoop), in this allaphbed! Can you rede (since We and
Thou had it out already) its world? It is the same told of all.

FW, 18.17–19

With simultaneous gestures of inclusion and of separation, the discourse in this selection from *Finnegans Wake* acknowledges a general
similarity in the aesthetic experiences produced by a piece of art while
it leaves ambiguous the precise nature of the referents. As a consequence, we derive a sense of the declaiming voice reaching each of us
in a register that differs from that heard by anyone else. The passage
emphatically rebuffs linear-minded attempts to discover definitive interpretations. Despite such warnings, however, most readers instinctively resist accepting this proposition here or in any of Joyce's other
works, for its implications prove frankly unsettling to the presuppositions that we bring to a piece of literature. In abstract terms we may
acquiesce to the concept of the mutability of language and of the indeterminacy of meaning, but, despite our postmodern conditioning, the
application of such views, even to overtly innovative fiction, proves extremely difficult.

To a large degree, a habituation to thinking in terms of the principles
of Newtonian physics still conditions our perceptions. Consciously or
not, most of us have come to rely on the reassuring consistency derived
from impressions of an apparently ordered world governed by the patterns—natural and artificial—of cause-and-effect logic that we impose
to conjoin our experiences. When lights unexpectedly go out, we assume that a fuse has blown. When we hear strange noises coming from
an empty room, we tell ourselves that the building is settling. A quest
for certitude dominates our intellectual responses, and any view that
questions such an approach by extension questions everything that we
think we see.

Nonetheless the ineluctable modality of *Finnegans Wake* stands as a process of writing that does just that.[1] The multiplicity of its images continually assaults the comfortable limits that we have assigned to signifiers. Its discourses offer encouragement to a number of diverse strategies for reading, while frustrating any approach sustained solely by the consistent, predictable systems of linear thinking. Although we all begin with the same physical artifact, "this claybook . . . the same told of all," its "curios of signs" produce a plethora of signifieds from determinedly ambiguous and inconsistent signifiers. When we fall back on cause-and-effect logic, Joyce's book leaves most of us vaguely disturbed about where to direct our attention and about what significance we should give to various aspects of the work. "Thus the unfacts, did we possess them, are too imprecisely few to warrant our certitude, the evidencegivers by legpoll too untrustworthily irreperible where his adjugers are semmingly freak threes but his judicandees plainly minus twos" (*FW,* 57.16–19). Alternatives abound, but certainty eludes us.

This condition does not inevitably insure the failure of every attempt to unify the apparently disparate elements of *Finnegans Wake.* It does, however, suggest that the traditional application of either/or questions in a binary, discriminatory pursuit of meaning will not exhaust the possibilities of the work. Unfortunately, the security that linear thinking promises makes it difficult to give over this approach. As a result impulses for stratifying and for patterning can continue to impair our initial response. This in turn produces an imperative towards interpretive hegemony, and that impulse frustrates any alternative attempts that we might make at understanding.

I do not believe that a definitive interpretation lies buried in *Finnegans Wake*—or for that matter in any of Joyce's works—awaiting discovery by some industrious critic. On the other hand, neither do I believe that his writing exists as an elaborate objective correlative for the sterile waste land of intellectual solipsism. Rather, each work in Joyce's canon invites and sustains a range of valid but provisional readings, yet no work gives itself over completely and forever to a single interpretation. As a consequence, any intelligent response will provide its own immediate aesthetic rewards, and the best have the potential to enhance other readings. At the same time, all remain transitional—each inevitably giving way to subsequent responses—for the antithesis of certitude is not confusion but provisionality.

I have not attempted in this study to foreground any specific response to Joyce's writings or to form a hierarchy of interpretive strategies open to readers. Instead, I have concentrated attention upon factors that enable and empower the derivation of valid alternative meanings:

the apparently disjunctive elements conditioning both Joyce's process of composition and the reader's act of apprehension. My goal quite simply is to articulate the range of potential meanings inherent in the makeup of any aesthetically satisfying artistic creation.

Theoretical diversity has already become a prominent feature of contemporary literary studies, and this condition has naturally led to a greater interpretive openness. As readers have become more self-consciously aware of the viability of multiple perspectives informing the interpretation of any piece of literature, any notion of broad intellectual certitude has come to carry less and less significance, seeming more likely to lead to oversimplification than to enlightenment. These impressions have prompted many to move increasingly further from methods whose theoretical biases most overtly aim at the derivations of a single, hegemonic interpretation. Instead, these readers have come to concentrate with growing attention on methodologies overtly opposed to the quest for definitive meaning.

While many critics would readily accept the generalizations regarding the application of literary theory that I have outlined in the preceding paragraph, I suspect that a number would disagree over which methods have become more useful because of this shift in attitudes. Chronological biases have tempted some to follow a reductivist logic, linking New Critics and Historicists with reactionary attitudes and Marxists, Feminists, Deconstructors, Semioticians, and Neo-Historicists with innovative views. Such delineations, however, relying as they do on ephemeral distinctions or upon pragmatic differentiations often prove less rigorous, and consequently less useful, than they initially appear. In fact, the methodologies of most successful critics and critical schools display surprising affinities for one another.

Long before French became the language of choice in English literary criticism, Hugh Kenner betrayed signs of proto/crypto poststructuralism in *Dublin's Joyce*. And, despite his assertions of "différance," Jacques Derrida has repeatedly shown himself to be one of the most adept and most brilliant close readers. Other less accomplished critics display an even greater tendency to elide dissimilarities while ostensibly maintaining the theoretical integrity of a specific movement. In some respects one can understand this impulse towards leveling. The methods of the New Critics have proven their ability to yield greatly enhanced reader appreciation for any number of works, and our appetite for greater comprehension makes seductive defamiliarized approaches to familiar literature.

My disagreement with this disposition toward amalgamation certainly does not stem from specific opposition to the interpretive results that it can produce. Rather I am opposed to the dominant hermeneutical assumption that undermines the epistemological integrity of a particular methodology—whatever its idiosyncrasies—in a grail quest for critical certitude. Whether its announced goal is to discover the author's true meaning implanted in the labyrinth of his writing or to establish the absence of ascertainable meaning in the language of the work, each of the methods alluded to above still rests on the assumption of the possibility of articulating a specific aesthetic response that will hold primacy over all others.

This study begins with a basic premise antipathetic to such a view. Instead of generating yet another isolated interpretation struggling towards literary hegemony, I wish to consider strategies for perceiving a range of options: the choices offered to both author and reader for forming any of a variety of possible imaginative constructs—that is, texts—stimulated by the images of a particular work. Obviously individual, often idiosyncratic preferences constitute the formation of any text, yet the self-conscious subjectivity of this gesture should not diminish for us the significance of the reading that results. In fact, our understanding, however imperfect or incomplete, of the range of factors informing these preferences allows us to derive a more complete sense of a work's potential for generating meanings. Articulating some of these options will not make the creation of specific texts inevitable. It will, however, clarify some of the issues that any interpretation must engage.

I realize, of course, that my own goal may seem to vary from the aims of those whom I have criticized only in its breadth. My examination presumes that certain amorphous but finite limitations, outlined by the work itself, circumscribe one's possible responses to a piece of literature, and I seek to define those limitations through close examination of Joyce's canon. Nonetheless, I feel that I am making important distinctions in my approach to a piece of art. While I may show elective affinities for degrees of certitude, I emphatically reject closure. I am not attempting, through semantic camouflage, to deny the need for a single interpretive approach while simultaneously supplanting all others with my own. Nor am I seeking to advance an anarchic attitude, embracing all idiosyncratic views as equal. Rather I wish to draw attention to the polymorphous possibilities of any particular artistic expression. This awareness seeks to accommodate both/and rather than either/or thinking, relying on the assumption that one can enjoy completely whatever immediate response one makes to the aesthetic experience without incurring the limitations of unquestioning commitment to a single view.

Although inevitably my own texts will intrude into many of my remarks, I have tried to highlight not interpretations but motivations: the
portions of a work calculated to compel the reader to make decisions
which subvert the objectivity and permanence of any specific response.

These views derive their intellectual foundation from reader response theories, especially the studies of Wolfgang Iser,[2] but my own
approach diverges from established lines of inquiry in several significant
ways. In working to counter the impulse toward extremes of solipsism
or of positivism inherent in many applications of the method, I have
emphasized the dynamics of writing/reading as defined by broad artistic
parameters and not simply by the boundaries laid down by the consciousness of the individual. Consequently, I have directed my efforts
toward descriptions of how the author and the author's milieu function
in tandem with the reader's own to form the aesthetic experience. I believe that the terms of the relationship between artist and audience
while unstable remain complementary. Although the level of engagement fluctuates throughout the duration of a reading, an individual can
achieve the most satisfactory aesthetic experience only by acknowledging the both/and provenance of the text. Because the major work already
done on reader response theory has not centered attention on this relationship, I have concentrated on extending my investigation along
lines that they suggest but do not pursue.[3]

From its conception to the moment a piece of art ceases to exist, the
process of creation itself repeatedly shifts, with the loci of creativity determined by the movement of responsibility for choice. The writer exercises an initial prescriptive influence by constructing the paradigm—
influenced by the artist's cultural and intellectual milieu—describing
the limits of valid interpretation. As the aesthetic condition moves from
act to artifact, the role of the author becomes progressively less dynamic
and more static. Successive readers endeavor to apprehend the paradigm, but they operate under the influence of contemporary cultural
and intellectual attitudes.

Joyce himself outlined this process in the creative model described
by Stephen in *A Portrait of the Artist as a Young Man*: "The artist, like the
God of the creation, remains within or behind or beyond or above his
handiwork, invisible, refined out of existence, indifferent, paring his fingernails" (*P,* 215). While the discourse invites the reader to discern a
great deal of irony in those lines, one can also derive from them an
understanding of the delicate balance that must exist in the relationship
between author and reader. Although the author presents a work unified by specific paradigmatic assumptions, once the reader's engage-

ment begins to create a text, he or she assumes the power to shape the significance of the immediate aesthetic experience. The power has some restrictions, for to attain legitimacy the reader's text must justify every response in terms of the constraints imposed by the writer's paradigm. Within those limitations, however, the reader takes on full creative control, assuming the function of the arbiter of provisional meaning.

Nonetheless, as Stephen implies, after the completion of the writing process the artist's influence over the meaning(s) that one can derive from a work does not disappear. At this point, the author's control over the evolving shape of a published work has neither a fixed nor a readily determinable position, but, because of the continuing impact of the paradigm, artistic stasis should not be confused with the absence of influence. Balancing the creative responsibilities of the writer and of the reader stands as a crucial aspect of responding to literature. Unlike E. D. Hirsch, I do not believe that one should invoke ideas of authorial intentionality, no matter how far displaced from direct consideration, to justify a search for an ideal reading implanted in the work.[4] At the same time, I strongly believe that the delineation of the paradigm laid down by the author remains a central concern, especially as it manifests itself as stylistic manipulation. By developing a sense of the diverse forces shaping the act of creation, one can begin to determine the limits of the artifact that this writing has produced. By extension, when the reader has a very specific awareness of the paradigm, he or she more securely exercises latitude in a given response.

What I am proposing, then, is a dialectic equilibrium: a both/and condition that does not assign either to the author or to the reader the position of sole arbiter of meaning. Rather, the perspectives of artist and of audience conjoin to produce a text. As a consequence intentionality must not become either an anathema or an icon. It stands as an ambiguous but undeniable feature encountered in the process of writing and in the act of reading, seen in terms of the limits that the author imposes upon the formal process of creation. Whether these limits enable the author to achieve the work he or she intends to bring into existence does not matter, for we are confronted by the artifact and not by its Platonic ideal. Intentionality remains ephemeral. No reader, no matter how pliant, can hope to recover completely the author's aims (nor for that matter could the author), yet no reader, no matter how independent, can fully escape the shaping influence of the author's consciousness. Necessarily, then, the impulses governing the act of composition remain an important consideration, for they establish guidelines for the constitution of any text derived from the finished work. Thus, the tension between constitution and comprehension—both in terms of the author and in terms of the reader—stands as the centerpiece of my study.

Before proceeding further, I should clarify my use of certain terms. Although my methodology derives its basis from concepts that one generally associates with reader-response theories, I have felt the need to give a special significance to a number of already familiar terms and to introduce others not already in use. My approach to reading applies a very precise meaning to the word *text*. (In a general way, I use it in a manner analogous to Iser's term *gestalt*.) I see the term as a verb rather than as a noun: an imaginative (re)construction stimulated by the way one perceives images within the work and not as the artifact of wood pulp, paste, and ink that we have before us. Further, I do not believe that in viewing an intellectually complex and gratifying piece of art one will ever arrive at a definitive or complete text, and so I am opposed to the limitation of possibilities inherent in Iser's impulse to describe an ideal, implied, or hypothetical reader "upon whom all possible actualizations of the text may be projected."[5] Such a hypothetical reader, constituted from the subjective perspective of what one individual or some group of individuals construes as ideal could hardly be less idiosyncratic than its creators. In my opinion, the range of potential texts extends far beyond that of a single, consistent benchmark. Rather, since the text is a product of an evolving imagination, any intellectually vigorous individual will create a series of provisional readings corresponding to each encounter with the work. Each will necessarily draw upon past interpretations, and each will inevitably give way to subsequent modifications. Any particular text stands as only one of a variety of possible responses, conditioned but not prescribed both by the reader's experiences (retentions) and by his or her expectations (protentions). Over a number of readings and rereadings the mutability of all of these factors becomes evident: experiences accumulate and recede in our consciousness, and we shift or emend our expectations as our perceptions of specific situations change. This flux circumvents the possibility that one would ever arrive at a final or complete text for a work, but, equally, it holds the promise of continual rejuvenation of prior readings. Consequently, in each encounter the individual creates a provisional reading, subject to continuing revision. Each one draws upon past interpretations, and each one gives way to subsequent modifications.

As I have already noted, this process evolves in a manner much less chaotic than it might seem to at first glance. The paradigm—the elements which define the creative limits of any imaginative representation of the material in the work—imposes constraints by the aesthetic frame it places around possible readings. One perceives the paradigm relatively. Its genesis takes place in the convergence of the artistic values and influences shaping the author's process of composition. Its apprehension evolves through a series of modifications and amalgamations as successive readers work to reconcile the presuppositions that they bring to a work with features defined by their own experience of reading and by those of others.

Paradigm definition and reconstitution operates every time someone reads a work, but its precise features remain difficult to discern. Literary precedent provides a useful starting point and allows one to move beyond mere instinctual response. Basic stylistic and thematic features announce association with broad conventions of reading. They allow one to assign varying significance to those features based on his or her expectations. In the course of reading, however, the text that emerges will retain its coherence only as long as one can continue to reconcile the characteristics inherent in the work with the expectations brought to it. When irresolvable discrepancies arise, one must adjust expectations relating to the paradigm. This process of reconciliation both defines the paradigm and traces its application, so that on the level of intellectual contact which the reader/audience has with the artifact, the terms "artwork" and "paradigm" become synonymous.

Let me try to clarify my meaning anecdotally. Most of us would rebel at the notion that the best view of the Mona Lisa could be attained only from a single spot on the floor of the Louvre and that visitors to the gallery should be prohibited from looking at it from any other location. Instinctively, we would feel that one would derive the greatest sense of Leonardo da Vinci's painting by being able to move around it, to see it from a range of attitudes. At the same time, few would subscribe to the idea that one could take aesthetic pleasure from the picture by facing away from it and gazing at a blank wall at the opposite end of the gallery. The materials, the dimensions, the colors, and the forms within the work direct without defining the response that a viewer can make to it. The paradigm of the Mona Lisa begins with the physical boundaries laid down by the artist: the size of the canvas, the shape of the figures, the range and intensity of the brush strokes. It evolves to encompass social and cultural assumptions implicit in the composition within the picture: costume, expression, gesture, and background to name just a few. While all of these elements certainly contribute to the paradigm, their characterizing features, as even this short list suggests, do not remain limited to concrete attributes. Denotative and connotative elements function intellectually to produce possible readings. These features will not submit to reification; they lack the stability to adhere to the discipline of a specific system or code.

Any work of literature establishes a similar paradigm, inviting one to construct a variety of responses or texts within the literal limits which it lays down. The challenge in reading is to delineate at least an approximation of the paradigm and to articulate options for responding to the work which fit logically into the limits which that paradigm defines. To derive a more complete sense of the structure of the paradigm implicit in a particular work, one must attend to the specific application of artistic elements by the author while matching them against a range of personal aesthetic responses, justified by elements of the work itself, which that author may not have foreseen or even intended.[6]

Stated most simply, then, the approach that I propose to follow in this study seeks to balance the intellectual context of the author against that of the reader. Each artist, indeed every individual, perceives the repertoire on a personal, idiosyncratic level. A common cultural heritage may produce broad agreement in some areas, but individual taste and idiosyncratic inclinations cause each of us to give a great deal of attention to particular elements while completely ignoring others. This exercise of selective emphasis and suppression produces a fluctuating apprehension of the social paradigm against which we measure our experiences, and it causes our perceptions to be at variance even with those of others who share a similar cultural background. Additionally, diverse intellectual and artistic forces equally influence the writer's literary paradigms. As a result a critical interpretation striving to engage the complexities of a sophisticated piece of writing must maintain an openness to the possibility of a range of external features shaping the aesthetic boundaries of the work.

Based on this premise, my study necessarily involves the formation of a flexible methodology to accommodate a broad, extraliterary perspective, yet it does not go so far as to wish to include, unselectively, any material accessible to Joyce as open to association with his work. Consequently, to limit extrapolation or digression, I have focused my attention on specific literary associations, presuming a connection between Joyce and his general social environment but delineating only the most significant points of contact between the two. Inquiries into the links between one of Joyce's works and his intellectual ambiance, source studies, as they are generally and sometimes condescendingly called, have always played an important part in the interpretation of his canon, for, to a greater degree than any other Modernist, he successfully combines in his art highly derivative and highly innovative impulses.[7]

Artistic influence, however, remains an evanescent element in the creative process, and it rarely takes the form of overt imitation. Furthermore, the impact of any specific forebear on Joyce's creative process will necessarily reflect only a small and contingent portion of the forces shaping his work. Thus, although in subsequent chapters I will refer to creative analogues between Joyce and particular authors, my intent is not to establish the dominance of any particular artistic antecedent. Indeed, a useful study of Joyce's social paradigm should not focus exclusively on the precise application of particular features borrowed from other authors. Rather, in noting similarities between Joyce and specific predecessors, I have examined selected artists to exemplify the broader intellectual climate that contributed to the formation of a particular literary work. These analogues in turn provide one with a clearer sense of the limits, the denotations and connotations that Joyce intended to impose on various narrative elements within his canon.

Harold Bloom's theories of artistic influence forcefully underscore both the relevance of and the problems inherent in any study of artistic interaction. Bloom's metaphoric conception of anxiety and struggle, however, overdramatizes and oversimplifies the situation. He posits an overt and direct confrontation when, more often than not, the interaction is muted and inferential.[8]

As always, detecting evidence of broad influence forms the preamble to the more difficult task of assigning to each its proper significance. Despite Joyce's well-documented concern for his personal and cultural pasts, artistic sources served only as touchstones for his creative process. Nonetheless, Joyce could no more deny their impact on his consciousness than he could deny the formative influence of his Catholic childhood. The artistic and intellectual traditions from which he emerged coalesce to form a social repertoire circumscribing all of his writing in much the same manner that aesthetic paradigms delineate his individual works. While Joyce never acknowledged more than suggestive roles for his literary antecedents, he could not escape the influence of the tradition created by their work, for his predecessors defined the artistic ambiance that left its mark on his work. Consequently, our awareness of what he borrowed and of what he rejected from authors who preceded him allows us to give greater subtlety to our views of those more concrete, quantifiable elements of his works—character, plot, discourse.

Attentiveness to nuance is perhaps the most useful trait that one could bring to a study of Joyce's canon. It has long been a critical commonplace that *Ulysses* is a book teaching us, among other things, how to read *Ulysses*. Like many received ideas, this view combines an incisive assessment with a deceptive simplicity that can lead an ingenuous reader to an artificial sense of closure. On one level the observation acknowledges a fairly obvious aspect of Joyce's style, his overt manipulation of the responses of his readers. More subtly, it suggests the complex relationship between reader and writer that this approach necessarily creates. It calls upon us to recognize in ourselves a function well beyond the role of passive receptor of an unchanging work. Instead, in foregrounding the act of reading, it characterizes a dynamic, reciprocal, mutable relationship between reader and writer that makes presumptuous the assignment even provisionally of hegemony to a specific reading or interpretation.

I do not find this relationship unique to *Ulysses*, and so this study, tracing the evolution of his style from the technically polished but highly derivative examples of his earliest prose fiction up to the purely idiosyncratic form of *Finnegans Wake*, sketches the range of associations between reader and writer included in the bulk of Joyce's canon. As an artist, Joyce acted always both as writer and as reader, and throughout the process of creation he remained attentive to both roles. Reading informed his view of the world and of his craft, as he adopted and adapted techniques that he found in the writings of others. Similarly, the act of writing reformed his sensibilities as a reader, and he consciously attempted to continue that evolution by reshaping the expectations of his readers. Consequently, a sensitivity to the interpretive potential inherent in Joyce's art involves both acknowledgment of the way that his intellectual milieu manipulates his aesthetic sense and consideration of the way that he directs readers to exploit the work: creating texts suggested though not prescribed by the paradigm growing out of contrasting but not ultimately conflicting presumptions.

The narrowness of Joyce's thematic range immeasurably increased the pressure for multiplicity of expression. From the very first words that he wrote, Joyce was sure of his subject. His books rehearse the same themes time and again, yet they continue to engage our attention—not because of the originality of their topic but because of the growing novelty offered in the structures of successive works. Paradigmatic and stylistic development progressed simultaneously. As a result, I have examined the transformation of Joyce's writing from a heavily derivative form into a fiercely innovative style, and analyzed the potential for reader response contingent upon those changes. Just as I have organized my assessment of his canon's paradigmatic development around a single prominent feature—the influence of artistic predecessors—I have centered attention on a specific stylistic trait—free indirect discourse—as the element that most fully characterizes his formal evolutions. Neither, of course, can encapsulate the variety of Joyce's growth, but taken together they serve to summarize its salient features.

In much the same manner as the paradigm, free indirect discourse operates suggestively. It integrates into a dominant narrative voice the linguistic traits of another, leaving to the reader the choice of determining the source. It can be characterized as a form of stylistic ventriloquism, but in its most sophisticated manifestation neither the lips of the ventriloquist nor those of his dummy move. Rather it falls to the reader to decide who at any one time is speaking and what the implications of that choice are. As options multiply and their consequent effects begin to influence the possibilities for further differentiation, what may have at first seemed a relatively minor event becomes the characterizing force of one's (provisional) comprehension of a text. (Free indirect discourse has held the interest of linguists for most of this century, but it has only recently come to receive widespread consideration in literary criticism. An outline of the salient features of free indirect discourse appears in appendix A.)

With the composition of *Dubliners,* Joyce laid down the terms of his artistic evolution, articulating his perception of his intellectual and cultural heritage while honing his technical ability. He drew freely and heavily upon the works of his predecessors, testing his own ideas against the literary tradition which still exercised a pronounced influence on his work. At the same time, over the course of forming his stories he made tremendous artistic advances.

Although still rudimentary in terms of his later achievement, the use of free indirect discourse in the stories reflects a marked development of Joyce's ability to manipulate the formal elements of prose. It endows *Dubliners* with a sophistication absent in his earliest efforts. Still uncomplicated by the ambiguities of diction that it will assume in *Portrait,* the free indirect discourse of *Dubliners* gives little doubt as to the identity of each speaker who insinuates his or her voice into the narrative. Moving from story to story, we readily accustom ourselves to the variance of rhythm producing a duality of two clearly identifiable voices speaking more or less simultaneously. This does not, however, diminish its artistic significance or blunt its aesthetic impact. As evidenced by the striking evolution from the drafts of the earliest stories to the final versions of the latest ones, even in its most rudimentary manifestation free indirect discourse exerts a powerful impact upon how one reads a piece of literature.

Nonetheless, with a meticulous attention to detail and a monocular view of the world, Joyce's stories present readers with the fait accompli of his characters' lives and little more. In writing the bulk of *Dubliners* he came to see the inadequacy of that approach, and he radically reformed subsequent stories and later reshaped his incipient novel into *A Portrait of the Artist as a Young Man.*

To achieve changes in the form of *Dubliners* Joyce did not, like the God of creation, work ex nihilo. Instead with measured calculation he turned to his literary antecedents to learn the craft of writing, and echoes of the techniques characterizing the works of Balzac, de Maupassant, Wilde, and others obtrude throughout his stories. As he became more immersed in implementing the process of free indirect discourse into his prose and in refining and intensifying its application, Joyce continued to draw upon these figures and upon other models like Dickens, Conrad, and eventually Flaubert. Reading these writers cumulatively reinforced earlier impressions, but the experience pushed Joyce beyond emulation. It gave him the confidence to apply free indirect discourse not simply periodically in the fashion of his forebears but in an intense, unrelenting manner that would distinguish his next work, *Portrait,* from any of the fiction that had preceded it.

The movement away from the habits of composition influencing earlier work to the techniques applied to *Portrait* underscores the central concern of this study. It signals Joyce's emergence as an artist cognizant of his cultural tradition but functioning without full acquiescence to any prescribed influence. Creative strategies bringing the reader to a comparable level of awareness characterize its disposition. In *Portrait* Joyce changes his approach to narrative structure on two levels: He drastically diminished the directive force of the independent views of the third person narrator of *Stephen Hero*—the prototype for *Portrait*—while integrating the attitudes of a range of characters into the discourse. He also obscures the features that in *Dubliners* allowed one to distinguish unambiguously the sources of specific voices.

The most striking change, and one that would continue to evolve in all of his subsequent work, lies in the role of the narrator. In the self-contained world of each story in *Dubliners* the characteristics of the narrator remain relatively fixed and manifestations of the narrative voice assumed a predictable consistency. In *Portrait* a mutability begins to appear. The narrator remains a dominant consciousness, chronicling the development of Stephen Dedalus from infant to adult, but the tone changes progressively. In a parallel to the maturing process that Stephen undergoes, the narrative voice modulates, resonating an increasingly sophisticated tone in each chapter. The narrator's basic perspective remains the same, but he shows an ever-developing facility for assuming linguistic characteristics most appropriate to the context in which he appears. In *Ulysses* Joyce will extend this fluctuation to suggest a palpable paradigmatic tension between a narrative voice straining for conformity within a particular context and discourse and the reader's sense of a consistent narrative consciousness. In *Portrait* the narrator's impact on the paradigm has not progressed so far, but he nonetheless exerts a marked impact upon our perception of the discourse.

Ambiguity generally engages the reader's attention far more forcefully than it had in *Dubliners*. The discourse of *Portrait* no longer simply alternates attention between the views of the narrator and those of a specific character, for in many instances one must assign identities and not simply recognize the speaker. Those decisions make one realize the temporality of whatever choice one makes. Free indirect discourse moves the reader to the foreground of the work, overtly engaging one with the creation of meaning. At the same time it confronts us with the provisional nature of any text derived from a paradigm apparently so malleable.

Paradoxically, the significant change in *Portrait* is the movement from the implicit to the explicit: In *Dubliners*, when the reader creates texts, the decisions predicating their formation do not foreground the ambiguity upon which they are based. By contrast, in *Portrait* the discourse itself continually reminds one that uncertainty persists after every decision. In subsequent writing Joyce would exploit this condition, employing his formal skill to increase the involvement, indeed increase his dependence upon the involvement of the reader. Before attempting this, however, he had to achieve a fluency in a final form that he had not yet taken up: multiple perspectives.

Despite the liberal use of free indirect discourse and the broad range of thematic alternatives that he had offered in earlier works, Joyce still must have felt a gap in his mimetic abilities. For the first decade of his artistic career, his writing fixed its attention on a single figure and filtered the narrative discourse through the consciousness of that character or through narrative consciousnesses highlighting that individual's nature. In planning *Ulysses*, Joyce determined upon a radical departure, featuring a range of figures acting independently and in polyvocal competition with the narrative voice. To work through the difficulties of balancing the demands that this new approach would place upon him, he temporarily set aside his work on *Ulysses*, switched genres, and wrote a drama.

Many critics see Joyce's play *Exiles* as an unwanted, even embarrassing, appendage to an otherwise forceful artistic canon, but to view it in such a way ignores an important feature of its construction.[9] To a large degree *Exiles* served as a sketch for the more ambitious characterizations that would follow. Thus, the experience of composing this work prepared him to write *Ulysses*, just as the experience of viewing it prepares us to read *Ulysses*.

Superficially patterned on the stark naturalism of Ibsen, *Exiles* in fact stands as a precursor to the dramas of Beckett and of Pinter. The play's central features intentionally turn upon an ambiguity that serves as an implicit demand for the participation of the audience. The indeterminacies that fill the scenes of the drama, verbally inverting the conventions of free indirect discourse, invite us to participate in the completion of its meaning. No figure articulates complete or consistent standards for judging the action, and so we must integrate our own attitudes and experiences into the action, assuming a role analogous to the response that one makes to the increasingly detached narrator of Joyce's mature prose fiction.

When he turned to *Ulysses*, Joyce no longer needed to draw upon his literary antecedents to borrow forms for implementing his ideas. In writing *Dubliners* and *Portrait*, he had to master the repertoire of his predecessors and to show his ability to introduce innovative contributions to that tradition. Consequently, in *Ulysses* Joyce could feel less bound by the conventions of his craft, and so he became increasingly concerned with the function of the reader. Joyce knew that he could form aesthetic experiences from whatever model he chose to use, and he directed his efforts to enhancing the participation of the reader in the creation of meaning within his works. Involvement rested on a delicate balance between material with enough cues to give the reader some sense of possible reactions yet constituted in such a way as to avoid prescriptive responses. Consequently, he turned to a variety of familiar modes—including clichéd forms and nonliterary styles—to constitute the chapters of *Ulysses*. He examined a range of pedestrian works to fix the expectations which these forms had conditioned, and then he inverted them in *Ulysses* to produce a re-viewing and a re-creation of banal characters, concepts, and acts.

In *Ulysses* free indirect discourse dominates the narrative in a manner more evident and more diffused than its manifestations in *Portrait*. A series of characters—Stephen Dedalus, Leopold Bloom, and Molly Bloom—and a range of shifting forms condition and then recondition our responses. Vivid depictions of the consciousnesses of Stephen and of Molly provide strong contrast to the attitudes that Bloom brings to the novel, and they threaten to rupture all but the most flexible para-digmatic assumptions. A shifting of stylistic approaches and a conse-quent shifting of the narrative presence introduce additional alterna-tives for perceiving events, and they leave to the reader the task of forming a coherent sense of the action. Each individual and each form compete for our attention, and yet no style and none of these figures emerge as the centering influence of the work. Nor is there a shared hegemony, in Bakhtin's sense, in the determination of meaning. Rather the differing forms and the differing views of each figure enforce, through free indirect discourse, the polymorphous possibility of the work. More than anything he had written up to that point, *Ulysses* denies the existence of a hegemonic reading and affirms the obligation of the reader to continue to create and to recreate meaning from what is pre-sented.

Finnegans Wake exfoliates all of these efforts. It becomes the coda of Joyce's artistic development: a discourse operating not in the conven-tional diachronic manner but instead in a synchronic simultaneity of voice that presents all of the work's possibilities in a series of coinci-dental, concurrent discourses. Consequently my study ends not with a detailed examination of the *Wake* but with a comment on how Joyce's final book reintroduces the aesthetic aims of all that preceded it. There the author initiates the narrative discourse and sets the boundaries of the work while denying responsibility for any interpretation, and the reader becomes the final arbiter of meaning and the self-conscious den-ier of closure. In this collaboration Joyce foregrounds the relationship standing at the center of each of his works, and he points up the strategy for recuperating meaning by which any of his works can be understood.

II | Aesthetic Evolution: The Shaping Forces behind *Dubliners*

Although in the introduction I have proposed an examination of Joyce's canon primarily based on principles articulated by reader response criticism, my announced aim to broaden consideration of the repertoire of both Joyce and his audience also necessitates close attention to elements of historicist criticism. I do not intend to integrate into my study a wide-ranging survey of the period, but, taking a cue from Hayden White's views on the subjectivity of intellectual history, I will highlight specific elements in Joyce's creative ambiance that had a shaping impact on the constitution of his writing.[1] Identifying these influences, of course, can only set down the broadest limits of the paradigm—the frame for da Vinci's canvas. Nonetheless, such an examination of the protentions and the retentions brought to a specific work must form the basis for any rigorous investigation of this nature. To comprehend the scope of potential readings, while avoiding entanglement with prescriptive methods of interpretation, one must undertake a balanced consideration of the alternative perspectives open to the reader and to the writer. Since the paradigm itself evolves within and out of broader intellectual milieus, one comes to a full sense of its alternatives only through an awareness of salient features of the artistic contexts associated with its evolution.

To provide a context for subsequent analysis, this chapter will necessarily focus on Joyce and on his artistic background. It will examine Joyce's own intellectual and cultural environment as reflected in his readings, in his observations, and in his initial efforts at composition. From this scrutiny will emerge the features of his social repertoire that will obtain throughout his career as a writer. This in turn will highlight, in later chapters, the protocols shaping a reader's derivation of meaning.

Perhaps I should digress to reaffirm the differences between this approach and those more traditional sources studies. I do not propose to undertake an analysis of the forces shaping the composition of *Dubliners* in an effort to prove beyond all doubt that a particular figure exercised a dominant creative influence on the formation of Joyce's fiction. Nor

17

do I intend to advocate a meta-view of authorial intentionality—so far as that term designates an approach leading to an interpretation that has hegemony over all other meanings. As I stated in my introduction, I feel that the concept of an ideal reading oversimplifies the artistic value of any piece of literature. Rather I mean to use various authors synecdochically—as representatives of intellectual movements or creative methods that at one time or another engaged Joyce's imagination. My goals are to define significant aspects of the creative aims guiding Joyce in the constitution of a particular work and to use this delineation to identify the range of valid responses that one may make to his writing.

Because of its chronological position in Joyce's canon (he had published the initial versions of certain stories as early as 1904), some readers see *Dubliners* as an apprentice piece separate from the achievement of his more mature writings. This may be marginally true in terms of the technical control and the artistic inventiveness that he would later display, but *Dubliners* nonetheless stands as the fully finished product of a capable craftsman, deservedly considered on the same plane as all his subsequent writing. I wish to emphasize the significance of this bond, for through the formation of these stories Joyce committed himself to a basic creative perspective that would govern the evolution of the remainder of his canon. A more precise description of the temporal development of *Dubliners* will underscore this relationship, for as Joyce's letters make clear, the process of its composition coincides with a period of intense examination of his aesthetic values, clarifying for him the mature artistic vision that he would adopt.

Joyce formed the stories over several distinct creative stages: The initial composition and a series of crucial revisions took place between 1904 and 1907. Subsequent revisions, notably in "Eveline" and in "The Boarding House," occurred around 1909. And additional changes, less elaborate than previous ones, came even later, probably between 1910 and 1912. (For a detailed chronological breakdown of the initial compositions and revisions of the stories, see appendix B.) On 29 January 1914, just four days before *Portrait* began to appear serially in *The Egoist*, Grant Richards agreed to publish *Dubliners*. By that time strong parallels already obtained between *Dubliners* and *Portrait*, prefiguring elements that would figure prominently in *Ulysses* and in *Finnegans Wake*.

These events support the supposition that from his initial endeavors onward the process of rewriting formed an important aspect of Joyce's creation and must take an equally prominent place in any attempt by a reader to engage his work. Through his effort to create and to refine these stories, the ideas and the values that would constitute all subsequent writing coalesced. More importantly, from the experience of writing *Dubliners*, Joyce derived the rudiments of the narrative technique and the artistic perspective that would define all of his subsequent paradigms. To derive some sense of the issues that he confronted and of the paradigmatic structure that resulted, one must step back from the completed work to examine the process of composition and retrace the creative stages in the stylistic development of *Dubliners* during this formative period between 1904 and 1907 when Joyce made major revisions in his stories. Such an analysis foregrounds the features supporting the intellectual ethos of *Dubliners* and, by extension, defines those that will inform the remainder of the canon.

Joyce began composing both *Dubliners* and *Stephen Hero* early in 1904. Work proceeded in tandem until around June of 1905 when concern for crafting his short stories took primacy over the production of his incipient novel. He shifted his attention from the solipsism that marked the narrative of *Stephen Hero*, and centered his interest instead on the broader scope of the lower-middle-class life of his city, confronting creative considerations that he had previously avoided in *Stephen Hero*. Work on his short stories led him to characters and situations outside the range of his personal experiences, and it prompted him to adopt perspectives that extended beyond the fictionalized autobiographical recollections of *Stephen Hero*. He still projected his own impressions of his city into the actions and feelings of diverse individuals in *Dubliners*, but with an increased sensitivity to broader narrative demands. By September of 1907 when he completed the first draft of his final story, "The Dead," his artistic powers had so evolved that he chose to abandon the formal structure used in writing *Stephen Hero* for innovative methods closer to those that would characterize *Portrait*.

(A full treatment of Joyce's artistic break with his early creative efforts appears in chapter three, an examination of *Stephen Hero*. Although Joyce's ultimate rejection of the paradigm that formed *Stephen Hero* has important implications for the composition of *Dubliners*, its most significant impact fell on the writing of *Portrait*. Consequently, I have deferred my examination of *Stephen Hero* in order to juxtapose it with a consideration of *Portrait*.)

Identifying the forces within Joyce's mind while he was composing and refining *Dubliners* rests necessarily on supposition, and, as noted in the introduction, the paradigms to which I have been referring must by their very nature remain approximate rather than definitive constructs. To see them as anything more would lead one towards a deceptive sense of certitude similar to that gripping the characters of the short stories.

Even while acknowledging this necessary ambiguity, however, one can draw upon biographical information and textual evidence relating to the development of various stories to gain some insight into the changes in Joyce's perspectives and thus into his approach toward writing: Manuscripts of various drafts reflect the maturation of ideas and of techniques. Passages from his letters written during this period articulate specific artistic and aesthetic problems that may have prompted these changes. And evidence from the books that he read during this time provides an indication of the nature of the sources that molded his response to these problems.[2]

A number of fine studies have already examined the thematic importance of the reformation of individual stories, and Robert Scholes has ably summarized the stages of manuscript development.[3] These analyses, however, generally concern themselves with the significance of the impact of Joyce's revisions in terms of specific stories and of their relation to the entire collection. I want to emphasize the broader effect of the evolution of *Dubliners* on Joyce's artistic consciousness by tracing the path of his revisions back to their most probable sources. From this inversion of methods of previous scholars, I intend to outline the nature of the artistic paradigms characterizing not simply his short stories but all his subsequent work.

Joyce wrote *Dubliners* during intermittent periods of hectic activity. Although ideas for his short stories may have been forming in his mind over several years, he began actual work in June or July of 1904 at the request of George Russell, editor of *The Irish Homestead* (*Letters*, II.43). He wrote the initial versions of "The Sisters," "Eveline," and "After the Race" in Dublin during the summer and early fall—shortly before he left Ireland for the Continent. While he spent some time working on ideas for what would become his story "Clay," from October of 1904 to June of 1905 evidence in his correspondence (*Letters*, II.67–91) indicates that Joyce devoted most of his energy to composing chapters of *Stephen Hero*.[4] Between July and October of 1905, he wrote nine additional stories in a form markedly different from the three that had already appeared in print, and he prepared the collection of twelve for submission to the English publisher Grant Richards. For much of 1906 he continued to develop the scope of *Dubliners*, adding two stories—"A Little Cloud" and "Two Gallants"—in January and April. Under pressure from Richards to remove material that might give offense to the middle-class sensibilities of an English readership, Joyce drastically revised five others between June and August.

In the fall of 1906 negotiations with Richards broke down, but Joyce continued the process of reformation given initial impetus by the objections of Richards, making additional revisions in October and November. In 1907 he composed "The Dead" and probably refined other stories over the next two years. By 1909, when he submitted his manuscript to Maunsel and Co. in an unsuccessful attempt to get his collection into print, available evidence indicates that Joyce had completed the major revisions for the stories, although he continued to polish his work until it was finally published in 1914 by Grant Richards.

The features distinguishing Joyce's artistic evolution emerge sporadically throughout the compositional stages of *Dubliners*, yet development remains relatively easy to identify and to assess because of the collection's unvarying topical backdrop. "Eveline," for example, one of the first stories written, went through significant revisions between its initial publication in *The Irish Homestead* on 10 September 1904 and its appearance in 1914. Nonetheless, like "The Sisters" and "After the Race," the *Homestead* "Eveline" presents the same narrative framework—the basic plot, action, and characterizations—that would constitute the final rendition. Further, even in its earliest form, it articulates concerns that would stand as central themes in all of Joyce's works—claustrophobia, parochialism, oppression, freedom, and desire. At the same time, this first version lacks the sharp dialogic focus and the subtle characterization of the story published in 1914. With the other two pieces that appeared in *The Irish Homestead*, "Eveline" affirms Joyce's sense of thematic purpose even as it reveals the paradigmatic limits of his early writing.

In 1912 an emended and expanded "Eveline" appeared in the late page proofs of the edition proposed by Maunsel. In his study of the textual evolution of the stories, Scholes summarizes the shaping force of these revisions. "Through countless little changes of this kind, Joyce carefully eliminated his own personality from *Dubliners*, as he developed a system whereby the events and characters presented in the narrative rather than any assumed narrative persona determine the diction and syntax of the narrative." In light of his subsequent work on narrative theory Scholes would now probably take such observations a bit further. Here I would like to anticipate that critical development to extrapolate on the form Scholes has identified without labeling—free indirect discourse, for the changes encapsulate significant creative advances reflecting the much broader paradigm now constituting *Dubliners*.[5]

As Scholes rightly points out, Joyce's process of emendation markedly restructures the discourse of the story, but those revisions do something much more sophisticated than imitating the putative Flaubertian gesture of "eliminat[ing] his own personality." The movement tends toward accretion rather than abnegation, and it greatly enhances the creative alternatives open to both the author and the reader. In this later version of the story, free indirect discourse undermines one's sense of a discrete narrative voice, operating outside the influence of the natures of any of the characters in the work. The striking change that results—the modulation of the narrative—comes not so much from Joyce's elimination of his own personality from the discourse as from a refusal to give primacy to a single point of view. Increasingly, the revisions amalgamate the attitudes of Eveline within the perspective of the narrator. The changes go beyond the simple supplanting of the narrative persona. They reform the reader's perspective of Eveline's character, changing it from the view of a rather predictable type into the apprehension of figure whose complexity adumbrates the nature evinced by Gerty MacDowell in *Ulysses*.

Specifically, with the incorporation of free indirect discourse, the story combines diegetic and dialogic impulses, detached description and highly personal feelings. In this way it calls the reader's attention to the paradoxes in Eveline's personality, and it makes more ambiguous her motivation for rejecting Frank. The exhausted diction of cliché persistently fuses the reader's sense of Eveline's vulnerability with a new awareness of her penchant for melodrama conjoined with a clear-eyed pragmatism. Initially she simply "was going away"; in the later version she experiences a pang of sentimental nostalgia: "Perhaps she would never see again those familiar objects from which she had never dreamed of being divided" (*JJA*, IV.3b). At other points in the story, constructions become less elaborate, emphasizing more overtly the calculating elements in Eveline's temperament. Contemplating her elopement, she no longer wonders "Was it wise—was it honourable?" but merely "Was it wise?" And, in considering the impact that her departure will have on her coworkers at the Stores, she no longer worries about what they will think of her but rather about what they will say (*JJA*, V.132). This elaboration of perspective and the consequent intensification of character and tone can obtain because the viewpoint of the reader can move back and forth between Eveline's personal attitudes and the more aloof perspective of the narrator. More to the point, however, the significant difference between the early form of "Eveline" and its final version reflects the broader imaginative revaluation that came to condition Joyce's style throughout *Dubliners*.

Conventional approaches do not readily yield a full sense of the assumptions informing the readjusted paradigm and leading to the radical modification of the formal construction of Joyce's stories. Although his application of free indirect discourse shows an affinity for methods that had already gained attention through the work of writers like Gustave Flaubert and Henry James, little evidence exists to show that Joyce consciously attempted to emulate their efforts. In fact, a critic attempting to ascertain the range of literary influences on Joyce's fiction during this period faces the problem of having no overt point of reference.

As a young man in Dublin, Joyce had ardently supported the drama of Ibsen and the verse of a succession of poets including James Clarence Mangan. By 1904, when he left Dublin for the Continent, fiction had become as important to him as poetry or drama, yet he singled out no particular novelist as a model and followed no fixed pattern of inquiry in his approach to what he read. Despite his familiarity with the works of leading contemporary writers, their books seemed only to engage his attention tangentially. Certainly no author or movement earned the unreserved admiration that he had previously given to Ibsen and to Mangan. In fact, in a gesture that one might logically expect from an emerging artist, Joyce's initial impulse appears to have been to turn away from established figures in fiction.[6]

Still, Joyce's letters to his brother Stanislaus, one of the early "whetstones" for his artistic sensibilities, give one a sense of Joyce's perception of the creative issues conditioning his response to what he has read. Often they betray impatience, and Joyce's dissatisfaction with the approaches of various authors reflectively highlights concerns emerging in his own writing. One letter, for example, composed while he was still working on *Stephen Hero*, criticizes George Moore's *The Untilled Field*, and it provides a negative correlative for the idiosyncratic details informing the fragment of Joyce's first novel that still survives.

> I have read Moore's "Untilled Field" in Tauchnitz. Damned stupid. A woman alludes to her husband in the confession-box as "Ned." Ned thinks &c! A lady who has been living for three years on the line between Bray and Dublin is told by her husband that there is a meeting in Dublin at which he must be present. She looks up the table to see the hours of the trains. This on DW and WR [the Dublin, Wicklow, and Wexford Railway] where the trains go regularly: this after three years. Isn't it rather stupid of Moore. And the punctuation! Madonna! (*Letters*, II.71)

The competitiveness he felt with other Irish writers certainly had some influence in shaping these remarks, but more significantly the passage also points up a near compulsive attention to naturalistic accuracy. Joyce's correspondence indicates that he had already formed the habit of giving meticulous attention to detail that would remain a hallmark of all his subsequent work. (See, for example, *Letters*, II.109.) Naturally enough, this emphasis carried over to *Stephen Hero*. There, however, its manifestations show Joyce's still incipient grasp of the technique, often producing undifferentiated particulars buried in a suffocating series of independent clauses, as in the following description of Simon Dedalus. "Stephen's father was quite capable of talking himself into believing what he knew to be untrue. He knew that his own ruin had been his own handiwork but he had talked himself into believing that it was the handiwork of others. He had his son's distaste for responsibility without his son's courage. He was one of those illogical wiseacres with whom no evidence can outreason the first impression" (110).

By the time he wrote *Portrait*, Joyce could produce a description of Simon Dedalus through a series of elaborations and condensations that presents a much more evocative picture than the outline made in *Stephen Hero*:

> Stephen began to enumerate glibly his father's attributes.
> —A medical student, an oarsman, a tenor, an amateur actor, a shouting politician, a small landlord, a small investor, a drinker, a good fellow, a storyteller, somebody's secretary, something in a distillery, a taxgatherer, a bankrupt and at present a praiser of his own past. (*P,* 241)

In 1904, however, he had not yet acquired such a fine sense of balance, but indications of a growing sophistication began to appear well before Joyce decided to recast *Stephen Hero* as *Portrait*.

The form of the short stories of *Dubliners* enforced limitations on descriptive extravagance while allowing an attention to detail that produced stunning effects. The opening lines of "The Dead," for example, convey a very precise sense of Lily's nature in a hurried but not forced rhythm that matches her movements up and down the hall. "Lily, the caretaker's daughter, was literally run off her feet. Hardly had she brought one gentleman into the little pantry behind the office on the ground floor and helped him off with his overcoat than the wheezy halldoor bell clanged again and she had to scamper along the bare hallway to let in another guest" (175). The difference between this selection and the one from *Stephen Hero* indicates the degree of creative growth that Joyce achieved over the three years separating their composition, but noting stylistic contrast marks only the first stage of efforts to determine the full implications of such a change.

Biographical information offers a basis for additional inquiries. During the initial stages of work on his novel, other writers seemed very much on Joyce's mind. In a letter to his brother Stanislaus written three weeks after the one containing the remarks on Moore, he gives some indication of the impact of his exposure to specific literary sources. After sardonically dismissing a story by Henry James, "Madonna of the Future," as "very pleasant reading," Joyce presents, in an equally cavalier fashion, a thumbnail sketch of the French writer Ernest Renan. "I am reading the Souvenirs of Renan. Damme if I understand him. 'Une Celte, mêlé de Gascon, mâtiné de Lappon' 'un prêtre manqué'. He professes romanticism, love for Brittany, affection for old masters, regret at having to abandon dear old Grandmother Church—I fancy his life of Jesus must be very maudlin stuff. No wonder Huysmans calls him a comedian" (*Letters*, II.72). The parallel thematic concerns raised by *Stephen Hero*—a novel that also features a Celtic protagonist, "un prêtre manqué," with a predilection for romanticism and ambivalence towards the Catholic Church—make this disavowal less clear-cut than it may initially seem.

Mary T. Reynolds has undertaken a detailed examination of the nature of the artistic relationship between Joyce and Renan, and she has traced imaginative convergences that Joyce's remarks would not have led one to expect. Arguing that Renan's work served as an important model for elements of the discourse within *Stephen Hero*, Reynolds sees Stephen as suffering "doubt in much the same way that Renan portrays himself in his reminiscences (the *Souvenirs*, or *Recollections*): that is, balancing the intellectual pressures of secularism and doubt with the claim of orthodoxy that came from his upbringing and appreciation of institutional values." Reynolds then goes on to highlight close associations between the ideas that Renan depicted in his work and elements within the consciousness of Stephen Daedalus.[7] Her observations illuminate salient aspects of the imaginative framework of *Stephen Hero*, but more significantly, at least in terms of this study, they underscore intellectual and creative tendencies that would be counteracted by Joyce's subsequent artistic development: a dependence in his efforts at writing upon the overt contextual support, through allusion, of his literary antecedents, and an early ambivalent association with an obtrusive, heavy-handed approach like Renan's.

As Joyce's attention began to turn more and more to his short stories, comments in his letters increasingly suggest a search for formal models to guide the construction of his work. At the same time initial efforts were rather tentative and extremely cautious. In a February 28th letter to Stanislaus, for example, Joyce shows an interest in the short stories of J. P. Jacobsen, a Danish writer who displayed a talent for presenting minute descriptions through a lyrical form free of sentimentality (*Let-*

ters, II.82–83). Jacobsen is not a radical stylistic innovator but, as indicated by the passage below from a description of Provence in Jacobsen's short story "Fru Fonss," one intimately aware of the impact of topos. "The city on either side [of the river] seemed built up of silence, with all these noon-hushed streets, and all these deaf-mute houses with every shutter closed, tightly closed on everyone, houses that could neither hear or see!"[8] Here Jacobsen deftly evokes the same constrictive atmosphere that Joyce would infuse into stories like "Araby," written over the summer of 1905. "North Richmond Street, being blind, was a quiet street except at the hour when the Christian Brothers School set the boys free. An uninhabited house of two storeys stood at the blind end, detached from its neighbours in a square ground. The other houses of the street, conscious of decent lives within them, gazed at one another with brown imperturbable faces" (*D*, 29). I hardly wish to credit Jacobsen with inspiring the opening paragraph of "Araby," but the juxtaposition does show Joyce's growing sensitivity to the nuances of impressionistic detail. As the composition of *Dubliners* continued, the increasing refinement of this sensitivity became a characterizing feature of Joyce's revisions.

Nonetheless, the formal diversity that one finds in versions of stories written during this period refutes the idea that a particular literary model had a prescriptive influence. As Joyce's letters to Stanislaus show, he was carefully scrutinizing the works of a number of other authors for materials that could be adopted to his own ends, and each reference contributes elements to a broad picture of his aesthetic concerns. "Have you read Turgenieff's 'Lear of the Steppes'. He does many things well and is useful technically but in European literature he has not so high a place as you seem to think he has" (*Letters*, II.91). Like the circular that Bloom receives in Lestrygonians announcing the coming of Elijah (a.k.a. Alexander J. Dowie), Joyce's pronouncement seems at first glance to be nothing more than a throwaway. The statement provokes, almost inevitably, the petulant questions of why Turgenev, and what does he do well, for by 1905 few readers would see Turgenev as a creative innovator.

A close look at *A Lear of the Steppes* suggests some answers. Even now his stories retain a singular, ingenuous charm that on some level would have appealed to Joyce, but more specifically Turgenev's writing evinces a narrative playfulness quite similar to the tone that Joyce was himself cultivating. In the following lines a moment of self-deflating irony undercuts the bourgeois sensibilities that the narrator has so carefully insinuated into the passage.

My mother did not like Harlov's elder daughter; she called her a stuck-up thing. Anna Martinova scarcely ever came to pay us her respects, and behaved with chilly decorum in my mother's presence, though it was by her good offices she had been educated at a boarding-school, and had been married, and on her wedding-day had received a thousand roubles and a yellow Turkish shawl, the latter, it is true, a trifle worse for wear.[9]

This movement from self-righteous indignation to an unconscious revelation of wounded pride and spitefulness presents, in truncated form and with much less self-awareness, the same ambivalence pervading the consciousness of many characters in *Dubliners*. The overriding bitterness of Turgenev's narrator, however, enforces a much less ambiguous attitude than those characterizing individuals in Joyce's stories. Despite acknowledging the condition of the shawl, the narrator has a faith in his own certitude that none of Joyce's characters enjoy. Nonetheless, the invocation of *A Lear of the Steppes* serves as a useful benchmark for tracing Joyce's development. His allusion to it shows that naturalistic detail still remains important, but he also begins to give increasing attention to narrative complexity. During 1905 Joyce would further clarify his perspective to expand the potential for a diversity of texts inherent in his collection of short stories.

This new interest in multiplicity conjointly led Joyce to a much more sophisticated sense of his role as an artist. In an often-quoted passage from a letter written to Grant Richards in June of 1906, Joyce defended "the odour of ashpits and old weeds and offal" that pervades *Dubliners* by invoking, albeit through inflated diction, the aims of his work. "I seriously believe that you will retard the course of civilisation in Ireland by preventing the Irish people from having one good look at themselves in my nicely polished looking-glass" (*Letters*, I.64). Admittedly, these lines and other remarks that he made (cf. *Letters*, II.110) suggest that a degree of vindictiveness intruded upon the tone of his collection. The opinion that an impulse to castigate his homeland had come to dominate the stories, however, oversimplifies Joyce's emotional attitudes towards his country and unjustly circumscribes the artistic potential of the pieces. The letter to Richards summarizes a view arrived at by Joyce after long consideration, but, when viewed in the context of the stories themselves, it more clearly represents the desire to reflect the multiplicity of Dublin than simply a wish to condemn the city peremptorily.

Joyce very carefully chooses as the objective correlative of his art a "nicely polished looking-glass," and not the cracked one purloined by Buck Mulligan from the room of a servant (*U*, 1.138–40). Through this image he asserts not an interest in vilifying Ireland but a desire to present an honest, artful depiction of the complex human condition of his country. Ireland provides the source for the degraded incidents that give shape to his observations. At the same time, the paradigm conditioning the collection now allows the reader the freedom to discern a good deal of pathos that could not be found in the events depicted in the 1904 stories appearing in *The Irish Homestead*.

One cannot fix specifically the moment of change in Joyce's attitude, but outlines of the specific character of his paradigmatic adjustment begin to appear a year prior to the letter to Richards quoted in part above. In correspondence written to Stanislaus between July 19th and September 24th of 1905, through observations on the character of various fellow artists, Joyce gives an indication of his own struggle to articulate the precepts upon which he would rely in formulating his artistic sensibilities. The views expressed in these letters have not moved beyond the formative stage and are generally brief to the point of terseness. They do, however, show a self-conscious concern for expanding the features of his artistic consciousness—balancing moral detachment and ethical awareness.

Nonetheless, interpretation remains problematic, for Joyce is not concerned with presenting a manifesto or with justifying his ideas to others. Rather he is using Stanislaus as a sounding board. We are eavesdropping on a conversation, hearing only half of the dialogue and doubtless missing many of the nuances. The comments consequently remain open-ended, but they do offer certain insights on Joyce's thinking. Individually, they draw attention to specific issues of artistic commitment, and taken together they reproduce "the curve of an emotion," Joyce's evolving paradigm for *Dubliners*.

In a letter written to Stanislaus on 19 July 1905, for example, one finds a particularly rich and diverse series of remarks. Joyce successively compares himself to Goldsmith, articulates doubts about "the excellence of my literary manners," and notes that "[i]t seems so improbable that Hardy, for example, will be spoken of in two hundred years." Continuing his observations on the artistic consciousness, he remarks that "Maupassant writes very well, of course, but I am afraid that his moral sense is rather obtuse." Joyce sums up his own position by saying "[t]he struggle against conventions in which I am at present involved was not entered into by me so much as a protest against these conventions as with the intention of living in conformity with my moral nature" (*Letters*, II.99). In another letter written on September 1st, he makes an oblique reference to the ameliorative power of Ibsen, asking "[i]s it not possible for a few persons of character and culture to make Dublin a capital such as Christiana has become" (*Letters*, II.105). And then, in a third letter composed in late September Joyce compares his own artistic temperament to those of Rimbaud, Renan, and Newman. He finds that he and Rimbaud "who is hardly a writer at all" truly have it, while Newman's and Renan's temperaments are divided between art and other disciplines (*Letters*, II.110).

Like Virginia Woolf's "orts, scraps, and fragments," these passages give a highly impressionistic and diverse view of Joyce's artistic attitudes, yet cumulatively they suggest a pattern for discerning at least one of the characterizing elements important to the cultivation of a proper artistic temperament. Joyce framed his remarks reflexively, in terms outlining his specific views of other writers. Most of these writers represent formal influences that Joyce had already rejected, yet they remain features of his artistic consciousness because of the alternative imaginative paradigms that they personify. Goldsmith, Ibsen, Rimbaud—artists with divergent concerns writing in different genres—all provide highly personal commentaries on their societies. The letters make clear the affinity that Joyce feels with the distinct features of their natures: Each shows a deep awareness of the forces acting upon an individual, forces which ultimately bring about the individual's downfall, and each emphasizes the importance of the individual following dictates inspired by an inner vision. Hardy and de Maupassant, on the other hand, receive a much harsher assessment, suggesting the limitations that Joyce wished to impose on the range of social expression. At this point in his development, Joyce has little patience for thinking dominated by sweeping social commentary or for writing that allows sentimentality or melodrama to obscure the definition of character. The criticism of Renan and Newman underscores this point. Despite whatever admiration he may have had for the technical proficiencies of both men, he obviously felt that a dedicated artist must eschew didacticism and concern himself primarily with the perfection of his art.

Although these remarks seem at times to veer toward contradiction, Joyce's subsequent writing enforces his dedication to achieving this delicate balance between artist and environment. The declaration with which Stephen closes *Portrait*, for example, affirms a willingness to be acted upon by the cultural ambiance as much as it demonstrates a desire to react to it: "Welcome, O life! I go to encounter for the millionth time the reality of experience and to forge in the smithy of my soul the uncreated conscience of my race" (*P,* 253). In this statement neither Stephen nor his creator embraces the role of a didactic writer. Instead, what becomes manifest is, to return to the mirror metaphor, an impulse to reflect and, through reflection, to re-view the human condition artistically. These attitudes do not touch upon the stylistic growth in Joyce's abilities. (De Maupassant, for instance, would have a marked impact on Joyce's formal development, as I show later in this chapter.) But they do show an inclusiveness informing his own temperament and by extension his paradigmatic concerns.

The connection between Joyce's general perception of the attributes that should characterize an artist—his moral purpose and temperament—and the contextual concerns of *Dubliners* becomes evident in a letter sent to Stanislaus shortly after he had written those quoted above. In it Joyce singles out Mikhail Lermontov's novel *A Hero of Our Time* as a work having an artistic goal similar to his own, and by analogy he sets forth his own sense of the function of art. "The only book I know like [*Dubliners*] is Lermontoff's *Hero of Our Days*. Of course mine is much longer and Lermontoff's hero is an aristocrat and a tired man and a brave animal. But there is a likeness in the aim and title and at times in the acid treatment" (*Letters*, II.111).

As Joyce says, the social context defining Lermontov's central character could not be further removed from that surrounding the individuals of Joyce's short stories, yet in terms of his creative growth the differences carry relatively little significance. At this point in his artistic development, Joyce was attuned to stylistic, not thematic, similarities. Since, as the letter plainly states he viewed the "acid treatment" in *A Hero of Our Time* as paralleling stylistic elements of *Dubliners*, an examination of some of the novel's narrative features clarifies Joyce's sense of the paradigm characterizing *Dubliners*.

A Hero of Our Time consists of five episodes originally published serially in the Russian journal *Fatherland Notes*. It centers around the life of a young Russian officer, Grigory Alexandrovich Pechorin, depicted as a decadent, Byronic adventurer. Lermontov's prose evokes the same precise yet detached tone that one finds in many descriptions in *Dubliners*, and while Joyce's letter never clearly defines Lermontov's "moral sense," the passage quoted below, commenting on Pechorin's nature, gives us some indication of the formal elements that attracted Joyce:

> I became convinced of the innocence of the man who brought his own weaknesses and vices so mercilessly to light. The story of a human soul, even the smallest of souls, is hardly less interesting and useful than the history of a whole nation especially when it is the result of self-examination on the part of a mature mind and written without any vain desire to arouse sympathy or surprise.[10]

The description implicitly sketches an ethos that the novel later attempts to articulate, and from this perspective the disparities between the settings and the events of *A Hero of Our Time* and those of *Dubliners* mean relatively little. The narrative fixes its attention not on wide-ranging societal pressures but on the self-reflexive examinations of a particular individual, and the sentiments that it expresses could as easily relate this analysis to the central concern of any of Joyce's stories as to Lermontov's Pechorin.

The structure of *Dubliners,* of course, presents a more elaborate depiction of this condition, and Lermontov probably reinforced rather than inspired the methods that Joyce adopted. The allusion remains significant, however, because it underscores the sense that by 1905 Joyce had abandoned the presuppositions governing the composition of *Stephen Hero* and the earliest versions of *Dubliners* to embrace a much less restrictive paradigm. This revised approach would endow the struggles of even the most mundane of individuals with a complexity that demanded far more from the reader than the passive reception of details. Two decades after this process began, Joyce, in remarks to Arthur Power that unconsciously answer the charge that he used *Dubliners* simply to scourge the Irish consciousness, touched on these aims. ''For myself, I always write about Dublin, because if I can get to the heart of Dublin I can get to the heart of all the cities of the world. In the particular is contained the universal.''[11]

The clarification of artistic purpose that Joyce reached in 1905 gave him a contextual frame for his thematic interests. It also had a contingent stylistic effect upon the constitution of his stories. The passage below, from a draft of ''The Boarding House'' composed during the summer of 1905, reflects this new-found pleasure in ambiguity. It also balances an interest in banal domestic tragedy with an ability to transcend an apparently stereotypical situation. Joyce endows the narrative with an emotional complexity that blunts any interpretive impulse within the reader to turn to stock responses for meaning, evoking polyphonic resonances similar to those that Mikhail Bakhtin found in Dostoevski.[12] The narrative plays out the significant events of the story indirectly, through the thoughts and the recollections of a series of characters: Polly Mooney, Mrs. Mooney, and Bob Doran. Their multiple voices deflect any impulse in the reader toward easy generalizations or simplistic interpretations.

Even when the discourse concentrates on presenting the attitudes of Bob Doran, its language insinuates traces of the competing emotional contexts dictating the terms of his struggles.

> Mr Doran was very anxious indeed this Sunday morning. He had made two attempts to shave but his hand had been so unsteady that he had been obliged to desist. Three days' reddish beard fringed his jaws and every two or three minutes a mist gathered on his glasses so that he had to take them off and polish them with his pocket handkerchief. The recollection of his confession of the night before was a cause of acute pain to him: the priest had drawn out every ridiculous detail of the affair and in the end had so magnified his sin that he was almost thankful at being afforded a loophole of reparation. (*JJA*, IV.31)

From the opening sentence, pivoting on the fussy interjection "indeed," Joyce anchors the syntactic development of the paragraph with phrases capturing the bathos and hysteria surrounding Doran's fruitless efforts to avoid facing the inevitable resolution of his dilemma. The narrative toys with multiplicity. It contrasts language and action to invite readers to see simultaneously the seriousness of the situation and the ludicrousness of the character. By withholding an explanation of the specific source of uneasiness while concentrating attention on Doran's unsuccessful attempts to shave, the discourse causes us to suspend our judgment. Developing the image of a supercilious man endeavoring to suppress his growing anxiety, agitated descriptions of an "unsteady" hand and a sweaty forehead combine to undercut the petulant bravado of "obliged to desist." By the time Doran does confront "the cause of acute pain to him," the diction of the narrative, mixing pomposity and slang, has heightened the reader's sense of Doran's confusion and priggishness. It leaves us to decide upon the amount of irony and of sympathy we wish to assign to the situation.

The passage relies heavily, of course, on free indirect discourse as a vehicle for this intensifying reader engagement. The first two sentences neatly convey what later in the story will become Doran's characterizing trait: fretfulness. The next sentence introduces by contrast the dispassionate tone of a disinterested third party. The final sentence—with its measured insinuation of the voice of the priest in the confessional box—alternates between detachment and involvement, allowing the reader the latitude of interpretation already noted.

The deft alternation between the narrative presentation of descriptive details and Doran's account of his emotional turmoil demonstrates a marked improvement over the constitution of stories first composed during the previous summer. Unfortunately, Joyce at this time did not have the ability to sustain this technique, and other segments of this initial version reflect a linear singularity in the discourse that remained unchanged until later revisions. Nonetheless, the initial description of

Bob Doran's emotional turmoil testifies to an early commitment to narrative techniques devoted to overturning the hegemony of a single perspective. While the application in *Dubliners* of this process never equaled the inventiveness that would be displayed in the styles of *Portrait*, many of the subsequent revisions of the short stories approximated these techniques.

Throughout the remaining stages of the composition of *Dubliners* Joyce, now secure in his sense of purpose, treated style as a central element, and his revisions evince a continuing effort to identify forms suitable for incorporation into his own work. This impulse for borrowing probably grew out of his early inclination, outlined in the passages quoted from letters to his brother Stanislaus written in 1904 and in 1905, to comment, generally in a desultory manner, on the work of various other authors. Once he had achieved a measure of confidence in his own sense of artistic identity, he could afford to view the relative strengths and deficiencies of other writers less antagonistically. Nevertheless, Joyce initially appears to have been content to allow stylistic growth to evolve independently and at its own pace. Consequently, despite selected instances of formal virtuosity, drafts of stories composed during the summer of 1905 remained unfocused and without the features of a consistent stylistic direction. This condition began to change in the spring of 1906 when Grant Richards, the publisher who had agreed to bring out *Dubliners*, precipitated a major development in Joyce's form by attempting to censor several of the stories.

Controversy over the manuscript revolved around matters of taste and public morality. It began innocuously enough, but it soon escalated into a bitter struggle.[13] Shortly after Joyce learned, late in February of 1906, of the agreement to publish *Dubliners*, he sent Richards a copy of the just-completed story "Two Gallants." On April 23rd Richards wrote to Joyce stating that because of its subject matter he could not possibly include the new piece in the collection. He also objected to certain passages in "Counterparts" and "Grace." An epistolary debate ensued that continued into the fall, expanding beyond the original points of contention to encompass parts of "Ivy Day in the Committee Room" and "The Boarding House" and all of "An Encounter." Joyce understandably felt concern for the integrity of his collection, but he also was anxious to get his work into print. His correspondence with Richards reflects his efforts to satisfy the objections of his publisher without doing irreparable damage to his stories. Although Joyce concentrated most of his energy on defending passages threatened by Richards's blue pencil, he did modify portions of *Dubliners* in an effort to reach a compromise.

In a July 6th letter Joyce announced that he had reworked "Two Gallants," "Ivy Day in the Committee Room," "Grace," and "Counterparts," rewritten "The Sisters," rearranged the order of the stories in the middle of the book, and "corrected a few small errors" (*Letters*, II.143). The changes ultimately had little impact on Richards who in October decided against bringing out *Dubliners*, but they have a great significance for anyone interested in an examination of the evolution of Joyce's artistic ability. The pattern of the revisions suggests that something beyond a desire to mollify his publisher motivated Joyce. While some revisions address directly certain objections that Richards had made, others rework material that had never come under criticism. Furthermore, despite Joyce's statement that he had "injured these stories by these deletions," the emendations consistently reflect the growing sophistication of his creative powers.[14]

The most elaborate alterations appear in "The Sisters" where, as Florence Walzl demonstrates with meticulous precision, the extensive revisions reshape the story and strengthen the unity of the entire collection. Although it does not touch on the matter directly, Walzl's detailed analysis, focusing attention on Joyce's concern for formal consistency throughout *Dubliners*, lends support to my theory that alterations made in the stories developed less from pressure from his publisher than from new attitudes of his own toward the text. Richards's impact ultimately was neither destructive nor superfluous, for it spurred Joyce to hone the connotative and denotative power of his prose. At the same time, while Richards's censoriousness acted as an important goad for revision, it was Joyce's own emerging artistic maturity that stood as the shaping force behind the changes.

"Counterparts" serves as a prime example of how the development of Joyce's stylistic sensibilities and the modifications precipitated by urging from Richards converge to focus attention on the central character. In the revised version of this story, through free indirect discourse, the degree of influence exerted by mimetic forms begins to correspond more closely with that of diegetic ones. Farrington's consciousness comes to dominate the reader's perceptions of the action, and at only a few points does the narration move forward free of the shaping impact of his voice. This shift of perspective particularly stands out in the passage that Joyce inserted to replace the one to which Richards objected. As first composed, the offending lines read as follows:

> Farrington said he wouldn't mind having the far one and began to smile
> at her but when Weathers offered to introduce her he said "No, he was

only chaffing" because he knew he had not money enough. She continued to cast bold glances at him and changed the position of her legs often and when she was going out she brushed against his chair and said "Pardon!" in a Cockney accent." (*JJA*, IV.85)

Contrasting the original with his subsequent version illuminates techniques used to enhance the characterization of Farrington and to adjust the woman's function in the episode. In his revision Joyce expands selected details and removes references that might distract attention from the mood developing within Farrington. Weathers's offer to play the pander and Farrington's concern for the state of his finances disappear, as do all traces of direct discourse. Intransitive verbs—"wandered," "gazed," "glanced"—and present participles—"striking," "reaching," "staring"—combine with an accumulation of adjectives and prepositional phrases to evoke a languid, sensual atmosphere. These changes heighten the mimetic effect of the account of Farrington's aroused interest.[15]

Farrington's eyes wandered at every moment in the direction of one of the young women. There was something striking in her appearance. An immense scarf of peacock blue muslin was wound round her hat and knotted in a great bow under her chin; she wore bright yellow gloves, reaching to the elbow. Farrington gazed admiringly at the plump arm which she moved very often and with much grace; and, when after a little time she answered his gaze, he admired still more her large dark brown eyes. The oblique staring expression in them fascinated him. She glanced at him once or twice and, when the party was leaving the room, she brushed against his chair and said *O, pardon!* in a London accent. He watched her leave the room in the hope that she would look back at him but he was disappointed. (*JJA*, V.218–19)

From a pragmatic point of view, the new paragraph satisfies Richards's objections by removing descriptions of the woman's "bold glances" and of her tendency to shift "the position of her legs often," but it has a deeper aesthetic impact. It realigns the dynamics of the action. In reworking the narration, Joyce replaces a description that alternates attention between the man and the woman with one that centers the reader in Farrington's consciousness, the structuring perspective of the story. The discourse slowly unfolds the details of dress and gesture that arouse the man's sexual interest. Each article or action builds upon the impressions that precede it. Joyce need not expand upon Farrington's lust. The reader experiences its development with him. Farrington's attitudes have so informed the constitution of the scene that they work subtle changes on the woman herself. She no longer sounds like a Cockney, but, in keeping with Farrington's expectations, she speaks with a possibly more sophisticated if less specific London accent. She behaves not as an aggressive flirt but as a passive beauty. In short, she has ceased to function as an independent character. Instead she becomes a standard, allowing the reader to measure the drunkenness that causes Farrington to see even the most casual of glances as an invitation.

When confronted with the prospect of having to revise significant portions of *Dubliners* to satisfy the public scruples of his publisher, Joyce took the opportunity to integrate sophisticated formal innovations into the discourse. Drawing inspiration from artistic predecessors proved the most familiar and efficient way to achieve such a radical restructuring in a relatively short time. (As an inexperienced writer in Dublin, Joyce had composed several closet dramas modeled on the works of Ibsen, so the process was not entirely new to him.[16]) While controversy with Richards makes clear the immediate impetus for the contextual changes, the motives prompting the numerous stylistic changes prove more difficult to pinpoint.

Joyce's own abilities as an artist refute any suggestions that he needed to copy the methods of others to improve his own works. At the same time, he had a very clear sense of the techniques of his predecessors, and it would be fatuous to assert that none exercised any sort of influence on his revisions. In any case a search for precise sources of borrowings only obscures the real issue. To trace the path of Joyce's expanding paradigm for *Dubliners*, one needs to comprehend the changing artistic aims that lay behind his emendations. Cultivating a sense of the range of writers whose work conditioned these changes will greatly contribute to efforts to clarify the scope of this evolving imaginative repertoire.

Joyce's previous use of free indirect discourse and his fascination with "le mot juste" naturally bring to mind Gustave Flaubert as a model, and Joyce, who probably read *Madame Bovary* while he was a young man in Dublin, certainly was aware of Flaubert's stylistic abilities. He does not, however, seem to have had the opportunity in 1906 to refamiliarize himself with Flaubert's methods. Joyce did not acquire a personal copy of *Madame Bovary* until 1912 or later, and, in the stream of letters to Stanislaus discussing the work of contemporaries, he makes no mention of Flaubert. Instead evidence from Joyce's letters and from his personal library suggests that other writers exercised a more immediate influence.

As noted above Joyce had read some de Maupassant during the summer of 1905 (*Letters*, II.99), and despite reservations about de Maupassant's "moral sense" Joyce had already acquired several volumes of that author's work.[17] Generally, elements of de Maupassant's style present, in rougher form, techniques similar to those Joyce used to revise his work. That very roughness added to de Maupassant's attractiveness as a model, for, while laying down general guidelines for the use of free indirect discourse, the infelicities of de Maupassant's prose encouraged Joyce to exercise a measure of innovation in their application. More particular convergences, however, underscore de Maupassant's usefulness.

Many of Joyce's emendations of *Dubliners* augment the reader's sense of a particular individual, and de Maupassant's artistic strength lies in just this skill for intensifying descriptions of figures in his stories. His characterizations reveal the frailties and tawdriness of human nature through a scrupulous regard for detail. Henry James commented on just such a trait in the introduction to *The Odd Number*, one of the de Maupassant volumes that Joyce owned. "His most brilliantly clever tales deal with the life pervaded, for the most part, by a strong smell of the barnyard and the wine-shop, of the Norman cottage and market-place."[18] More specifically, as indicated by the selections below, taken from *The Odd Number*, de Maupassant had an ability to convey the features of desire—a woman's attractiveness and a man's incipient lust—through a grammar of objectification. De Maupassant's vocabulary suggests a protocol for describing eroticism, outlining for Joyce a pattern for rewriting his depiction of Farrington that would not diffuse the sexual tension of the scene.

> They soon perceived the girl, the only human being who came walking across the land. And they felt themselves rejoiced by the brilliant reflections thrown off by her tin milk-pail under the flame of the sun. They never talked about her. They were simply glad to see her, without understanding why.
>
> She was a great strong wench with red hair, burned by the heat of sunny days, a great sturdy wench of the environs of Paris. ("Two Little Soldiers," 190–91)

> * * * *

> She had such a droll way of speaking, of talking, of laughing, of understanding and of not understanding, of raising her eyes to ask a question (eyes blue as deep water), of stopping her drawing a moment to make a guess at what you meant, of returning once more to work, of saying "yes" or "no"—that I could have listened and looked indefinitely. ("The Wreck," 216)

As I have already intimated, however, suggestion and not prescription informed the influence. The revised paragraph in "Counterparts," through deft alternation between details of figures and dress, reflects the same sort of animal interest, yet it avoids the coarseness so close to the surface of so many of de Maupassant's descriptions.

At this point, Joyce still found much that attracted him in the methods of nineteenth-century French writers, but he also was aware of the limitations inherent in their approach. While *Dubliners* evinces a fascination for the depiction of lower-middle-class mores, it resists descriptions that would present the reader with narrow characterizations.[19] Whether or not these specific passages directly shaped the form of Joyce's short story will probably remain moot. Of greater significance, in terms of Joyce's artistic development, is the growing affinity that one can see, through analogues to de Maupassant's work, between Joyce's writing and particular experimental techniques of the fiction of the period.

Grant Richards's demands caused Joyce to reexamine an integral aspect of his paradigm, but this reassessment did not inevitably lead to the suppression. Instead, the experience seems to have sharpened Joyce's awareness of how contemporaries, through the judicious use of graphic detail, had produced effects similar to those he wished to achieve. Thinking through his publisher's objections with these options in mind encouraged Joyce's impulse towards multiplicity as he decided which passages he could allow himself to change and which had to be kept intact. Additionally, in revising the procedure for using explicit descriptions and for relying on suggestion, he also refined his concept of the role that the reader would play in forming a text for the stories.

A passage added to "The Boarding House," providing the details of Bob Doran's seduction, gives a precise sense of how Joyce had come to view the use of explicit detail in his work:

> Then late one night as he was undressing for bed she had tapped at his door, timidly. She wanted to relight her candle at his for hers had been blown out by a gust. It was her bath night. She wore a loose open combing jacket of printed flannel. Her white instep shone in the opening of her furry slippers and the blood glowed warmly behind her perfumed skin. From her hands and wrists too as she lit and steadied her candle a faint perfume arose. (*JJA*, V.179)

Like the passage from "Counterparts," this selection uses techniques reminiscent of de Maupassant to underscore the sensual power of physical elements within the description. At the same time, as in the "Counterparts" revision, Joyce balances details of Polly's dress and figure as he describes her standing at the door. He suppresses the blunt sexuality common in de Maupassant, Zola, and other contemporary French writers by emphasizing her "white instep" and "perfumed skin" and not her more obvious attractions, yet the juxtaposition of vivid description and restrained action charges the scene with erotic tension.

Biographical and bibliographical evidence shows that this reassessment had a permanent impact on Joyce's process of composition. Even after negotiations with Richards came to an end, Joyce continued this pattern of narrative revaluations in reworking portions of the stories in *Dubliners*. The earliest manuscript version of "The Boarding House," for example, a holograph composed in July of 1905, does not contain the lines quoted above. They first appear in the late Maunsel page proofs. No intermediate versions of the story exist, and so one cannot fix the date of the addition more precisely than sometime between 1905 and 1911 or 1912. Its frank tone and explicit detail parallel the form of the lines from "Counterparts" that Richards wished Joyce to delete, but Richards makes no reference to this particular passage in any of his letters. This suggests that Joyce composed the addition after his technical powers had matured, probably during revisions noted in his correspondence made in the final months of 1906 (cf. *Letters*, II.182.186.192–93).

Even at this stage, however, the growth of Joyce's stylistic sensibilities did not trace a linear path of evolution. Rather his impulse seems to have been to embrace forms eclectically instead of following the dictates of a clearly defined school or movement. His attitude towards the writings of Oscar Wilde illuminates some of the principles guiding his survey of the works of a variety of authors for forms suitable for achieving specific effects. Most of Wilde's thematic and formal interests diverge sharply from Joyce's own concerns. Nonetheless over the years that he lived abroad Joyce acquired a number of Wilde's books, including a heavily marked copy of *The Picture of Dorian Gray*,[20] and, as a fellow Irish artist and iconoclast, Wilde subsequently received a great deal of allusive attention in both *Ulysses* and *Finnegans Wake*. I believe, however, that Wilde exerted an even earlier influence on Joyce's style.

In an August of 1906 letter, Joyce analyzes *The Picture of Dorian Gray*, detailing what he found satisfying and dissatisfying in the work: "Some chapters are like Huysmans, catalogued atrocities, lists of perfumes and instruments. The central idea is fantastic. . . . Wilde seems to have had some good intentions in writing it—some wish to put himself before the world—but the book is rather crowded with lies and epigrams" (*Letters*, II.150). The letter provides ample clues for ascertaining the specific targets of Joyce's criticism. Allusions to hedonistic excesses recur throughout *Dorian Gray*, and Basil Hallward catalogues Dorian's in a long indictment immediately before his murder.[21] The "lists of perfumes and instruments," taken directly from Huysmans's *A Rebours*, make up most of chapter eleven (*DG*, 133–40). And the "lies and epigrams" that crowd the book, presented through the vapid philosophizing of Sir Henry Wotton, appear almost every time that he speaks: "Faithfulness is to the emotional life what consistency is to the life of the intellect— simply a confession of failure. Faithfulness! I must analyze it some day. The passion for property is in it. There are many things that we would throw away if we were not afraid that others might pick them up" (*DG*, 49). The precise nature of Wilde's "good intentions" remains less clear, but Joyce's previous remarks on other writers provide some likely answers.

Wilde, no less than Joyce, took pride in his artistic temperament, but Wilde chose to use a calculated artificiality to outline the paradigm of his novel. Although one result produced a form antithetic to the Hardyesque methods that Joyce had already disparaged, it evinced a subtler, though no less insistent, didacticism. In qualifying his admiration for the concept with an account of the flaws that he perceives in its execution, Joyce draws attention both to the problem of the delicate manipulation of sensuous detail and to the close relationship between style and artistic temperament. While the remarks indicate an admiration for Wilde's candid depictions of creative freedom, Joyce also recognizes the drawbacks of undisciplined elaboration. His comments do not suggest that he saw Wilde's work as a model for his own, but they do indicate that he may have learned important lessons from Wilde.

In the following excerpt from *Dorian Gray* one can clearly see these contrasting strengths and weaknesses. Its extravagant language balances gesture and rhythm to create a suggestion of languid license, but the selection also points up the excesses that Joyce avoided in his own refinements of *Dubliners*.

> A week later Dorian Gray was sitting in the conservatory at Selby Royal talking to the pretty Duchess of Monmouth, who with her husband, a jaded-looking man of sixty, was amongst his guests. It was tea-time, and the mellow light of the huge lace-covered lamp that stood on the table lit up the delicate china and hammered silver of the service at which the Duchess was presiding. Her white hands were moving daintily among the cups, and her full red lips were smiling at something that Dorian had whispered to her. Lord Henry was lying back in a silk-draped wicker chair looking at them. On a peach-coloured divan sat Lady Narborough pretending

to listen to the Duke's description of the last Brazilian beetle that he had added to his collection. Three young men in elaborate smoking-suits were handing tea-cakes to some of the women. The house-party consisted of twelve people, and there were more expected to arrive on the next day. (*DG*, 193)

The Duchess of Monmouth's "full red lips" and "the delicate china and hammered silver" accentuating her hands work on the reader's perception of static voluptuousness. The succession of images conveys an ennui congruent to the context, but their repletion forces the reader to struggle against glut. While the result may have suited Wilde's intentions, the indulgence produces sensations too narrow for Joyce's paradigm. As Joyce noted, *Dorian Gray* has an exaggerated richness of detail that flirts with self-parody. Much of the force of Wilde's narration comes out of a self-conscious, syntactical prodigality that Joyce in his own work chose to eschew in favor of more focused descriptive details.

In his own revisions of *Dubliners*, Joyce avoids this paralysis through a sensitivity to the juxtaposition of verbal resonances. By fusing gesture and rhythm, he produces descriptions that set in motion normally inanimate objects. In "Counterparts" the force and the cadence of the description of the woman whom Farrington admires direct the reader through the paragraph with the same efficacy as curves and colors that guide one through the typography of a painting. Through Farrington's eyes the putatively static scene remains animated, moving from the "peacock blue muslin" scarf "knotted in a great bow under her chin" to "bright yellow gloves" serving to highlight "a plump arm." Likewise, in "The Boarding House," as Polly Mooney stands at Bob Doran's door, "furry slippers" call attention to her "white instep," and perfume rises "[f]rom her hands and wrists" as she relights her candle. Like the rising desire it suggests, the description rivets attention on the figure while ranging over its features.

Identification of artistic models can generally go no further than informed speculation, and others may see different authors as more significant sources for Joyce's techniques in his revisions. Such disagreements are, however, of secondary importance. In Joyce's creative responses to the prose of his immediate predecessors, one finds the principles constituting the artistic sensibilities that would govern all of his subsequent writing. In his drive to unify his aesthetic and artistic standards, Joyce was selecting parameters that would both evoke and deny the tradition from which he emerged. Thus one cannot escape analogues between Joyce and the work of his literary antecedents, for his writing acknowledges its intimate relation to the milieu from which it emerged even as it asserts its independence.

Although he continued to develop his craft throughout his life, at the time he had composed the first draft of "The Dead," Joyce's creative powers had reached a level that significantly surpassed the form of his inchoate novel *Stephen Hero*. His decision to abandon it in favor of the more innovative style of *Portrait* coincided with writing "The Dead," but it came as the culmination of a series of artistic choices made over the three years spent working on *Dubliners*. During this period Joyce had developed a firm control over his technical skills and had evolved a unified concept of his collection. He continued to refine "The Dead" after his initial draft and polished the form of other stories as well, but by early 1907 he had recognized the crucial features of his artistic temperament and his creative abilities and brought them into harmony. They had acquired the characterizing features that would shape his mature work, and they demand our attention if we hope to exploit the imaginative potential of the remainder of the canon.

LEEDS METROPOLITAN
UNIVERSITY
LIBRARY

III | *Stephen Hero*: From the Nineteenth Century to Modernism

The stylistic modifications introduced into the stories in *Dubliners* bring to the foreground creative powers in Joyce's writing markedly beyond those evinced in the narrative of *Stephen Hero*. The demands that these forms place upon the act of comprehension suggest that, through the process of composing these works, Joyce came to a profound understanding of the dynamics of the relationship between reader and writer. As a result, the narratives of his stories articulate artistic perspectives that overtly rely upon the reader to bear a considerable measure of creative responsibility for defining the factors governing any texts derived from his work.

This virtuosity in *Dubliners* might cause one to dismiss an examination of *Stephen Hero* at this point in the study as anachronistic. Yet, as I noted in the previous chapter, *Stephen Hero* marks a crucial stage in Joyce's artistic development, and it would be a mistake to relegate it to an ancillary position in Joyce's canon—either as a piece of juvenilia or as the rough sketch of later work. Rather it takes on reflective significance in relation to Joyce's other work. Thus, despite its preceding *Dubliners* in order of composition, one comes to a clearer apprehension of the traits characterizing *Stephen Hero* by juxtaposing it between *Dubliners* and *A Portrait of the Artist as a Young Man*. In terms of creative force, for example, one can read in the *Dubliners* stories stylistic gestures that move away from the traditional monologic discourse precisely because they stand out from the narrative patterns established in *Stephen Hero*. As such, the factors distinguishing Joyce's first attempt at prose fiction from his subsequent work form a benchmark, testifying to the aesthetic attitudes, the artistic temperament, to which Joyce subscribed at the beginning of his career. Examining it in light of the revisions made on *Dubliners* allows one to understand more clearly the paradigmatic advances that Joyce had to make before he could begin to compose *Portrait*.

I have already presented examples of how the influence of selective artistic antecedents led to the discrete employment in *Dubliners* of stylistic traits that would come to dominate the structure of *Portrait*. At the same time, I have asserted that Joyce's creative evolution did not proceed solely through the imitation of his literary predecessors. Calculating the balance between the inspiration of others and the growth of personal talent has become the central task of the opening chapters of this study, and *Stephen Hero*, with its reminders of Joyce's early aims and its hints at his later achievements, acts as a crucial nexus between the parallel tracks of this investigation. In the fragment of the novel still extant one finds early instances of formal experimentation adumbrating techniques that Joyce would later apply with much greater consistency. In addition, the work's paradigmatic suppositions outline an approach to artistic considerations, later modified in *Portrait*, not specifically dealt with in the structure of *Dubliners*. Thus *Stephen Hero* holds out the possibility of illuminating the stylistic protocols, especially those relating to free indirect discourse, as well as the broader aesthetic assumptions directing the evolution of Joyce's subsequent works.

Despite this promise, however, a number of the facts relating to the composition of *Stephen Hero* converge to discourage one from seeing it as more than an extremely remote ancestor to *Portrait*.[1] Joyce began writing the novel early in 1904, even before he had begun creating the first stories of *Dubliners*.[2] By the time that he ceased work on it in June of 1905, he had written 914 pages, in his own estimation "about half the book."[3] All existing evidence suggests that, in its basic constitution at least, *Stephen Hero* took a form strikingly different from that of *Portrait*. Although most of the original manuscript of the novel no longer exists, in the portion still remaining the narrative style bears evidence of the strong influence of traditional nineteenth-century novelistic conventions. By extrapolation, the sheer bulk of what had been written, presumably tracing in detail the life of Stephen Daedalus from birth through his first year at the university, suggests none of the gaps, the evocative omissions, that have come to characterize Joyce's emergence through *Portrait* as a modern writer. Nonetheless, as I will show in the remainder of this chapter, while the surviving episodes of *Stephen Hero* certainly give one a profound sense of the conventions that Joyce later chose to abandon when writing *Portrait*, they also present instances of a narrative undercurrent offering a subtler view of the discourse: evidence of the stylistic impulses that would come to maturity in the later work.

Admittedly, disparities in structure and in emphasis make any connections that one would care to posit between *Stephen Hero* and *Portrait* problematic. From what can be determined from the eleven surviving chapters making up the "university episode" (XV–XXV, following Gabler's revised numbering system),[4] the narrative of *Stephen Hero* concerns itself primarily with the chronicling of day-to-day events and not with the depiction of radical shifts in consciousness—like those occurring between chapters in *Portrait*. Yet, although such a divarication between tight linear progression and loose episodic development makes the framework of the two novels appear antithetical, one can still mark stages in the evolution of specific stylistic inclinations through an examination of the forms of the two works. Passages within *Stephen Hero* that present examples of Joyce's early manipulation of narrative voice, when contrasted with selections from *Portrait*, allow one to see a progressive development in the sophisticated manipulation of narrative possibilities—primarily through an increasing use of free indirect discourse. Further, as the emphasis of narration shifts from expansive description to dramatic concentration, one can discover frequent instances of the stylistic modulation that will characterize the rhythm of the discourses of Joyce's subsequent writing.

A fluency for shaping complex stylistic elements to mirror contextual diversity stands as one of the signal qualities of the compositional process of *Portrait*. In fact, one might argue that the consistent virtuosity of the narrative so conditions the reader that one tends to take its achievement for granted. *Stephen Hero*, on the other hand, with only selective evidence of the emergence of this trait allows the reader to remain sensitive to the nuances of Joyce's prose. Its discourse does not yet demonstrate the consistent ability to combine precisely the extent of description essential for the presentation of coherent images and the concentration or distribution of perspective needed to produce a range of satisfying readings. Further, although in discrete instances the structure of the discourse shows some awareness of the impact that the application of innovative stylistic methods can produce, the narrative does not yet establish a command of the full potential of such techniques.

Passages that appear in the initial pages of *Stephen Hero* describing Stephen's expository talents reflect examples of both these strengths and these weaknesses in Joyce's early efforts at integrating free indirect discourse into the narrative: "Stephen's style of writing, though it was over affectionate towards the antique and even the obsolete and too easily rhetorical, was remarkable for a certain crude originality of expression" (*SH*, 27). The discourse goes on to elaborate upon the description of Stephen's creative consciousness, and "antique and even obsolete" terms creep into the exposition. As a result, the tone of the narration, following the pattern set by Stephen's own essays, shifts from the descriptive to the rhetorical and introduces a competing voice to counterpoint the one already established.

> He gave himself no great trouble to sustain the boldnesses which were expressed or implied in his essays. He threw them out as sudden defence-works while he was busy constructing the enigma of a manner. For the youth had been apprised of another crisis and he wished to make ready for the shock of it. On account of such manoeuvres he came to be regarded as a very unequilibrated young man who took more interest than young men usually take in theories which might be permitted as pastimes. (*SH*, 27)

This modulation of diction affects the whole rhythm of the passage, and in turn it encourages the attentive reader to begin to engage the question of the perspectives shaping the discourse. The intrusion of traits associated with Stephen's nature and with his view of the world compels one to give some consideration to the possibility that the narrative has begun to act as an ironic commentary upon itself. To my mind, the fact that such a conclusion is not patently obvious strengthens rather than undermines the formal impact of the passage, for the ambiguity enhances the scope of possible responses by the reader. Furthermore, since this stylistic gesture stands as one of the central elements of the formal structure of *Portrait*, its appearance in *Stephen Hero* provides one with the opportunity to contrast some of Joyce's early efforts with his fully developed versions of this technique.[5]

Throughout the descriptions of Stephen's university experiences, alternative stylistic elements continue to intrude episodically into segments of the discourse. Each appearance necessarily contributes to the tempering of the reader's perception of the dominant narrative view, as it inculcates traits closely reflecting Stephen's own perspectives into the discourse. The process, however, does not yet show the smoothly fluctuating design evident in later works. In fact in some instances one might even feel that this technique exercises an influence on the discourse at once too profound and too subtle.

As noted above, the narrative often manifests discursive inclinations paralleling the tendency to overwrite noted in Stephen's prose. This intensifies the impact of Stephen's nature upon the reader's perceptions of the work, but Joyce has not yet mastered the ability to balance the tension created by the resultant competing voices. Consequently, specific portions of the discourse on occasion blur the distinction between weaknesses of the central character and those of the author. To illustrate my point, allow me to cite two passages drawn from chapter XVI describing Stephen's feelings as he walks across Dublin. The first deftly integrates into the narrative perspective the painful, pedantic self-consciousness of Stephen's emerging artistic nature. "The damp Dublin winter seemed to harmonize with his inward sense of unreadiness and he did not follow the least of feminine provocations through tortuous, unexpected ways any more zealously than he followed through ways even less satisfying the nimble movements of the elusive one" (*SH*, 37). Near the end of this passage, however, a second selection suggests a much more tenuous sense of the direction the narrative should take. "One day he passed on his homeward journey through Fairview. At the fork of the roads before the swampy beach a big dog was recumbent. From time to time he lifted his muzzle in the vapourous air, uttering a prolonged sorrowful howl" (*SH*, 38). While the discourse seems in its context to be a description disassociated from the consciousness of any character, it still labors under the influence of the pedantries and the infelicities of expression linked to Stephen. The inflated language depicting the mundane scene—"homeward journey," "recumbent," "vapourous air," "a prolonged sorrowful howl"—invites one to respond to an apparently ironic gesture. At the same time by not providing more specific guidelines for the ironic interpretation, it leaves the reader with the difficult task of separating awkwardness from artifice.

More often than not, however, applications of free indirect discourse lead to interpretive complexities that adumbrate the more aesthetically satisfying forms of Joyce's later work. In general the results tend to be less polished than the manipulations of *Portrait*, but they do demonstrate a similar ability to undermine narrative detachment with the contrapuntal voices of a range of characters. In the opening pages of chapter XV, for example, the consciousness of the university bursar enters into the narrative in a passage that undergoes a subtle metamorphosis from description into exposition.

> He performed his duties with great unction and was often to be seen looming in the hall watching the coming and going of the students. He insisted on punctuality: a minute or so late once or twice—he would not mind that so much; he would clap his hands and make some cheery reproof. But what made him severe was a few minutes lost every day: it disturbed the proper working of the classes. (23–24)

This segment opens with an apparently detached depiction, but even in the first sentence consciously ambiguous touches—words like "unction" and "looming"—color our perception of the bursar. A position more intimately engaged with the nature of its subject begins to evolve in the third sentence. The narrative continues to enforce upon the reader a sense of the bursar's ludicrousness, but it does so by allowing the fussy tone of his speech patterns to control the development of the discourse: "a minute or so late once or twice—he would not mind that so much; he would clap his hands and make some cheery reproof. But what made him severe was a few minutes lost every day: it disturbed the proper working of the classes." As in the selection cited earlier, the integration into the discourse of voices with apparently competing aims blunts distinctions between the object or person being observed and the voice providing the description. As a consequence, the determination of the precise ironic implications of the passage becomes the responsibility of the reader, and presumably can vary with each encounter with the work.

Despite the uneven quality of the passages quoted above, they provide insights crucial to evaluating the creative changes that Joyce underwent in 1905 and 1906. One can discern in them the imaginative power that would consistently inform the structure of his subsequent writing, but these initial efforts lack the self-confidence necessary for prolonged application. Writing *Stephen Hero* gave Joyce a sense of his artistic potential, but it also emphasized his need to cultivate models that would offer guidance without circumscribing personal growth. The transformation of *Stephen Hero* into *Portrait* reflects his efforts to achieve that balance. For the remainder of the chapter, I propose to outline the specific stylistic changes that grew out of work on *Stephen Hero*. In chapter four I will examine the paradigmatic influence of other writers.

With regard to free indirect discourse in particular, Joyce did not so much alter the mode of its application in *Portrait* as accelerate the process by which the narrative confronted the reader with alternative approaches to thematic recuperation. The impact of free indirect discourse upon Joyce's style and upon the reader's perception of the work calls to mind the distinctions made by Roland Barthes. In *S/Z* Barthes differentiates between the innovative, *scriptible* (writerly) fiction and the classical, *lisible* (readerly) fiction. Barthes emphasizes the tendency of *lisible* fiction to put the reader in the passive position of merely receiving information. "To end, to fill, to join, to unify—one might say that this is the basic requirement of the *readerly,* as though it were prey to some obsessive fear: that of omitting a connection."[6] From this perspective, it would seem that *Stephen Hero* captures a moment of Joyce's aesthetic transition. It maintains a commitment to the production of *lisible* works, but it also evinces a desire to begin the implementation of *scriptible* fiction.

Despite the flexibility produced by discrete instances of free indirect discourse, the general narrative line of *Stephen Hero* appears to have been tightly plotted with relatively few opportunities for interpretive variation. The discourse of *Portrait*, on the other hand, with its fragmented, accretive rebellions against family, church, and state, depends upon the active engagement of the reader to unfold completely. Intentional ambiguity stands at the center of each episode of *Portrait*, inviting and denying each provisional reconciliation of antinomy. In composing it Joyce has expanded the reader's alternatives and responsibilities. Instead of being confronted with a linear chronology that one must recuperate as a *lisible* text, gaps in the narrative that can be bridged in a variety of ways endow the reader with the freedom to construct a range of *scriptible* texts. When one contrasts these gaps with the surfeit of information of *Stephen Hero*, both the achievement of the later work and the contribution of the earlier one become apparent.

Although I will discuss them in greater detail in chapter five, let me for now simply touch upon the impact generated by the pattern of significant omissions that work to engage us in the active creation of a text for *Portrait*, omissions conspicuously avoided in the composition of *Stephen Hero*. The Icaran form of *Portrait*, characterizing the end of one chapter and the beginning of the next, has become a critical commonplace. Each chapter ends with Stephen at an emotional highpoint, soaring like Icarus. Subsequently, each following chapter opens with Stephen in a depressed or degraded frame of mind, metaphysically analogous to Icarus's fall into the sea.[7] What seems to me most significant is not the flux of Stephen's emotions but the marked change in emotional, intellectual, and artistic development that each instance brackets. Each episode ends with Stephen on the brink of a new discovery about himself and his relation to the world he inhabits. Each subsequent chapter begins with Stephen so accustomed to his new level of maturity that it has become a source of oppression rather than of delight. The period encompassing the transition from Stephen's initial wonder to his sated ennui occurs in the gap between the chapters. To continue with the narrative, we readers dexterously, and perhaps unconsciously, bridge these gaps between episodes by adjusting our perception of Stephen's nature. These adjustments necessarily affect our continuing perception of his consciousness as free indirect discourse reintroduces his point of view into the narrative.

The movement requires one to do more than simply elide elements marking a break in narrative chronology, for it involves a continual reacquaintance with a re-formed Stephen, determined by the reader and not by prescriptive descriptions within the narrative. The discourse defines the gap through parameters so large as to allow one the choice of a range of strategies for responding to the new elements of Stephen's nature, and as a consequence it enables one to participate in the creation of the subsequent interpretive path of the work. In terms of this study the specific choices are less significant than the possibilities affirmed by the condition itself, for the gaps between and (in a somewhat diminished form) within the chapters reflect both Joyce's new mastery of the discourse and an increased confidence in the reader's ability to deal with a more overtly *scriptible* text.

It would be an oversimplification, however, to see the discourse of *Portrait* as enforcing a revaluation of the role of the reader simply through the omission of details supposedly essential to the linear comprehension of various descriptions. Joyce's mature sense of the creative potential inherent in his thematic material rested on a deeper artistic awareness, relating to the impact to be derived from a fluctuating structure within the discourse. The variety of this approach becomes evident when one examines the manipulation of passages borrowed from *Stephen Hero*, whether through expansion or contraction, to accommodate dramatic tension within a significantly broader paradigm.

In *Stephen Hero*, for example, Joyce devotes five pages (*SH*, 42–47) to a scene at the Daniels's house where Stephen reencounters Emma Clery. There the narrative uses the meeting as a vehicle for presenting a detailed account of the emotions that Stephen feels towards his society: a desire for the acceptance and approval of those around him crossed with a disdain for their bourgeois mentality and forced familiarity. Although the discourse highlights Stephen's conflicting impulses, it consists basically of a rather straightforward account of these emotions, leaving little room for anything but a *lisible* response by the reader. In *Portrait* the narrative shifts the scene to Emma's own house, and condenses it into a single paragraph, relegating it to a recollection that punctuates Stephen's composition of his villanelle:

> Having written [the lines] out he lay back on the lumpy pillow, murmuring them again. The lumps of knotted flock under his head reminded him of the lumps of knotted horsehair in the sofa of her parlour on which he used to sit, smiling or serious, asking himself why he had come, displeased with her and with himself, confounded by the print of the Sacred Heart above the untenanted sideboard. He saw her approach him in a lull of the talk and beg him to sing one of his curious songs. Then he saw himself sitting at the old piano, striking chords softly from its speckled keys and singing, amid the talk which had risen again in the room, to her who

leaned beside the mantelpiece a dainty song of the Elizabethans, a sad and sweet loth to depart, the victory chant of Agincourt, the happy air of Greensleeves. While he sang and she listened, or feigned to listen, his heart was at rest but when the quaint old songs had ended and he heard again the voices in the room he remembered his own sarcasm: the house where young men are called by their christian names a little too soon. (*P,* 219)

Stephen's somewhat nostalgic remembrance retains the naturalistic detail that had characterized the earlier version of the episode, but in this subsequent form the reader must draw impressions from a discourse that is greatly abbreviated and much more ambivalent. Although the narrative borrows key phrases from *Stephen Hero,* they lack the discursive support provided in the previous work. They stand in relative isolation and must now convey the full significance of impressions previously developed over entire paragraphs: "[L]umps of knotted horsehair in the sofa" and "the print of the Sacred Heart" imply rather than establish a scene of middle-class shabbiness unfolding according to unspoken parameters derived from the influence of Catholicism; "one of his curious songs . . . a dainty song of the Elizabethans" obliquely invites one to recognize Stephen's position as an aesthete without prescribing it unconditionally; and "the house where young men are called by their christian names a little too soon" suggests without confirming the priggish aloofness of Stephen demonstrated so clearly in the earlier novel.

In brief, the revised scene discards the declamatory asides of the longer version that had blunted the subtle features of the conflicting feelings causing Stephen's discomfort. This new form testifies to Joyce's increased artistic confidence: both in his ability as a writer to define strong and contrasting emotions in a few deft phrases and in our power (and our willingness) as readers to create a range of texts within the broad parameters defined by the episode. Because the passage omits the conventional lexical clues that would signal a clear expression of Stephen's consciousness, the reader, conditioned by the accumulation of instances of free indirect discourse elsewhere in the work, can derive meanings according to the weight he or she chooses to assign to the voices of Stephen and of the narrator in the descriptive account. In *Portrait* Stephen's bemused questioning of his own motivations for visiting the Clery house, Emma's request that he play the piano, his bitterness when he had finished his performance, all advance the basic action much as they did in *Stephen Hero,* but by the incorporation of the perspectives of Stephen with those of the narrator, the significance of those gestures and feelings always remains open to the provisional response of the reader.

When Joyce integrated into *Portrait* material originally composed for *Stephen Hero*, his revisions did not deal exclusively with compression. In fact, in a number of instances, prosaic segments of his earlier work became the kernel for elaborate lyrical descriptions underscoring Stephen's emotional turmoil. One such mundane passage appears at the close of chapter XV of *Stephen Hero* where the narrative tersely outlines the routine of Stephen's daily journey from the Daedalus home to the university:

> Every morning he rose and came down to breakfast. After breakfast he took the tram for town, settling himself on the front seat outside with his face to the wind. He got down off the tram at Amiens St Station instead of going on to the Pillar because he wished to partake in the morning life of the city. This morning walk was pleasant for him and there was no face that passed him on its way to its commercial prison but he strove to pierce to the motive centre of its ugliness. It was always with a feeling of displeasure that he entered the Green and saw on the far side the gloomy building of the College. (*SH*, 30)

The description of a similar scene in *Portrait* occupies fully the first ten pages of chapter V, following Stephen as he leaves the depressing atmosphere of his family's kitchen to walk across the city.

The cursory allusions to Stephen's mood found in the passage from *Stephen Hero* undergo elaborate expansion, and his feelings modulate the tone of the narrative. The details of city life produce a number of often conflicting responses as a multitude of succeeding images confront him. After some initial vacillation, Stephen's fascination with Dublin overbears his contempt for his surroundings, and a range of emotions dilutes the force of the misanthropy expressed in the passage from *Stephen Hero*. "He drove their echoes even out of his heart with an execration: but, as he walked down the avenue and felt the grey morning light falling about him through the dripping trees and smelt the strange wild smell of the wet leaves and bark, his soul was loosed of her miseries" (*P*, 176).

The change in the rhythm of the discourse, in some ways less complex than that of preceding episodes, does not represent a stylistic regression. Rather it demonstrates a willingness to engage the consciousness of the reader in a prolonged encounter with the Dublin milieu that has shaped Stephen's nature. Through this retrospective gesture the narrative allows us to balance Stephen's final attitudes toward his environment, harshly articulated in the remainder of the chapter, against our own impressions developing under the influence but not under the complete control of Stephen's views.

As the account of Stephen's sensations unfolds, control of the descriptions deftly moves between narrator-bound indirect discourse and free indirect discourse. While the narrative voice continues to assert its presence, it also draws heavily on Stephen's feelings in developing impressions of the scene. One instance, for example, appears in a paragraph of descriptions alternately presented in the accents of Stephen and of the narrative voice. From the opening sentence Stephen's own sardonic opinions begin to insinuate themselves into the introduction of his confidant, Cranly. Near the end of the passage Stephen's rhetorical presence takes control of the discourse, offering insights related as much to Stephen as to Cranly.

> Why was it that when he thought of Cranly he could never raise before his mind the entire image of his body but only the image of the head and face? . . . the face of a severed head or deathmask . . . a priestlike face . . . priest-like in the lips that were long and bloodless and faintly smiling . . . it was the face of a guilty priest who heard confessions of those whom he had not the power to absolve. . . . (*P,* 178)

The description says little directly about the elements of Cranly's temperament, but it infers a great deal from Stephen's physiognomical response to Cranly's features. The elements of Stephen's attitude that are revealed make us aware of the simultaneous attraction and repulsion that he feels not just for Cranly but for everything in Dublin society that his friend represents. At the same time, the filtering of some of the descriptions preceding it in the paragraph through the mediating consciousness of the narrator enhances the legitimacy of the impression: it becomes more than the isolated opinions of a petulant young man for a friend who does not share his iconoclastic views.

Joyce, of course, is aware that an extended description informed by Stephen's nature would disrupt the balance of competing views that he wishes to create. Consequently, after accustoming the reader to descriptions conditioned, through indirect discourse, by Stephen's voice, Joyce introduces an aura of ambiguity that disrupts expectations and impels an active engagement with production in the *scriptible* text. In the paragraph following the description of Cranly, the narrator records five lines of bad poetry extemporaneously composed by Stephen.

> The ivy whines upon the wall
> And whines and twines upon the wall
> The ivy whines upon the wall

> The yellow ivy on the wall
> Ivy, ivy up the wall.
> (*P.* 179)

Then a gloss appears.

> Did any one ever hear such drivel? Lord Almighty! Who ever heard of
> ivy whining on a wall? Yellow ivy: That was all right. Yellow ivory also.
> And what about ivory ivy? (*P.* 179)

The open-ended quality of the comments leaves to the reader the
task of identifying the source of the voice. If one settles upon the narrator, the passage becomes ironic. If the choice falls upon Stephen, it
becomes self-reflexive. And if Cranly is selected, it becomes a reflection
of the harsh environment opposing Stephen's clumsy attempts at creativity. Because of the alternatives, any decision that we make necessarily remains provisional, for it exists under the influence of the alternative
possibilities of interpretation. As a result the selection demonstrates a
level of ambiguity that makes it infinitely more complex than the ur-
version in *Stephen Hero*.

The indeterminacy of this passage reminds readers of the provisionality of any effort to impose a hegemonic view on a portion of the narrative, but Joyce has still other structural variations in mind. In the final
four pages of this description, as Stephen walks with Davin and thinks
of the latter's story of his encounter with a woman in the Ballyhoura
hills, indirect discourse temporarily gives way to dialogue. When the
recollection of the story comes to an end, the dominant narrative voice
seems to reassert itself to present for the reader a summary of the competing emotions that ran through Stephen's consciousness throughout
the walk:

> But the trees in Stephen's Green were fragrant of rain and the rain-
> sodden earth gave forth its mortal odour, a faint incense rising upward
> through the mould from many hearts. The soul of the gallant venal city
> which his elders had told him of had shrunk with time to a faint mortal
> odour rising from the earth and he knew that in a moment when he entered
> the sombre college he would be conscious of a corruption other than that
> of Buck Egan and Burnchapel Whaley. (*P.* 184)

This impression, however, does not last long. Free indirect discourse appears again, but only obliquely, near the end of the passage—"he
knew"; "he would be conscious." Nonetheless, its residual influence,
drawing force from the preceding pages, resounds though the paragraph
and underscores the delicate equilibrium formed by the overlapping of

alternative perceptions. These variations remind us of the more ambivalent, more sophisticated depiction of Stephen that has unfolded, enforcing a much more ambiguous relationship with the institutions of his city than that presented in the conclusion of the original version in *Stephen Hero*.

In the description of the walk across the city, qualitative more than quantitative changes mark the significant development in Joyce's style, and they can well serve to distinguish the contrasting paradigms forming the structures of *Stephen Hero* and of *Portrait*. Joyce's revisions do not simply reflect a search for the mot juste. They signal his intention to convey the conflicting feelings arising within Stephen from a progression of dialectic confrontations taking place at every stage of Stephen's growth.

As one would expect, a reciprocal relationship obtains between the increasingly sophisticated stylistic structure of *Portrait* and the growth in scope and variety of its paradigmatic concerns. Throughout the narration the diversification and the complexity of the formal constitution of the novel encourage the reader to examine a very broad range of potential interpretations inherent within the parameters of its contextual frame. This condition greatly enhances one's creative participation in the formation of texts, especially when compared with the alternatives offered by *Stephen Hero*. A number of parallel sections in the two works reflect this difference, but one scene in particular, the informal debate between Stephen and the dean of studies on the character of language (*P.* 184–90), foregrounds the evolution of ambivalence within the consciousness of Stephen as it appears in *Portrait* from the certitude that had been depicted in the earlier work.

The episode's structural source can be traced to a similar discussion with Father Butt that occurs in *Stephen Hero* (*SH*, 26–29). In each of the two selections, the central events of the action unfold in much the same manner, although the interchange in *Stephen Hero* unfolds over three separate discussions with Father Butt while in *Portrait* the entire conversation takes place during a brief encounter in the Physics Theatre of the university as the dean of studies lights a fire. The striking difference lies in the emotional undercurrent that conditions each scene, for *Portrait* reflects social tensions and emotional equivocations that produce a much subtler rendition of the clash between Stephen and the dean of studies.

In *Stephen Hero*, although the ideas articulated represent polar extremes in attitudes, the discussion remains polite. So great a gulf separates the worlds inhabited by each of the men that it prevents any genuine intellectual engagement from occurring. Father Butt's remarks indicate that he never truly takes Stephen's disagreements seriously. At the same time, Stephen maintains an aura of detachment from Father Butt's good-natured, pragmatic views that never wavers, and his thoughts reflect no hostility towards his opponent.

In *Portrait*, on the other hand, the dean of studies presents a suave but aggressively patronizing figure, not just advocating an alternative perspective but posing a direct threat to Stephen's artistic growth. The dean takes Stephen's views very seriously and does his best to demolish them. With equal poise and determination Stephen confronts this effort to bring his attitudes into line with the quotidian views held by most, and, while inwardly raging, struggles vigorously to blunt the priest's arguments with a veneer of calm:

> [The dean's] courtesy of manner rang a little false, and Stephen looked at the English convert with the same eyes as the elder brother in the parable may have turned on the prodigal. A humble follower in the wake of clamourous conversions, a poor Englishman in Ireland, he seemed to have entered on the stage of jesuit history when that strange play of intrigue and suffering and envy and struggle and indignity had been all but given through—a late comer, a tardy spirit.
>
> *   *   *   *
>
> The little word seemed to have turned a rapier point of [Stephen's] sensitiveness against this courteous and vigilant foe. He felt with a smart of dejection that the man to whom he was speaking was a countryman of Ben Jonson. (*P.* 188–89)

Stephen's anger and contempt grow out of a complex interplay between frustration and alienation, and the condition reflects the conscious application of contextual and formal ambiguity distinguishing the structure of *Portrait* from that of *Stephen Hero*. From the contrast we realize that contextual as well as formal ambivalence characterizes Stephen's relations with his environment. Dissonance both in language and in concepts prevents either man from feeling even the most rudimentary empathy for the other's perspective. Yet while the dean remains comfortably unshaken in his beliefs, Stephen is torn by conflicting doubts.

Stephen will not risk his integrity through even outward conformity, but he cannot help longing for the esteem that such conformity would bring. The priest, with his parochial attitude, personifies the intellectual stagnation of Dublin (paradoxically so since, as Stephen sardonically notes, the priest is an English convert). At the same time the dean of studies also represents one of the institutions that confers the formal, public recognition and encouragement that Stephen desires. Stephen himself indicates the significance of this position by the fact that, throughout the discussion, he never oversteps the bounds of courtesy, never lets his contempt jeopardize the possibility of acceptance. Although he jealously guards his independence, he still retains enough respect for the society against which he rebels to wish for its approval.

In *Portrait* the independence of the narrative voice matched with the force of Stephen's nature creates an atmosphere of ambiguity, as free indirect discourse permeates the narrative to a degree significantly surpassing its presence in *Stephen Hero*. Descriptions neither follow a monological pattern detached from any character, nor do they invariably echo the attitudes of Stephen. Instead, free indirect discourse leads to an expressive polyphony that in turn imposes qualifications on the apparently privileged narrative voice. Stephen's character is not the subject of a detached exposition by an independent narrator, nor is it the revised summation of a mature individual reconciling a series of disparate events into a pattern to suit the personality that has evolved. Rather, the narrative follows the path of Stephen's maturation, clarifying the stages of his development while underscoring the subjectivity of his perceptions.

Consequently, identifying elements of *scriptible* fiction intruding into the generally *lisible* format of *Stephen Hero* helps one recognize the subtler features of the *scriptible* fiction emerging in the structure of *Portrait*. As the next chapter will show, a continuing commitment to stylistic experimentation enabled Joyce to move from a reliance upon a prose style dominated by the conventions of his literary antecedents to an expressiveness characterized by a form that articulated the central elements of Modernism. As one would expect in *scriptible* writing, the most important new feature differentiating the protocol regulating the composition of *Stephen Hero* from that governing the writing in *Portrait* deals with omissions rather than with additions to the narrative structure. These evolutions are evident both in Joyce's shift in concern for temporal conjunction within the discourse and in his realignment with his artistic antecedents.

IV | The Intellectual Heritage of
A Portrait of the Artist as a Young Man

The preceding chapter dwelt upon the way changes in aesthetic and artistic attitudes manifested themselves in Joyce's writing. It highlighted his movement from the position defined by *Stephen Hero* as that of an author stylistically attuned to the literary traditions embraced by his age to the stance adopted in the composition of *Portrait* of a writer operating beyond the limits of those conventions. The innovative narrative features of *Portrait* foreground the elements that most forcefully assert the independence of Joyce's artistic vision, and at first glance they seem to render the differences noted between Joyce and his literary antecedents both stark and absolute. In considering aspects of Joyce's paradigmatic assumptions, however, one should not posit a strict dichotomy between the values shaping Joyce's consciousness and those guiding the writers who preceded him.

In twentieth-century criticism an interest in tradition and individual talent has been under scrutiny since T. S. Eliot and the Leavises began reminding readers of the relevance of the topic. More recently Harold Bloom has reaffirmed the importance of intertextual impulses that lead writers to borrow and to reshape from predecessors whatever methods they feel would assist them in creating new forms of their own. With respect to Joyce, however, as a number of post-structuralist critics have already implied, a great deal of additional work remains to be done before the significance of this relationship is clarified. Specifically, the multiplicity and the variability of allusiveness need to be given greater attention.

The influence of literary antecedents endows *Portrait* with a cultural overlay having a profound impact on the shape of the imaginative responses of both Joyce and his readers. The texts that Joyce derives from reading other authors shape his own writing, not in a linear, analogous fashion but in mutable associative gestures that suggest potential interpretations rather than prescribe a single meaning. In much the same way as each of us reads Joyce, we draw our texts for his work, in degrees varying according to the background of the individual, from texts that he has derived from writings of authors that he has read. Therefore, understanding our own responses to *Portrait*, our sense of how the work can be perceived, involves coming to some sense of Joyce's responses to other artists. To establish the motivations and the assumptions directing the pace of his development, I would like to elaborate upon the intellectual forces connecting Joyce with the literary tradition from which he emerged.

As part of his process of composing *Portrait*, Joyce self-consciously sought to capture the tempo of Dublin life by writing the novel in a series of styles running directly counter to the parochial literary prejudices of his native land. The basic premise of this approach put him in opposition to the conventions laid down by Yeats and the other writers of "the Celtic twilight," for it aligned Joyce both formally and contextually with authors, generally though not exclusively Continental, whose methods sharply diverged from those of the central features of the Irish literary revival and ultimately from the traditional modes of nineteenth-century English prose fiction. One stylistic approach in particular—free indirect discourse—offers a means for establishing both the retrospective and the proleptic elements of this process. Its presence in *Portrait* authorizes consideration of particular writers whose works may have inspired Joyce, and its specific application charts Joyce's paradigmatic growth beyond the innovations of his predecessors.

Tracing Joyce's awareness of free indirect discourse, however, immediately raises problems of association, for it most likely developed accretively as impressions gradually accumulated from exposure to a variety of writers. Since authors had been employing free indirect discourse in forming their narratives for at least one hundred and fifty years before Joyce began writing, the very diffuseness of this condition stands as an impediment to the development of a precise sense of his borrowings.[1] Additionally, because authors apply free indirect discourse to varying degrees and under diverse paradigmatic constraints, one needs to outline, at least in a general way, definite patterns of reading before commenting on the forces shaping Joyce's stylistic development. Fortunately, Joyce's intellectual background offers certain clear guidelines for discerning his paradigmatic impulses.

Joyce's Trieste library, formed between his departure from Ireland in 1904 and his move to Paris in 1920, provides a chronological record of the growth of particular intellectual and creative concerns.[2] Of course, as in any personal library, titles and topics within the collection can in themselves only operate suggestively. Ownership cannot guarantee interest, and interest does not always lead to reading. Nonetheless, when viewed representatively, the catalogue of Joyce's books offers illuminating information relating to his artistic and intellectual inclinations. In simple quantitative terms the accumulation of specific books denotes obvious preferences for certain topics and for particular writers. In addition, marginalia in a select number of the books that Joyce owned call attention to particular features that evidently held his interest. Further, both internal and external evidence—printing information, bills from booksellers, and references in letters—make it possible to determine with a fair degree of precision the approximate date of purchase of many of these books. Those known to have been acquired through 1913 (and possibly some of the books that Joyce bought early in 1914) provide an especially credible starting point for forming a list of authors who attracted his interest while he was reconstituting the paradigm of *Stephen Hero* into the more diverse paradigm of *Portrait*.

When one combines impressions derived from this material with biographical commentary—most notably information detailing the duration and methods of his writing and records of the views that Joyce expressed regarding specific works or authors—the investigation of which figures prove most useful in tracing the growth of his artistic consciousness becomes much less problematic. Patterns of selection emerge, highlighting particular types of writing that held his attention and, derivatively, that exerted the strongest influence. While the identification of specific sources must still remain a matter of speculation, the process described above makes it relatively easy to distill from examinations of various artistic works and figures found in the library the creative issues engaging his attention. This in turn enables one to project formal correlations between traits characterizing both Joyce's reading and his writing, especially regarding the impact of free indirect discourse, and, by extension, of the stylistic protocol functioning in *Portrait*.

The task still, however, remains daunting. Joyce's clarification of his role as an artist and his confidence in his own creative power enabled him during the period between the composition of "The Dead" and the completion of *Portrait* to turn to other authors more freely and less competitively. At the same time identifications of discrete stylistic or contextual resonances based on Joyce's contemporaneous reading will in themselves not clarify the motives behind those borrowings or lead to a more precise sense of how they function in the work. Rather than following that approach, I intend to examine Joyce's writing during this period in terms of general creative inclinations analogous to those of five authors for whom he showed particular regard: Honoré de Balzac, Joseph Conrad, Emile Zola, Charles Dickens, and Gustave Flaubert. Whether or not Joyce derived specific compositional techniques directly from any of these figures stands as an open question. Nonetheless, his active interest in each encourages us to give attention to their writing in search of recurring formal elements that he may have wished to cultivate himself.

Variously, between 1907 and 1914 Joyce manifested a sustained interest in each of these men, but despite my chronological presentation of these authors, I am not asserting a programmatic development of artistic influence. The order that Joyce followed in examining the various works of Balzac, Dickens, Zola, Conrad, and Flaubert can be established only approximately, and the impact of each was certainly modified by exposure to previous and subsequent writers in this group. Additionally, one certainly cannot say with assurance that in each case Joyce went to the work of a particular author with the avowed intention of discovering formal models for his own work. What can be affirmed, as I have already suggested, is that similarities between the writers that I will note in this chapter evince Joyce's concern for diverse manifestations within a clearly defined stylistic tradition—especially in relation to free indirect discourse. Furthermore, these stylistic resonances suggest that these authors—and possibly others writing in a similar fashion—produced a reconditioning of Joyce's intellectual ambiance through a cumulative impact on his own habits of composition.

After a false start in *Stephen Hero*, Joyce amply demonstrates through the formation of *Dubliners* a masterful command of the idiom of naturalistic fiction. This interest must have remained strong during the initial stages of writing *Portrait*, for the catalogue of his personal library details the acquisition of a number of books written by authors committed to this approach. Since most often a particular writer is represented by one or perhaps two titles, one cannot fail to be struck by the significance of Joyce's ownership of thirteen volumes of one of the most prominent proponents of realism in the nineteenth century, Honoré de Balzac. The list includes *Béatrix, The Country Doctor, L'Enfant maudit, La Femme de trente ans, Histoire des treize, Louis Lambert, Mémoires de deux jeunes mariées, Les Paysans, Petites Misères de la vie conjugale, Physiologie du mariage, La Recherche de l'absolu, Les Rivalités*, and *A Woman of Thirty*. All of these works except possibly *A Woman of Thirty*, an English translation of a work Joyce already owned, *La Femme de trente ans*, would have been available to Joyce during the time that he was working on *Portrait*, and the sheer number of Balzac books points to a strong interest.[3] Admittedly, publication data alone stands as the least conclusive method for tracking influence. It can only show the earliest possible period for the acquisition of a particular edition, and it can provide no hard evidence showing when or even if a particular book was read. Complementary biographical information, however, does affirm Joyce's pronounced interest in Balzac.

Richard Ellmann has discovered that on 11 April 1908, at a time roughly coincidental with the completion of work on the first draft of chapters I–III of *Portrait*, Stanislaus Joyce recorded in his Trieste diary that his brother had recently read ten books by Balzac. This selective survey of Balzac's canon apparently gave Joyce little personal pleasure, for Stanislaus goes on to quote his brother as saying that the ten novels he had read were all "the same formless lumps of putty."[4] Nonetheless, his statement to his brother about reading Balzac and the proximity of these particular titles has led Ellmann to a close examination of Balzac for possible influence. Focusing his attention on *The Country Doctor*, he cites what he sees as a strong indication of the bond existing between the two authors. He identifies the passage from which he believes Joyce derived Stephen's epigrammatic assertion of his independence from the society that had dominated his childhood and his adolescence. "In bringing [*Portrait*] together Joyce found unexpected help in Balzac, who took for his own device and gave his hero in *Le Médecin de campagne* a book that Joyce owned in translation the Carthusian motto '*Fuge . . . Late . . . Tace.*' These Stephen translates as his own watchwords, 'silence, exile, and cunning.' "[5]

Although by no means conclusive, Ellmann's speculation shows a great deal of ingenuity, and it offers a rationale for Joyce's persistent interest in Balzac: Pragmatic considerations of contextual parallels seem to have provided the necessary justification for perseverance. The most obvious inducement would have been the usefulness of Balzac's novels as models for forming the setting and atmosphere of Stephen Dedalus's Dublin ambiance. Balzac filled his stories with vivid depictions of the *moeurs* of bourgeois society and with gritty descriptions of the details of urban living. His narrative discourses rely heavily on just the sort of presentation of naturalistic detail that would have still interested Joyce as he began to organize the material that he wished to bring into *Portrait*.

One can find similar, if somewhat broader-based support in portions of Balzac's novel *Louis Lambert*, another work in Joyce's library offering inducement to pursue further thematic associations. The opening scenes of *Louis Lambert*, like those of *Portrait*, are set in a private boys' school, Vendome, run by the Oratorian Fathers. The priests employ pandying, a punishment appropriated from the Jesuits, and Louis Lambert, intellectually aloof from the other boys, is often disciplined because of his supposed idleness. Subsequent chapters do not bear a close contextual resemblance to *Portrait*, but the book ends with a collection of journal-like observations comprising the mad thoughts of Lambert, similar in form though not in tone to Stephen's diary.

One might be tempted to expand upon such contextual analogues to clarify Joyce's thematic aims at points in the development of his novel. Joyce's parallel experiences, however, suggest to me that the similarities were of interest to him more for their coincidental nature than for their inspirational value. At the same time, the analogues do function significantly in terms of explaining Joyce's developing bond to Balzac, for they provide a rationale for a sustained interest that in turn led to certain stylistic influences on the formation of *Portrait*.

Despite the authority of the innovative gestures in the final version of *Portrait*, in the earliest stages of constituting the novel Joyce doubtless had less awareness of the evocative power of a broad application of free indirect discourse. Balzac, with his strong commitment to the same realistic tradition that informs *Dubliners*, serves to illustrate the formal impetus for initiating change. Specifically, I believe that the basic formal structure repeated in all of Balzac's works, a straightforward use of realistic detail enhanced by discrete applications of stylistic innovations, ultimately proved more suggestive than did thematic issues.

This connection may initially seem capricious in light of Flaubert's commonly acknowledged leadership in the great stylistic developments in nineteenth-century French writing, but I do not intend to dispute that position. Rather I am asserting that Joyce's own creative evolution admitted no concern for such a hierarchy and allowed him to proceed according to his own will. Furthermore, in the specific case of his composition of *Portrait*, limitations of what was readily available at the time abetted personal inclinations. By 1908 his library seems to have held a number of Balzac's works, but he did not come into possession of any books by Flaubert until 1912 at the earliest. I am certainly not denying the great impact of Flaubert's style on Joyce's own writing (I will, in fact, elaborate upon the connection shortly), but at the same time I feel it important to take cognizance of Balzac's immediate influence in disposing Joyce towards the development of free indirect discourse.

In any case, the association of Balzac with stylistic innovation is hardly so radical a proposal as it may seem at first glance. A number of critics have recently begun to discuss the manner in which portions of Balzac's writing adumbrate the technical sophistication that came to take on greater prominence in the work of subsequent novelists, with perhaps the best known instance of this reassessment being Roland Barthes's commentary in *S/Z* on the short story "Sarrasine." Throughout his study Barthes draws attention, as in the following example, to Balzac's methods of manipulating discourse in a manner clearly prefiguring the techniques central in the style of Flaubert. "Here it is impossible to attribute an origin, a point of view, to the statement. Now, this impossibility is one of the ways in which the plural nature of a text can be appreciated. The more indeterminate the origin of the statement, the more plural the text."[6] While Barthes does not specifically label these elements as free indirect discourse, the identification seems fairly clear. The manner adopted both by Balzac and by Joyce in establishing narrative plurality underscores this affinity between their techniques.

Despite Balzac's restrained employment of free indirect discourse, stylistic parallels between selections from his works and from *Portrait* affirm the potential for a potent formal influence. In the following passage taken from *The Country Doctor*, for example, the narrative incorporates the thoughts of the soldier, Pierre Joseph Genestas, into a description of his journey. "He had not expected that the journey would be a long one; but when, league after league, he had been misled as to the distance by the lying statements of the peasants, he thought it would be prudent not to venture any farther without fortifying the inner man."[7] What initially appears to be an objective depiction of the traveler's realization that he has become lost takes on a much subtler tone through the insinuation of his fatigue, resentment, and resignation—"league after league . . . misled by lying peasants . . . prudent not to venture farther." In much the same way, Joyce colors numerous descriptive moments with the intrusion of the consciousness of Stephen Dedalus. In chapter I of *Portrait*, for example, the discourse blends Stephen's thoughts into a description of a football game at Clongowes Wood. "He kept on the fringe of his line, out of sight of his prefect, out of the reach of the rude feet, feigning to run now and then. He felt his body small and weak amid the throng of players and his eyes were weak and watery" (*P*, 8).

Both passages display instances of free indirect discourse in its most elemental form. In each the relatively straightforward introduction of a voice in counterpoint to the basic description offers a subjective elaboration of the action without displacing the mood established by the narrator's basic description. Thus for both selections a fairly obvious bifurcation obtains, orienting the reader to the feelings of the protagonists while retaining the narrator's descriptive control of the discourse.

Even at this stage in his artistic development, however, these formal evocations of the style of Balzac or of other authors go beyond mere echoing. As the following examples illustrate, from his earliest efforts Joyce displayed a genius for style emphasizing his ability to extend the technical achievements that he has observed in others. In a passage from

La Femme de trente ans, Balzac develops a more sophisticated approach to free indirect discourse, animating a description of the Garden of the Tuileries by integrating into the narrator's perspective the point of view of a spectator watching a review of troops of the Grand Army of Napoleon.

> Le spectateur comparaît involontairement ces murs d'hommes à ces murs de pierre. Le soleil du printemps, qui jetait profusement sa lumière sur les murs blanc bâtis de la veille et sur les murs séculaires, éclairait pleinement ces innombrables figures basanées qui toutes racontaient des périls passes et attendaient gravement les périls a venir.[8]

> [Involuntarily the onlooker compared the walls of men with the walls of stone. The spring sun which threw its light profusely on the white walls erected the day before and on the centuries-old walls, shone fully on the numberless bronzed faces, all of whom related dangers of the past and gravely expected dangers to come.]

The discourse maintains a very delicate balance here. It moves from the narrator's point of view to that of the spectators, and then it blurs the final perspective. We cannot be sure whether thoughts of "dangers of the past and . . . dangers to come" originate with the soldiers or are projected upon them by the spectators or by the narrator. Ultimately, the discourse draws in the reader as arbiter. In a similar instance, at the close of chapter III of *Portrait*, the narrator describes Stephen contemplating the objects in his parents' kitchen. Just as Balzac had used the examination of inanimate objects as a springboard for merging the impressions of the spectator and of the soldiers with those of the narrative voice, Joyce makes Stephen's pious sentiments slant the depiction of his surroundings.

> He sat by the fire in the kitchen, not daring to speak for happiness. Till that moment he had not known how beautiful life could be. The green square of paper pinned round the lamp cast down a tender shade. On the dresser was a plate of sausages and white pudding and on the shelf there were eggs. They would be for the breakfast in the morning after the communion in the college chapel. White pudding and eggs and sausages and cups of tea. How simple and beautiful was life after all! And life lay all before him. (*P,* 146)

Stephen's happiness, announced in the first two sentences, insinuates itself unobtrusively into the discourse of the third to make the lamp "cast down a tender shade." The paragraph briefly reverts to straightforward description in the fourth and fifth sentences, but the rapture of the closing elevates them through retrospective arrangement. Sources of the sentiment are less diffused than in the Balzac passage, but the impact of the formal manipulation of temperament is, if anything, more telling.

The second example from Balzac shows a good deal more formal sophistication than does the passage from *The Country Doctor,* although it still reveals certain stylistic limitations. In *La Femme de trente ans* free indirect discourse deftly conjoins characterization and description while revealing Balzac's imperfect mastery of the technique. It expands the range of narrative control by enlivening, through an ingenious shift in perspective, what would otherwise be a rather typical description, but it also runs the risk of banality through the adjectives chosen to describe the soldiers. (In the following chapter I will discuss Joyce's adoption and elaboration of this technique.) The depiction in *Portrait*, on the other hand, traces a similar pattern, but it also reflects Joyce's greater sensitivity to its potential. Balzac's description ends with a clichéd reflection on the uncertainty conditioning the lives of soldiers. In *Portrait* the self-conscious depiction of the mundane environment of the Dedalus kitchen avoids evoking conventional impressions. By making Stephen's feelings both highly abstract and intensely personal, it enforces on the reader a sense of the transformational power of Stephen's burst of piety without prescribing its interpretation.

Certainly, despite these analogues, the stylistic differences between Balzac's works and Joyce's novel remain more apparent than do their similarities. In contrast to the structure of *Portrait*, instances of free indirect discourse in Balzac appear at sporadic intervals rather than following a regular pattern, and the formal aspirations of Balzac's writing seem much more restrained than Joyce's. (*The Country Doctor,* for example, concentrates free indirect discourse in the portion of the novel taking place before Genestas encounters Benassis. After that meeting, it occurs infrequently and contributes nothing to one's sense of the nature of the central character.) As a result, speculation connecting Balzac with the formation of *Portrait* can, of course, illuminate elements of the composition process, but the obvious technical disparities between the two authors necessarily enforce a sense that a range of sources rather than a single dominating influence must have contributed models to guide the shaping of the narrative discourse.

Various bits of information combine to demonstrate that Joyce probably began to devote serious attention to three works by Joseph Conrad shortly after the period he spent examining Balzac. The books were trade editions printed before 1914—*The Secret Agent* (1907), *A Set of Six* (1908), and *Tales of Unrest* (1898)—and sold at low prices on the continent by Tauchnitz, the German publishing house. Works from Tauchnitz often appeared in soft covers (as did many other books produced at the turn of the century), and readers wishing to preserve particular editions would have them rebound in hard covers. Physical evidence in the volumes shows that Joyce did in fact have *A Set of Six* and *Tales of Unrest* rebound in hard covers, probably some time in 1908 or 1909. In a 3 March 1910 letter, apparently after some sort of argument with his brother, Joyce specifically asks Stanislaus to return his copy of *A Set of Six* (*Letters*, II.283). Though pique may have prompted him to demand the volume in a peremptory tone, the fact that he singled it out and the date of his request remain significant. A final indication of usage comes from marginalia appearing in *The Secret Agent*, in *A Set of Six*, and in *Tales of Unrest* that follow the same pattern as marks found in other books that Joyce was reading at approximately the same time. (Joyce made similar notations in his copy of *David Copperfield*, a work that will be discussed later in this chapter.[9]) In each book Joyce's marginalia sustain the sense of his growing interest, throughout the period of composition of *Portrait*, in free indirect style and in the other formal techniques which grew out of his application of it. Taken together this information puts the period during which Joyce was most likely reading Conrad at some time between 1908 and 1911, coinciding roughly with his initial completion of chapter IV and the opening segments of V and his preparations for revision of the first draft of the now recast *Portrait* manuscript.

As with Balzac, one finds in Conrad an author employing stylistic innovations in a manner paralleling several of the forms that would appear in *Portrait*. A number of critics have examined Conrad's use of free indirect discourse, and one, Charles Jones, makes specific reference to its heavy application in *The Secret Agent*. "Much of the novel's strength and attractiveness lies in this shifting of the reader's viewpoint brought about by his constant uncertainty of the nature of the linguistic data confronting him—i.e., whether it represents the author's narration, a particular character's direct or reported utterance, or a mixture of all three."[10] Evidence in Joyce's copies of all three of these books indicates an interest in just this technique. I will not attempt here to discuss all his annotations, but I will use the following passages to exemplify his specific interest in Conrad and to outline the impact of that interest on his own work.

After making a number of discrete notations between pages 36 and 42 of *The Secret Agent*, Joyce highlighted, on page 61, the following description of Winnie Verloc's view of the nature of her younger brother.

There was no young man of his age in London more willing and docile than Stephen, she affirmed; none more affectionate and ready to please, and even useful, as long as people did not upset his poor head. Mrs. Verloc, turning towards her recumbent husband, raised herself on her elbow, and hung over him in her anxiety that he should believe Stevie to be a useful member of the family.[11]

Through a rather straightforward application of free indirect discourse, the passage specifically insinuates into the narrative the passionate concern of Winnie for the welfare of Stevie, but, more significantly, its structure foregrounds certain paradigmatic concerns that define the structure of the entire narrative.

Here and elsewhere Conrad uses free indirect discourse to explore the dialectic dilemmas facing the family, so that the style formally reminds readers of thematic issues: the unsuccessful attempts of Verloc and of Winnie to apply either/or thinking to accommodate the complexities of Verloc's position as pornographer, terrorist, husband, and household head. Further, it urges one to base any interpretation on a view of the both/and realities offered throughout the novel. Joyce's manipulation of the antipathy between either/or and both/and thinking will be examined fully in chapter five. What is of significance at this point of my study is his growing awareness of the imaginative potential inherent in the combination of formal and contextual concerns.

Joyce noted additional instances of Conrad's use of free indirect discourse in other books that he owned. His markings testify to a continuing concern for passages reflecting those dialectic conflicts that arise out of the competition of multiple perspectives for hegemony. In his copy of *A Set of Six*, for example, Joyce concentrated his markings in the story "Gaspar Ruiz," highlighting the conjunction of free indirect discourse and the incipient efforts of Ruiz to define himself. In one selection Joyce marked a paragraph describing Ruiz's efforts to impress an attractive young woman, Dona Ermina: "He had no feeling either way. But he felt a great devotion for that young girl. In his desire to appear worthy of her condescension, he boasted a little of his bodily strength. He had nothing else to boast of. Because of that quality his comrades treated him with as great a deference, he explained, as though he had been a sergeant, both in camp and in battle."[12] As he did with Verloc and, to a lesser degree, with Verloc's wife, Winnie, Conrad, through free indirect discourse, insinuates into the narrative the signifying traits and the ambiguities of the character of Ruiz. The resulting narrative, similar in tone to numerous passages in *Portrait*, allows Conrad to maintain an ironic distance even as he sketches a highly personal view of his central character.

In Joyce's copy of *Tales of Unrest* one finds perhaps the clearest evidence of his interest in Conrad's use of free indirect discourse. One of the stories, "An Outpost of Progress," focuses on the trauma of two white men in Africa who must face the disparity between their comfortable perceptions of their abilities to direct events and the constraints actually imposed upon their lives by the world around them. As the story unfolds, the action develops around previously suppressed elements of their characters that emerge from their responses to conditions over which they have no control. The following selection, describing Kayerts's vigil over the body of the murdered Carlier, exemplifies the type of passage that Joyce noted throughout the piece. "His heart [Kayerts's] thumped, and he felt hot all over at the thought of that danger. Carlier! What a beastly thing! To compose his now disturbed nerves—and no wonder!—he tried to whistle a little. Then, suddenly, he fell asleep, or thought he had slept; but at any rate there was a fog, and somebody whistled in the fog."[13]

Throughout Conrad's evocative prose, Joyce found stark depictions of the human psyche paralleling the efforts he had already undertaken in *Dubliners*. Free indirect discourse in *Dubliners* inevitably plays off the consciousness of a central character, and the short stories of *A Set of Six* and *Tales of Unrest* follow this pattern, reinforcing Joyce's predisposition towards the technique. In *The Secret Agent* Conrad imposed a broader paradigm on his depictions and extended the parameters of free indirect discourse. Its gesture towards multiplicity sets forth a model with which Joyce would experiment in *Portrait* and perfect in *Ulysses*. On the surface, Conrad's characters—saboteurs, renegades, colonials—have a more exotic aura than the shabby figures of lower-middle-class Dublin. Structurally, however, Conrad's emphasis on the conflicts within the consciousnesses of his characters and his precise integration of objective and subjective detail provided Joyce with a clearer sense than he had previously had of the significant dialectical movement available in free indirect discourse.

Many of the details of the artistic and intellectual bonds existing between Joyce and Conrad must necessarily come out of informed speculation. The pair of works by Emile Zola in the Trieste library reinforces more directly one's sense of the close relationship between Joyce's own experimentation and the inspiration that he drew from his predecessors. Unlike the authors considered above, Zola seems to have been a writer that Joyce, from a fairly early time, relied on as a benchmark for critical evaluation. In a 1903 review of T. Baron Russell's *Borlase and Son*, Joyce cites *Au Bonheur des dames* as "the supreme achievement in that class of fiction of which 'Borlase and Son' is a type''—a novel of tawdry, middle-class mercantilism (*CW,* 139). Later, in two letters written during his stay in Trieste, one dated 13 May 1906 and sent to Grant Richards and one of 11 February 1907 sent to Stanislaus (*Letters*, II.137 and 211), Joyce draws similar analogies between his work on *Dubliners* and Zola's writing.

In each of these three instances a wry tone belies admiration, but in every comparison it remains clear that Joyce saw Zola's writing as emblematic of a particular form. Doubtless it was this opinion that led him back to works from Zola's canon while recasting his own novel. A postal receipt, dated 5 November 1911 and found between the pages of Joyce's copy of *Nana*, suggests that he was reading it at about the same time that he was beginning to compose his initial version of the fifth chapter of *Portrait*, and passages from Zola's novel employ the same deft manipulation of narrative perspective that had attracted Joyce's attention in the books by Conrad.

Abundant examples of free indirect discourse appear throughout the work, but most interesting in terms of this study are the numerous occasions in which free indirect discourse underscores a dialectic conflict taking place within a character. In the first passage quoted below, Nana walks through the streets of Paris with one of her lovers, Count Muffat, and the narrative deftly employs free indirect discourse to form a polyphonic commentary on the scene. The narrative describes her as taking overt amusement from the trinkets on display in the shop windows. At the same time, it offers glimpses of Nana's mental turmoil as she rages to herself over the trouble that men give her and at the deplorable condition of her finances.

> Ca l'ennuyait à la fin, de n'être pas libre; et, dans sa révolte sourde, montait le furieux besoin de faire une bêtise. La belle avancé d'avoir des hommes bien! Elle venait de manger le prince et Steiner à des caprices d'enfant, sans qu'elle sût où l'argent passait.[14]

> [It bothered her immensely not to have her evening to herself, and, in her secret revolt, she felt a longing to do something foolish. What use was it to have well-off gentlemen! She had just run through the prince and Steiner, indulging all her childish caprices, without in the least knowing where the money had gone to.]

In two subsequent passages, bracketing a scene in which Nana agrees to resume her role as Muffat's mistress, Zola again employs free indirect discourse, this time in an even more sophisticated fashion: intensifying the reader's engagement with the conflicting emotions felt by both Nana and Muffat. Both selections begin with the same objective detachment quickly displaced by the unmistakable imprint of the personality of a particular individual that characterizes the methods Joyce himself would employ in *Portrait* to underscore the conflicts within Stephen's consciousness. The first passage conveys Muffat's increasing agitation as he prepares to enter Nana's room.

> Dans le corridor de droite, en effect, la porte de la loge se trouvait simplement poussée. Nana attendait. Cette petite Mathilde, un souillon d'ingénue, tenait sa loge très sale, avec une débandade de pots ébréchés, une toilette grasse, une chaise tachée de rouge, comme si on avait saigne sur la paille.[15]

> [In the passage on the right, the door of the dressing-room was in fact only half shut. Nana was waiting there. That little slut of a Mathilde kept her dressing-room in a slovenly state; there were cracked pots scattered all about, a dirty wash-hand basin, and a chair stained with rouge, as though some one had been bleeding on the rush seat.]

The second passage depicts Nana's initial reaction to Muffat's departure.

> Quand elle l'eût poussé dehors, après l'avoir chauffé d'une pluie de baisers sur les mains et sur la figure, elle souffla un moment. Mon Dieu! qu'il y avait donc une mauvaise odeur, dans la loge de cette sans soin de Mathilde![16]

> [When she had pushed him outside, after arousing him with a shower of kisses on his face and hands, she stood a moment to take a breath. My God! what a stench there was in the dressing-room of that untidy Mathilde!]

Both passages draw their emotional power as much from what remains unarticulated as from what they express. Each character transfers the ambivalence that the reunion produces to criticism of Mathilde, another actress. The reader, privileged by the distancing effect of free indirect discourse, balances their multiple responses into an evolving text.

The same modulating emotional rhythm within a character's mind appears in chapter III of *Portrait* in a passage describing Stephen's reaction to the first retreat sermon that had been preached by Father Arnall.

> He ate his dinner with surly appetite and, when the meal was over and the greasestrewn plates lay abandoned on the table, he rose and went to the window, clearing the thick scum from his mouth with his tongue and licking it from his lips. So he had sunk to the state of a beast that licks his

chaps after meat. This was the end; and a faint glimmer of fear began to pierce the fog of his mind. (*P.* 111)

Although Joyce's prose has a richness surpassing the selections from Zola, the structure of the passage adheres to the same patterns laid down in *Nana*. The narrative voice sets the scene and then recedes as the consciousness of the central character fixes on an objective correlative for the deep emotional ambivalence being experienced. Both in the selections from *Nana* and in the one from *Portrait*, free indirect discourse allows the reader to feel the mixture of contradictory impulses of banal and elevated emotions ruling the fictional characters. At the same time, it provides the distance necessary for one to appreciate the irony integrated among the range of attitudes depicted.

Not all of Joyce's literary associations, however, rely on such close creative resonances. Unlike the work of Balzac, Conrad, or Zola, Joyce's writing bears little obvious affinity (outside of broad parodic instances in *Ulysses*) to that of Dickens. Further, reminiscences of Stanislaus indicate that as a boy his brother had never cared for Dickens, and there is little reason here to suspect any change in Joyce's personal taste.[17] Nonetheless, the evidence of the library attests to an avid professional interest—of brief but intense duration—and consequently requires some explanation. Internal evidence in the books suggests that during the last few years of his residence in Trieste, Joyce purchased five of Dickens's novels—*The Adventures of Oliver Twist, Barnaby Rudge, Bleak House, David Copperfield*, and *The Life and Adventures of Nicholas Nickleby*. Publication data indicate that of the five works Joyce could only have acquired *Bleak House* before 1910 or 1911, some time after he had finished the initial reformation of *Stephen Hero* into the first four chapters of *Portrait*. Collateral information—marginalia and references in a 1912 essay on Dickens—further indicates that he probably had read a number of them, if not all, before the period in 1912 when he began work on chapter V and the novel's final revisions.[18] A close scrutiny of this secondary material leads one to the strong supposition that Dickens proved a more useful model for confirming the structure of *Portrait* than anyone has previously imagined.

In 1912 Joyce took a short trip to Padua in an effort to acquire certification to teach English in Italian schools. Louis Berrone discovered and published a series of examination papers that Joyce wrote as part of this process, including one of particular interest to this study, "The Centenary of Charles Dickens." (The topic itself was assigned rather than chosen by Joyce, but his recent reading made it an especially fortuitous selection.) Despite the artificial conditions under which the essay was written and the obvious qualifications in its praise of Dickens's work, "The Centenary of Charles Dickens" reflects Joyce's familiarity with the canon and his sense of the distinguishing features of Dickens's writing. Furthermore, specific comments in the paper draw attention to the aspects of Dickens that most likely prompted Joyce's reexamination.

One would naturally assume that the initial impulse Joyce felt to return to Dickens would be based on an interest in the latter's ability to render clearly and powerfully details of the English urban milieu, and in a portion of his examination paper Joyce touches on precisely this trait.

> If Dickens is to move you, you must not allow him to stray out of hearing of the chimes of Bow Bells. There he is on his native heath and there are his kingdom and his power. The life of London is the breath of his nostrils: he felt it as no writer since or before his time has felt it. The colours, the familiar noises, the very odours of the great metropolis unite in his work as in a mighty symphony wherein humour and pathos, life and death, hope and despair, are inextricably interwoven. . . . And yet it is certainly by his stories of the London of his own day that he must finally stand or fall.[19]

Here and elsewhere in the essay Joyce is obviously writing to please the examiner and not to articulate fully his own attitude, and he is far too experienced an examinee to mount an attack on the subject that had been assigned, no matter what his personal views. Nonetheless, the convoluted prose, full of the same circumlocutions employed by generations of students, obscures but does not eliminate evidence of Joyce's keen perception of the central aspects of Dickens's appeal. In his analysis of the importance of characterization, Joyce presents more directly and sympathetically a detailed view of Dickens's descriptive power.

> [W]e see every character of Dickens in the light of one strongly-marked or even exaggerated moral or physical quality. . . . It is precisely this little exaggeration which rivets his work firmly to popular taste, which fixes his characters firmly in popular memory. It is precisely by this little exaggeration that Dickens has influenced the spoken language of the inhabitants of the British Empire as no other writer since Shakespeare's time has influenced it [. . .][20]

Even after one allows for the necessarily synthetic tone of the essay, marked parallels emerge between aspects of Dickens's style singled out by Joyce and formal elements that Joyce employed in *Dubliners*. Berrone, in the introduction to his edition of Joyce's Padua essays, has tried to draw attention to the aura of self-reflexivity in the Dickens paper, but he leaves many of the richest implications of Joyce's statements unexplored.[21] Despite the cautious, predictable assessment of Dickens that we have seen in the selections quoted above, I believe that Joyce derives at least a portion of his attitude from the influence of passages in Dickens that he had already singled out as models for segments of his own work.

Annotations in one of the books, *David Copperfield*, support my contention by offering a more precise sense of what may have attracted Joyce's attention. They conform to the pattern of marking repeated throughout works in the Trieste library, especially in the Conrad works discussed above, with the bulk of Joyce's notations being centered on three parallel incidents in the book: David's leaving home (chapter V); his discussion with his aunt regarding Mr. Dick (chapter XIV); and his introduction to Doctor Strong's school (chapter XVI). Since each passage emphasizes David's youthful sense of isolation and his awkwardness as an outsider, they all bear thematic affinities with incidents in the first two chapters of *Portrait* which Joyce was revising around this time. Additionally, though not as obviously, the marginalia also suggest a significant formal conjunction between the two authors.

Because of Dickens's apparently conventional use of discourse, few readers in 1912 would have expected to find innovative narrative techniques in the straightforward, first-person chronicle of a work like *David Copperfield*. Over the past three decades, however, a number of critics have begun to explore sophisticated narrative elements in Dickens that most earlier scholars had overlooked. One, Roy Pascal, while acknowledging the limitations of free indirect discourse in a novel narrated in the first person, also argues for its limited use in *David Copperfield*. "The narrative form he uses postulates distance between himself and the other characters. Thus the chief source of free indirect speech is closed to him. The narrator can evoke through [free indirect discourse] what he himself is experiencing and has experienced at an earlier time; he can also use [free indirect discourse] for reporting the actual speech of characters."[22] Pascal is more assertive about the application of free indirect discourse in *Bleak House*, another book in the Trieste library. "In the narratorial sections [free indirect discourse] is almost always used for humourous-satirical purposes, and often seems to be an enlarged version of those fixed catchphrases through which many of Dickens's characters define themselves."[23]

The same narrational trait appears repeatedly in Joyce, as evident in one of its earliest instances, the passage from chapter I of *Portrait* describing Stephen's classmates at Clongowes Wood. After a sentence identifying two of the boys at the school, offhanded slang signals Stephen's and not the narrator's assessment of their personalities. "Rody Kickham was a decent fellow but Nasty Roche was a stink" (*P,* 8). The conjunction of free indirect discourse and character development through colloquialisms also calls to mind Joyce's praise of Dickens's ability to convey a rich subtlety within the cadences of ordinary speech, and it emphasizes the link that I have been developing.

W. J. M. Bronzwaer has made a particularly strong argument for the specific recurrence of free indirect discourse in *David Copperfield* that has even broader implications for the formation of *Portrait.* "The very fact that narrator and main character are one and the same person makes it imperative that the reader should be able to distinguish between the different points of view. In other words, in I-novels we constantly have to ask ourselves whether what we are reading represents the thoughts or feelings of the narrator-I or of the character-I."[24] In his copy of *David Copperfield,* Joyce demonstrates sensitivity to the very distinction that Bronzwaer emphasizes. In one instance, for example, Joyce's notations single out the following passage from chapter V describing David's departure for London.

> Looking out to ascertain for what, I saw to my amazement, Peggotty burst from a hedge and climb into the cart. She took me in both her arms, and squeezed me to her stays until the pressure on my nose was extremely painful, though I never thought of that till afterwards, when I found it very tender. Not a single word did Peggotty speak. Releasing one of her arms, she put it down in her pocket to the elbow, and brought out some paper bags of cakes, which she crammed into my pockets, and a purse, which she put into my hand; but not one word did she say. After another and a final squeeze with both arms, she got down from the cart and ran away, and my belief is, and has always been, without a solitary button on her gown. I picked up one of several that were rolling about, and treasured it as a keepsake for a long time.[25]

Although the I-character voice of the young David dominates much of the passage, parenthetical references to the retrospective attitude of the I-narrator fragment the discourses of the passage, coloring the description with gentle irony. "I saw to my amazement . . . though I never thought of that till afterwards . . . and my belief is, and has always been. . . ." The narrative modulation between the boy experiencing the event and the older man recollecting and weighing his youthful values traces a fairly common pattern of discourse, but in this instance Joyce's attentiveness to the technique highlights a key feature emerging in the narrative strategy of *Portrait.*

From the opening pages of *Portrait,* Joyce creates a rich range of textual possibilities by bifurcating the discourse into accounts of the complementary but independent attitudes of Stephen and of the narrative voice. I will take up the application of this feature of the discourse in greater detail in the following chapter, so for now I would like to concentrate on its paradigmatic implications. Joyce's interest in Dickens does not reflect a nostalgia for conventional nineteenth-century narrative. Rather, it suggests the turning point in his own conception of the bounds of fiction. By 1912 he had come to see how free indirect discourse can effectively overcome the hegemony of a single narrative point of view: Alternative voices need not simply counterpoint the dominant tone of the discourse. They can counterbalance it, so that the reader can assume the role of weighting the various elements.

One may well wonder at the apparent incongruity thus far of emphasizing the work of Balzac, Conrad, Zola, or Dickens as a force contributing to the shaping of Joyce's concept of style without mentioning the achievements of the nineteenth-century figure most commonly associated with free indirect discourse: Gustave Flaubert. Certainly Flaubert's vigorous application of structural experimentation provides a much broader guide for artistic development, setting standards for both other writers and for readers. Like many French writers of the period, Flaubert uses middle-class life as the contextual foundation of his work, but the power of his narrative structure extends the impact of his writing well beyond tightly defined social parameters to which his contemporaries adhered. In fact, much of the fiction of the period produces for readers indisputable echoes of the style of Flaubert. As a consequence evidence of experimentation in Balzac, Zola, or Conrad becomes apparent to many because Flaubert has made those techniques so familiar. Nevertheless, viewing Flaubert as the sole or even the primary force conditioning Joyce's decision to employ free indirect discourse oversimplifies the stages of his artistic evolution. Biographical and bibliographical evidence shows that Joyce delayed turning to Flaubert until a time fairly late in the writing of *Portrait,* and this somewhat tardy acknowledgment of Flaubert's work affirms the pattern of creative development that I have been tracing throughout this chapter. Free indirect discourse took on a central role in the narrative of *Portrait* through a series of incremental assimilations during the process of composition. Joyce could draw upon Flaubert for guidance ("return to" might be a better phrase since in Dublin Joyce had already displayed a strong interest) only after having committed himself to intense application of free indirect discourse in the structure of *Portrait.*

This is not to say that Flaubert did not have a profound effect upon Joyce's artistic perceptions, but during significant portions of his early creative period Joyce felt Flaubert's influence indirectly rather than directly. At a relatively early age Joyce must have come to some sense of the preeminence of Flaubert's artistic position. C. P. Curran recalls as much from informal discussions with Joyce on Flaubert when they were both students at University College Dublin,[26] and in his 1901 essay "The Day of the Rabblement" (*CW*, 71) Joyce specifically cites *Madame Bovary* as a work in diametric opposition to provincial Irish artistic conceptions. At the same time, close contact with Flaubert's work seems to have been sporadic. After the appearance of "The Day of the Rabblement," allusions to Flaubert disappear from Joyce's writings and conversations, and they do not reappear until 1914, when, in notes for his play *Exiles* (*E*, 115), Joyce refers to *Madame Bovary* as marking a shift in "the centre of sympathy" in a love triangle from the lover to the husband.

Joyce's pattern of book acquisitions supports my contention that he returned to a close examination of Flaubert's work only after the bulk of *Portrait* had been written. Joyce purchased a collection of Flaubert's short stories, *Premières Oeuvres*, from a Trieste bookseller on 8 April 1914, and he probably picked up *Salammbô* some time during his stay in Zurich. Although his copy of *Madame Bovary* was printed in 1905, an item advertised in the back pages of that particular volume was not available until 1912.[27] Joyce most likely acquired it around then, and probably reread it sometime in 1913 or early in 1914. I will describe in chapter seven how Flaubert's urbane and ironic treatment of Emma Bovary's adultery attracted Joyce's interest as he sought a starting point for the dramatic conflict in *Exiles*. In terms of *Portrait*, the French author's sophisticated application of free indirect discourse served less ambitious ends, allowing Joyce to consolidate his formal intentions as he shaped the final version of his novel. His obvious affinities to Flaubert clearly summarize (rather than project or prescribe) the growth of his creative paradigm.

Flaubert's writing foregrounded for Joyce the importance of free indirect discourse latent in the work of authors like Balzac and Dickens and encouraged its recuperation in Conrad and in Zola.[28] In its purest form, Flaubert's free indirect discourse conclusively demonstrated its ability to endow a discourse with a multiplicity that overturned authorial hegemony and transformed *lisible* prose into *scriptible* fiction. Joyce identified his debt to Flaubert in a previously quoted passage in chapter V of *Portrait* central to the work's structure: "The artist, like the

God of the creation, remains within or behind or beyond or above his handiwork, invisible, refined out of existence, indifferent, paring his fingernails" (*P,* 215). Stephen's remark about the artist paring his fingernails, paraphrased from one of Flaubert's letters, stands out as the best-known instance in *Portrait* of an allusion to Flaubert.[29] It shows the author as a figure setting strict parameters for the interpretation of a work but leaving the reader a great deal of room to create meaning within those boundaries. (I will discuss this aspect in greater detail in the next chapter.)

Nonetheless, *Madame Bovary* provides a much richer implicit resource for measuring Joyce's commitment to formal experimentation. Many critics have already commented at length on Flaubert's use of free indirect discourse, and Roy Pascal provides a summary particularly useful here for the obvious resonances with the form of *Portrait* that it suggests:

> Flaubert wanted to hide the very function of story-telling, as it were, to allow the story to tell and interpret itself, as far as this was possible; hence the narrator should, as he put it, "transport himself into his characters." This free indirect speech is not an occasional device, nor something employed for a specific situation or person; it is a major instrument for achieving the Flaubertian type of novel. Flaubert's realism did not imply the sort of objectivity that belongs to natural science, an objectivity founded on communicable skill and authoritative control over the (imaginary) object; on the contrary, it meant an imaginative self-submergence in the object, participation in the imagined character's experience, and communication of this intuitive experience.[30]

Further, as Henry H. Weinberg has observed, Flaubert combined with free indirect discourse a frequent use of irony "which greatly contributes to the novel's originality."[31] This same tendency to integrate ironic elements into narrative descriptions associated with a particular character appears frequently in *Portrait*, and, as noted previously, it allows readers to acquire an intimate sense of Stephen's consciousness while permitting a detached judgment of his nature.

Many examples would serve to establish the structural affinities existing between *Portrait* and *Madame Bovary,* but let me call attention to one in particular. In the well-known description of Emma's examination of the cigar case which may or may not have belonged to the "Vicomte" whom she met and admired at La Vaubyessard, Flaubert presents in intimate detail the isolation, the sentimentality, the naive romanticism that characterize Emma's nature. Free indirect discourse allows the reader to view her with a mixture of sympathy and sardonic amusement.

Often when Charles was out she went to the closet and took the green silk cigar case from among the piles of linen where she kept it. She would look at it, open it, even sniff its lining, fragrant with verbena and tobacco. Whose was it? The vicomte's. A present from his mistress, perhaps. It had been embroidered on some rosewood frame, a charming little piece of furniture kept hidden from prying eyes, over which a pensive girl had bent for hours and hours, her soft curls brushing its surface. Love had breathed through the mesh of the canvas; every stroke of the needle had recorded a hope or a memory; and all these intertwined silken threads bespoke one constant, silent passion.[32]

As the narrative unfolds, a rhetorical question—"Whose was it?"—signals an intrusion into the discourse. Speculations regarding the vicomte's putative lover assume the tone of Emma's sentimental romanticism, and the reader moves between the detachment and involvement of the two voices to fix a level of irony for evolving the text.

The same sort of imaginative projection integrated into the narration appears in a portion of a selection from *Portrait* dealing with Stephen's trip to Cork with his father. As the description of the scene in the anatomy theater unfolds, it becomes filled with Stephen's speculations about the students who have preceded him there. The scene turns on the irony, created through free indirect discourse, of the contrast between his sensitive rendition of student life and his resistance to the power of his father's nostalgic recollections.

On the desk before him he read the word *Foetus* cut several times in the dark stained wood. The sudden legend startled his blood: he seemed to feel the absent students of the college about and to shrink from their company. A vision of their life, which his father's words had been powerless to evoke, sprang up before him out of the word cut in the desk. A broadshouldered student with a moustache was cutting in the letters with a jackknife, seriously. Other students stood or sat near him laughing at his handiwork. One jogged his elbow. The big student turned on him, frowning. He was dressed in loose grey clothes and had tan boots (*P,* 89–90).

Stephen, like Emma Bovary, feels incipient dissatisfaction with his life and his surroundings. Each scene marks the beginning of efforts to resist the dictates of environment. Superficially, Emma's naive promiscuity bears slight resemblance to Stephen's intellectual rebellion, but at the core of their individual discontent remains the same dialectic impulse to resist the linear movements of their lives by expanding their alternatives for action. Likewise, whatever attraction or fascination a reader feels for either character comes out of the delicate balance, created by free indirect discourse and dialectic tension, between the intimate acquaintance and the ironic distance we feel in relation to his or her nature. Whether Joyce specifically relied upon this passage from *Madame Bovary* is not at all important. What is most striking is that the similarities between the two scenes testify to the degree of artistic competency that Joyce achieved through the process of writing *Portrait*.

As the central structuring force of *Portrait*, free indirect discourse draws its significance from intra- and intertextual relationships. In analyzing the stages by which it developed in Joyce's artistic consciousness, one discovers his methods of composition imbedded in the book to direct readers towards the paradigmatic bounds of his novel. One also senses the stylistic traces of those who pioneered the technique—reading in the manner that Jacques Derrida has termed "sous rature"—so that connections between Joyce and his intellectual antecedents clarify both his artistic aims and his technical achievement in refining and extending the formal advances of others. By drawing such a fine line in every descriptive paragraph between the nature of the narrative voice and that of the intruding consciousness of Stephen Dedalus, Joyce surpasses even Flaubert in the dexterity with which he matches subjective and objective depictions and in the sophisticated demands he places upon his readers.

A pattern of development going beyond the eclectic curiosity of an artist struggling to mature emerges from the borrowings that I have cited, but it does not reflect the reciprocal relationships of linear influences identified in conventional source studies. Joyce did not turn to other writers with the conscious intention of cutting and pasting together the best examples of writing that he could find in his literary antecedents to form his own novel. Rather, his interest in other authors mirrored his own evolving artistic consciousness, so that these figures become standards for measuring Joyce's growing commitment to formal experimentation. Specifically, as he examined the works of his predecessors, the most effective styles that he encountered—like free indirect discourse—became incorporated by sheer dint of repetition, into his own creative repertoire. While no single figure, even that of Flaubert, can claim to have exerted a dominating influence, the writings of a range of artists, for whom those noted in this chapter stand as representatives, did have a pronounced impact on his own technical development. An awareness of the echoes of the styles of those artists enhances in turn our own proficiencies as readers encountering Joyce's canon.

V | Et ignotas animum dimittit in artes: The Creation of the Reader in *A Portrait of the Artist as a Young Man*

With the completion of *Portrait*, Joyce finalized the terms of his relationship with his readers that would condition the rest of his creative output. *Exiles*, *Ulysses*, and *Finnegans Wake* all introduce innovative techniques, refine narrative strategies, and extend paradigms, yet each conforms to the basic protocols laid down in Joyce's first published novel. Consequently, with this chapter, the focus of my study turns from outlining the features conditioning Joyce's paradigms to examining the alternatives for response open to his readers.

Portrait completes the realignment of the discourse from *lisible* to *scriptible* fiction, offering the first instance of the balanced relationship between writer and reader characterizing the remainder of Joyce's canon. Nonetheless, many critics in their interpretations of this novel continue to follow their impulse to foreground the consciousness of the author while suppressing that of the reader. Over the years this tendency to privilege the putative views of the author has become more subtle but not less persistent. Growing critical sophistication has dispelled the initial responses to *Portrait* that elided the distance between author and protagonist, construing the novel as thinly disguised autobiography. Nevertheless, among contemporary readers the tendency remains to assume that the portrait of the title refers to a rendition of a Joyce-like artist figure, and, as a result, they limit their perception of the novel's paradigm to features that they assume confirm Joyce's intentionality.[1]

A more precise articulation of the work's epiphanic impulses must expand the range of compositional responsibility, for, in a significant way, the sense of self-portrait that we derive from the novel comes out of elements in its formal structure that persistently remind us of our role as readers. We do not simply apprehend in *Portrait* a recapitulation of a familiar form conditioned by assumptions of a strict separation of the functions of writer and of reader. Rather the novel insists on our full participation: we do not simply create an image of a text; we take responsibility for its extension and provisional completion. This condition does not bring about closure, for *Portrait* self-consciously rejects the hegemony of a specific reading. Instead by calling attention to our repeated re-formations, it makes us aware of the artistic traits developing within ourselves. Not Stephen, not Joyce, but each of us in turn provides the model for the features of the artist as a young man that we discern in the novel.

This condition of indeterminacy arises even before one begins to read the novel proper. I have borrowed the epigraph to *Portrait* (the only one that Joyce appended to one of his works) to serve as a title for this chapter, and I believe it encapsulates the intellectual posture that the novel encourages us to assume. It is a passage taken from the scene in Ovid's *Metamorphoses* describing the decision of the artisan Daedalus to defy King Minos and find a way to leave the island of Crete. Daedalus's determination, of course, leads to the construction of wax wings and prepares the way for the archetypal event which informs so much of the thematic structure of *Portrait*. In the context of Ovid's work the line seems to be clear enough—it can be roughly translated as "he turned his mind to unknown arts"—but as an introduction to *Portrait* it poses an interesting problem of reference. One could, with equal plausibility, decide that the antecedent to the pronoun acting as subject of the sentence—he or she—is Joyce, Stephen, or the reader. Each fits the sense of the epigraph, and whatever decision the reader settles upon informs all subsequent interpretations. (To a degree the pronoun itself, latent in the construction of the verb *dimittit*, demands of the reader an imaginative rendering to give it essence.) The point is not that one choice is invariably correct and that the other two are necessarily wrong but rather that from its first words *Portrait* self-consciously calls attention to the stylistic imperative that it repeatedly addresses to the reader to participate in the creation of meaning.[2]

This may be an opportune point at which to clarify some of the idiosyncratic aspects of my own approach to the application of theories of reception. Wolfgang Iser has offered a lexicon for discussing the various elements of reader response—figure, ground, succession, horizon, and latency—operating within the ostensive purport of an accepted repertoire of narrative segments, and I have adopted many of his terms to clarify the theoretical basis underlying many of my assumptions.[3] Iser's vocabulary alone, however, cannot sufficiently describe the formal multiplicity of *Portrait*. Consequently, I intend to develop the implications of examinations of intersections of protension and retension at the level of the "individual sentence correlate" that leads to Iser's "wandering viewpoint," to trace their cumulative impact on the reader's production of a text.

While the interplay of narrational forces within discrete portions of the work remains important, my central concern will be the protocol that encourages our efforts to conjoin episodic experiences. Every horizon prefigured in the mind of the reader, every projection interpolated into the work one reads, necessarily excludes a number of equally valid horizons. My aim in this chapter is to underscore the aesthetic power of *Portrait* by calling attention to the range of horizons, the multiplicity of texts, that it intentionally fosters.

The structure of Joyce's novel disrupts any conventional cause-and-effect assumptions that we might have regarding patterns of descriptive development, operating in a manner similar to what Gérard Genette has termed variable focalization. Genette explains this technique by using the example of *Madame Bovary* where "the focal character is first Charles, then Emma, then again Charles."[4] The method of *Portrait*, however, takes on a more elaborate nature than that implied by Genette's sense of a "focus of narration" shifting between characters.

The discourse commonly presents descriptive material in tandem, as the narrative advances through a voice keenly attuned to the nature of Stephen Dedalus but directed by a consciousness capable of greater insight. At crucial points, however, it reflects a paradigmatic expansion, and, as the focus of narration fluctuates, specific responsibility for the narrative act often remains open to conjecture. Reacting to the resulting ambiguity produced by an apparent overlapping of consciousnesses, a reader may feel the urge to clarify the condition through a series of choices that foreground a particular narrative representation, but emerging antinomies call into question the logical consistency of a single perspective. This tendency in *Portrait* frustrates simple either/or determinations. In its engagement of the reader it goes beyond even Flaubert's efforts to construct *scriptible* fiction. Form continually makes provisional the primacy of any single narrative presence through structural techniques—temporal gaps, incorporated genres, free indirect discourse—operating outside its hegemony. These methods introduce alternative perspectives, emphasize diegetic elements, and impose upon the reader the role of participant in the creation of narrative coherence, not after the fact but as part of the act of reading.

Examples illustrating the process by which *Portrait* continually reforms the reader's conceptions permeate the novel. For now I would like to concentrate on its first two pages to show how stylistic modulation confronts the reader, from the opening lines onward, with the imperative to choose specific readings from a range of textual options.

On one level this initial segment presents a series of false starts, for, as a rapid succession of forms compete for the reader's attention, none appears able to establish a primacy or narrative norm. The passage begins by introducing the convention of the fairy tale opening.

> Once upon a time and a very good time it was there was a moocow coming down along the road and this moocow that was coming down along the road met a nicens little boy named baby tuckoo. . . .

That mode is quickly brushed aside by two short paragraphs set in the style that will eventually come to characterize most of the narration within the remainder of the chapter.

> His father told him that story: his father looked at him through a glass: he had a hairy face.
>
> He was baby tuckoo. The moocow came down the road where Betty Byrne lived: she sold lemon platt.

This form, however, despite its ultimate durability, also gives way to two lines of a popular song, followed by two brief narrative sentences which are themselves displaced by Stephen's reinterpretation of the song.

> *O, the wild rose blossoms*
> *On the little green place.*
> He sang that song. That was his song.
> *O, the green wothe botheth.*

Two short descriptive paragraphs follow, only to be interrupted by a rendition, possibly Stephen's, of the piano music (described in the narrative) played by his mother.

> When you wet the bed first it is warm then it gets cold. His mother put on the oilsheet. That had the queer smell.
>
> His mother had a nicer smell than his father. She played on the piano the sailor's hornpipe for him to dance,
> He danced:

> *Tralala lala*
> *Tralala tralaladdy*
> *Tralala lala*
> *Tralala lala.*

Finally the narrative seems to assert itself in three successive paragraphs followed by three lines of dialogue,

Uncle Charles and Dante clapped. They were older than his father and mother but uncle Charles was older than Dante.

Dante had two brushes in her press. The brush with the maroon velvet back was for Michael Davitt and the brush with the green velvet back was for Parnell. Dante gave him a cachou every time he brought her a piece of tissue paper.

The Vances lived in number seven. They had a different father and mother. They were Eileen's father and mother. When they were grown up he was going to marry Eileen. He hid under the table. His mother said:

—O, Stephen will apologise.

Dante said:

—O, if not, the eagles will come and pull out his eyes.

but again it faces disruption when a children's rhyme modified, perhaps by Stephen, perhaps by Dante, perhaps by the narrative voice, parodies the threat.

> Pull out his eyes,
> Apologise,
> Apologise,
> Pull out his eyes.

> Apologise,
> Pull out his eyes,
> Pull out his eyes,
> Apologise
> (P, 7–8)[5]

In every instance the formal variations brought about by generic intrusions do not function apart from the environment of the novel; rather they present a reformation of that repertoire through the eyes of an outsider.

By leaving ambiguous the source or sources for significant portions of the passage, *Portrait* confronts the reader with questions of voice and of authority: Who is telling the fairy tale? Stephen? His father? The narrator? Does Stephen's mother sing the original verse of the song or does the narrative voice quote it? Is the apparent musical interlude appearing on page seven the narrator's mimetic rendition or a diegetic interpretation made by Stephen or his mother? Who creates the parodic nursery rhyme? While each question may appear banal in isolation, taken together they reflect alternatives that offer several significantly different possibilities for interpretation of the immediate tone of the passage and establish assumptions for comprehension of the succeeding discourse. Throughout the entire first section, variations delay the establishment or the recognition of the descriptive form that will shape narrative for the bulk of the chapter. They force the reader to confront initially the question of the nature of the mode and subsequently of the legitimacy of its depictions of the environment. The answers that one generates to these questions define the perspective from which an individual goes on to perceive the remainder of the work. One's response will establish the level of involvement of Stephen and of a range of other figures in shaping the novel's descriptive passages. This narrows the range of subsequent interpretations possible for a particular text, but it does not preclude the legitimacy of a range of other texts created through other readings.

Before examining the implications of my thesis that a definitive text of *Portrait* does not and cannot exist, I would like to explain in a more detailed fashion the logic supporting my position for labeling the voice of the narrator as a separate entity (with independent traits like those of any other character) rather than as a portion of Stephen's consciousness, for a number of readers have made serious attempts to identify Stephen as the narrative presence.[6] Admittedly, the work itself provides some justification for perceiving such an amalgamation, for many of its passages, without naming Stephen as their source, render images and events using a tone paralleling that associated with his intellect at various stages of his maturation. Further, the absence of markers signaling first-person narration and the presence of the stream of consciousness in *Ulysses* have led some critics to invoke this technique as a means of explaining Stephen's co-location in the direct and the indirect discourse of *Portrait*.

This approach, however, falters when one tries to use it to explain why descriptive segments bearing traces of Stephen's personality do not simultaneously establish his consciousness as the indisputable source of the narrative voice. Phrases from the opening episode, for example, mimic the disposition of the young Stephen.

> When you wet the bed first it is warm then it gets cold. His mother put on the oilsheet. That had the queer smell.
> His mother had a nicer smell than his father. She played on the piano the sailor's hornpipe for him to dance. He danced. (*P,* 7)

The lines certainly reflect an awareness of Stephen's nature, but the use of second- and third-person pronouns blurs direct association with Stephen's consciousness, yet the images do not present the complete conjunction of principal character and narrator that we encounter in the clearly defined stream of consciousness passages of a work like *Ulysses*.

There, whenever the stream of consciousness technique appears, linguistic markers clearly identify the source of the voice, as in the following example from the Proteus episode highlighting Stephen's thoughts on his origins. "Wombed in sin darkness I was too, made not begotten. By them, the man with my voice and my eyes and a ghostwoman with ashes on her breath. They clasped and sundered, did the coupler's will" (*U*, 3.45–47).

Later in the chapter I will address the question of whether the narrative voice represents the reconstruction of an immature consciousness by the mature Stephen. For now I wish to emphasize the ambiguity of the connection between Stephen and the narrator. As one begins to note the complexity of the impression created by the narrative beneath the simplicity of its initial tone, it becomes apparent that such a formal strategy could not function effectively within a single dominant perspective. These depictions present detached, critical views of the artistic impulse developing within Stephen in a voice that Stephen can understand but in language that he cannot yet reproduce.

The distinction I am making between the formal methods employed in *Portrait* and the stream of consciousness technique stands as a very precise but necessary one. The careful stylistic manipulation of *Portrait* establishes distinctive features for every voice contributing to the development of the discourse. Thus the narrative persona functions as an entity as distinct as Stephen or any other character. At the same time, descriptive methods at work within the discourse itself rely on a commingling of impressions, joining the voices of the narrator and of other individuals. Such an approach sharply conveys a particular personal perspective, while it simultaneously resists the impulse to confine the narrative to a single point of view. As a result, multiple views contribute to a shifting emphasis within the narrative and preclude the primacy of a single voice. Although the consciousness of Stephen certainly exerts the strongest influence on the development of the discourse, the perspectives of others, especially when they influence Stephen's thoughts, also have a pronounced impact. As the second paragraph of the work tells us, the commonplace introductory phrase, "once upon a time," does not emerge from Stephen's independent consciousness; the words are borrowed from a story told to Stephen by his father, Simon, who, in turn, borrowed them from the formulaic conventions of fairy tales. Throughout *Portrait* disparate narrative enunciations—a mixture of indirect and free indirect discourse—blur distinctions between descriptions emanating from the independent narrative voice and those tinged by phrases associated with the consciousness of Stephen or of other characters. The ambiguity of these articulations impresses on readers the polyvocal constitution of narrative description and the consequent provisional nature of any choices of emphasis they will make in their efforts to create texts from the novel.

None of Joyce's antecedents, save perhaps Flaubert, integrated alternative views into the narrative perspective with the density that he employed. Nonetheless, as noted in the previous chapter, authors had adopted free indirect discourse as a staple technique of prose fiction well before *Portrait* appeared. Despite the pervasive application of free indirect discourse, however, linguistic and literary critics have had some difficulty in reaching a consensus regarding general rules governing its identification and interpretation, often falling back on subjectivity to demonstrate its presence and on speculation to explain its function. In an essay on Joyce's use of free indirect discourse, Erwin R. Steinberg offers the following examples from *Ulysses*:

> By "Proteus," [free indirect discourse] is clearly in full operation: "They came down the steps from Leahy's terrace prudently, *Frauenzimmer*: and down the shelving shore flabbily their splayed feet sinking in the silted sand" [*U*, 3.29–31]. That sentence suggests an artist as a young man. The opening of "Calypso," however, though certainly having a different ring to it than the third-person sentences in "Proteus," does not sound very Bloomish: "Mr Leopold Bloom ate with relish the inner organs of beasts and fowls" [*U*, 4.1–2]. That is a little too formal for Bloom, a little too successfully literate.[7]

Steinberg accurately notes the difference in the styles of the two passages, but whether or not we must link the first to Stephen and disassociate the second from Bloom remains a matter of personal interpretation. Some readers might feel the tone of both segments to be in perfect resonance with the sardonic tone established by the narrator of the opening chapters of the work. Others might assign the conventional narrative voice of the first passage to an amorphous figure like "the arranger," David Hayman's ingenious term denoting the ubiquitous, polyvocal presence disrupting conceptions that a dominant narrative voice guides the discourse of *Ulysses*.[8] Still others might feel that the opening of Proteus perfectly captures the self-satisfied self-perception in which Bloom occasionally indulges in Calypso and elsewhere. My point is not that Steinberg is right or wrong but that he is engaging in the process that Joyce's application of free indirect discourse pushes all readers to: the creation of a specific text that excludes other equally valid readings.

Free indirect discourse in the passages cited by Steinberg does not simply integrate the consciousness of a character with that of the narrator. It blurs the distinctions between the two entities, forcing the reader into choices that time and again re-form the novel in the mind of that particular reader. The same conditions obtain in *Portrait* where free indirect discourse regularly occurs. In many instances the link between a particular character and elements within a narrative passage stands out clearly, but at a number of other points ambiguity obscures the identity of the voice, and this condition requires the reader to complete the sense of the passage. Far from contradicting the aims of the work, however, this ubiquitous (if ambivalent) application of free indirect discourse, in conjunction with other features of the narrative like parody and diegesis, enforces our awareness of the novel's central concerns.[9]

Hugh Kenner has drawn attention to important applications of free indirect discourse in *Portrait* by singling out one element, intonation, and eponymously calling it the Uncle Charles Principle, after the character whom Simon Dedalus exiles to the outhouse to smoke his pipe.[10] Kenner has provided a useful and witty label, but, as the categories listed in appendix A of this study make clear, his term touches only one facet of the technique. A more detailed discussion of free indirect discourse appears in John Paul Riquelme's *Teller and Tale in Joyce's Fiction.* In many ways Riquelme follows an approach analogous to mine, but in his conclusions he proposes an assessment of the narrative operation that generally conforms to received critical opinion. Riquelme feels that specimens of free indirect discourse evince the autobiographical presence of an older Stephen acting as narrator. From this perspective, as Stephen matures, his narration recapitulates his own past and presents Joyce's fictionalized autobiography.[11] Riquelme's reading represses important distinctions which, when taken into account, can lead to the production of equally valid texts.

Conjunction of the voices of Stephen and the narrator necessitates a circuitous means to explain the novel's complex ironic view of Stephen. Riquelme mutes the disparate tones of the consciousnesses of Stephen and of the narrative voice, projecting a narration founded on the retrospection of a mature writer. Through a series of stylistic regressions, Stephen presumably assumes a narrative voice set on an intellectual level comparable to that of the evolving consciousness of the central character while retaining the perspective of an experienced writer. Riquelme's thesis explains the marked contrast within the narrative created by free indirect discourse, but it also blunts much of the ambiguity that makes free indirect discourse such a powerful artistic technique. He posits a symbiotic relationship between the mature and immature minds of Stephen rather than a complementary one between the distinct but roughly equivalent consciousnesses of Stephen and the narrator. As a result the text he has created elides the very distance that free indirect discourse has worked so diligently to maintain. A less circumscribed view, and one more fruitful in terms of its potential for opening the novel to greater reader involvement, lies in a recognition of the separation that I propose between the narrator and the central character: a recognition that does not assume authorial hegemony or give primacy to the creation of a single text.

I realize, of course, that my approach directly contradicts the assertions of Wayne Booth, whose *The Rhetoric of Fiction* has had a pronounced effect on the critical sensibilities of several generations of American scholars. Booth describes his view of the relationship between writer and reader as follows:

> Regardless of my real beliefs and practices, I must subordinate my mind and heart to the book if I am to enjoy it to the full. The author creates, in short, an image of himself and another image of his reader; he makes his reader, as he makes his second self, and the most successful reading is one in which the created selves, author and reader, can find complete agreement.[12]

Readers conforming to Booth's characterization instinctively resist the abdication of authorial control inherent in a broad application of free indirect discourse, so for them the major difficulty presented by the opening paragraphs of *Portrait*, and one continued throughout the book, comes from competing voices delaying the establishment within the narrative of what Booth has termed "the norms of the work." Booth perceives this reluctance to depict in elaborate detail the exact configuration of the narrative discourse as a significant flaw in the novel, and this opinion leads him to mount a direct attack on the structure of *Portrait*.

> Whatever intelligence Joyce postulates in his reader . . . will not be sufficient for precise inference of a pattern of judgments which is, after all, private to Joyce. . . . We simply cannot avoid the conclusion that to some extent the book itself is at fault, regardless of its great virtues. . . . Even if we were now to do our homework like dutiful students, even if we were to study all of Joyce's work, even if we were to spend the lifetime that Joyce playfully said his novels demand, presumably we should never come to as rich, as refined, and as varied a conception of the quality of Stephen's last days in Ireland as Joyce had in mind. For some of us the air of detachment and objectivity [inherent in Joyce's style] may still be worth the price, but we must never pretend that a price was not paid.[13]

For Booth the distance between Joyce's world and the reader's world stands as an impediment to comprehension, one that must be surmounted before the work can be experienced fully. He grounds his thesis on the postulation of a linear approach to a piece of writing as the only valid response, assuming that all readers are willing to be led through a narrative to a conclusion that the author has already reached and that all writers are willing to exploit this passivity.

Such a concept, however, presumes a paradigmatic homogeneity to which authors simply no longer subscribe. Roland Barthes has offered a more viable assessment of the status of authorial intentionality in comments on Mallarmé's rejection of the role of explicator of the work, "suppressing the author in the interests of writing." This gesture of abnegation inevitably leads the reader to activities extending beyond speculations on what meanings lie hidden within the work, for, as Barthes notes, "[o]nce the author is removed, the claim to decipher a text becomes quite futile. To give a text an Author is to impose a limit on that text, to furnish it with a final signified, to close the writing."[14] Like Mallarmé, Joyce overturns constrictive modes of construing authorial presence in order to enhance the aesthetic impact of his work. He adopts the role of what Barthes has termed *scriptor.* This leaves the reader to exploit the very absences that Booth laments, not through glosses appended after the fact in the plodding manner of Melville's "painstaking burrower and grubworm of a poor devil of a Sub-Sub-[Librarian]," but through texts created as the work unfolds. Joyce does not, of course, refine himself out of existence by making us forget that *Portrait* is a story created by some writer. Instead he calls into question the primacy of a single voice assuming the authorial role of transmitting, either directly or ironically, "the norms of the work."

Because free indirect discourse permeates so much of the narrative and because so many instances of free indirect discourse reflect elements of Stephen's nature, the shift in descriptive style over the five chapters of *Portrait* closely corresponds to the process of intellectual and artistic maturation experienced by Stephen. Thus, arguments made by Booth, Riquelme, and others regarding the source of the narrative consciousness quite naturally focus on its relation to Stephen. At the same time, the novel's manipulation of narrational perspective through the recurrent use of free indirect discourse does more than simply enhance one's awareness of the distinctive form of the various chapters and call attention to the stylistic virtuosity of each incremental description of Stephen's growth. Free indirect discourse allows one to form a personal, subjective view of the growth of Stephen's consciousness while main-

taining the emotional distance necessary to achieve a sense of his surroundings more objectively than Stephen's own perceptions. This
objectivity, however, is really only relative. As I illustrated in my analysis of the opening pages of *Portrait*, free indirect discourse impedes the
emergence of a dominant style (arbiter of Booth's "norms of the
work"). As a consequence the reader may derive, indeed must derive,
some overriding formal structure to give coherence to a discrete text,
but he or she cannot ignore the provisional nature of that structure.

Successive lacunae, punctuating the sequential development of the
story line, serve as overt reminders of the options informing the reader's
continuing engagement in the process of creation. These gaps in the
chronological development of *Portrait* confirm the novel's episodic quality, and they impose upon the reader the responsibility for establishing
patterned continuity by fashioning conjunctions between its segments.
To facilitate this activity, the novel gives most scenes, with the exception
of Stephen's epiphanic moments, a quotidian rather than a develop-
mental aura. In reflecting this prosaic tempo of Stephen's life, *Portrait*
acquaints one with a range of alternatives for bridging any caesurae.
Thus one can follow the abrupt temporal displacement occurring from
chapter to chapter and impose a textual unity while retaining a sense
of the numerous other possibilities for interpreting the shifting tensions
between Stephen Dedalus and his environment.

I do not, of course, mean to suggest that an infinite number of texts
can legitimately be derived from Joyce's fiction. Whatever pattern of coherence the reader creates must develop within the paradigm of Joyce's
work and must reconcile competing and potentially conflicting impressions. Many other novels commonly encourage such a practice, and it
often consists of surreptitious elisions performed with little apparent
impact on interpretation. *Portrait*, however, foregrounds for the reader
this manipulation of the discourse, for the reconciliations required by
the narrative inevitably go beyond the maintenance of continuity to require a reconciliation of the discrepancy between an initial impression
and a subsequent attitude.

Thus, in moving from chapter I to chapter II of *Portrait* the reader
automatically supplies some sort of transition. One forges a concatenation between one's impression of Stephen on the playing field at Clongowes Wood, fresh from his interview with the rector, savoring his
moment of triumph over Father Dolan and the image of Simon Dedalus
banishing his pipe-smoking Uncle Charles to "a little outhouse" in a
garden in Blackrock. At this point in the reading the effort seems to
involve little more than an accommodation of the idiosyncrasies of

Joyce's style, for the thematic development of the novel still appears to accommodate a linear, cause-and-effect pattern of progression. A few pages later, however, an account of a meeting between Father Conmee, the former rector at Clongowes, and Simon Dedalus calls into question the presumption of a linear pattern of narrative development. Through the sardonic mediation of Simon Dedalus's retelling, Father Conmee gives a version of the aftermath of his interview with Stephen much different from the one that the closing events of the first chapter have urged us to construct. "Father Dolan and I, when I told them all at dinner about it, Father Dolan and I had a great laugh over it. *You better mind yourself, Father Dolan,* said I, *or young Dedalus will send you up for twice nine.* We had a famous laugh together over it. Ha! Ha! Ha!" (72).

This erosion in chapter II of Stephen's ostensible success in chapter I makes us conscious of the ambivalent nature of his achievement and forces a realignment of whatever text we have already formed. The satiric voice of Simon Dedalus comes from the same consciousness that had comforted baby tuckoo with the story of the moocow coming down along the road. Now, as he tells the family of his encounter with Father Conmee, Mr. Dedalus apparently undermines Stephen's satisfaction by rendering the boy's act of courage ludicrous. I use the word "apparently" because the episode ends equivocally, with the lines quoted in the passage above. Simon repeats Father Conmee's laughter, itself an ambiguous element whose significance changes with the emphasis in tone that the reader chooses to give it, and the reader must create Stephen's response as the work itself moves on to the next episode. The degree and the direction of this response, of course, will vary with every reader, and the conclusion that the reader supplies will determine the subsequent evolution of his or her text.

Further, the scene retrospectively introduces evidence, even before Stephen or the narrator acknowledges it, an early note of environmental discordance, making the change of fortunes that follow less emotionally abrupt. The removal of the Dedalus family to Dublin (*P,* 65) and Simon Dedalus's tone of bravado in his fireside speech to Stephen (*P,* 66) have already introduced a sense of impending financial disaster, but the backward glance at Stephen's meeting with the rector calls attention to how much information the novel leaves out and enforces its demand that we continually revise our own elision of events. The scene with Uncle Charles takes on deeper significance as we realize the degree to which it reflects greater tension within the family, and it guides the revision of our suppositions concerning what must have taken place during the significant silence between chapters I and II.

This process of encouraging the reader to review assumptions regarding the putative events that connect the experiences closing one episode with the markedly different ones beginning another continues throughout the work. As *Portrait* unfolds, the reader becomes habituated to the task of creating links, and the need for such prompting from Joyce diminishes. By the time chapter V opens, we have become fully attuned to the decorum of the work so that one naturally assimilates the shift in attitude from the aesthetic satisfaction of Stephen's epiphanic experience with the bird girl at the end of chapter IV to his postprandial depression in the Dedalus kitchen by a reconstruction of the evolving text.

In his efforts to stimulate the involvement of the reader, Joyce not only left out significant elements of the discourse but also added what at first glance appear to be superfluous ones. At various points, discrete segments—both artistic forms like Stephen's villanelle and extra-artistic ones like the retreat master's sermons—operate along lines not regulated by the characteristics that define the dominant generic scheme of the work. Each deviation disrupts the patterned rhythm and tone of the context which surrounds it, but in calling attention to itself it also underscores the features of the predominant genre. In addition, while none of the alternative genres incorporated into *Portrait* displaces the governing features of the novel, the introduction of each new construction demands a redistribution of the stylistic emphasis one gives to an incipient text. In brief, each of the variants remains an aberrant fixture, demanding attention without overtly signifying a specific, and hence limited, purpose.

In most early instances, the brevity of these generic disruptions causes their impact to be overlooked by all but the most scrupulous of readers. With the third chapter, however, the question of how to integrate shifts in generic form into a unified text begins to take on a dimension that cannot be ignored. The extended presentation of Father Arnall's retreat sermon, asserting itself over several dozen pages, stands distinctly outside the stylistic features that have up to this point characterized the work's narrative, and any assumptions that the reader has formed regarding the presumed structure of the discourse must necessarily change to accommodate this deviation in form. As the retreat master's homily struggles for primacy within the consciousness of Stephen against his incipient attitude of rebellion, it also struggles for recognition from a reader habituated to associating very different descriptive forms within the novel.

For readers who respond with skepticism to the logic supporting Father Arnall's sermon, the suggestion that one assign any lasting significance to the priest's remarks may appear naive. The work itself seems to provide ample evidence for dismissing Father Arnall's disquisition, for, although the sermon (*P,* 108) produces in Stephen a great deal of superficial, short-lived piety, it in fact embodies the kinetic approach to art that he will later condemn as pornographic (*P,* 205). Probably with this in mind, most critics have been inclined to take the religious devotion that follows the retreat at its face value, a period of recidivism in Stephen's development as an artist.

I believe, however, that it is a mistake simply to dismiss this generic intrusion as little more than a parody of Catholic ritual or as an attack on Catholic dogma. As James Thrane has shown, the Belvedere retreat conducted by Father Arnall follows a long-established penitential tradition,[15] and it reiterates approaches to doctrinal interpretation to which Stephen has been exposed throughout his life. Father Arnall's exhortations in fact restore to this dogma a (temporary) credibility in Stephen's mind because a decade of formal religious education has inculcated in him the sense of its efficacy. While the evocative images of the sermons may oversimplify the sophisticated doctrines which they attempt to exemplify (a flaw that Stephen is probably aware of), Father Arnall's homilies very lucidly remind him and the readers of the attractiveness of surrendering self-control to the direction of a social institution.

The retreat certainly represents for Stephen a temptation to embrace stability, trading conformity for certitude. (The invitation in chapter IV to join the Society of Jesus functions in much the same way.) Despite its formal and thematic separation from the dominant movement of the novel, the series of sermons operates effectively as a means of persuading Stephen to accept the viability of an environment governed by codes bound to the traditional values of his society. Although antithetical to the behavior inspired by the artistic impulse, its ritualized language and prescriptive behavior offer precisely the emotional satisfaction that will ultimately lead Stephen to dedicate himself to art: it outlines a perfectly justified response to the question of fulfillment. This strong and continuing attraction represents a portion of the beliefs and the perspectives that have contributed to the formation of Stephen's adolescent consciousness. Therefore, like the other conventional styles influencing the structural departures of *Portrait,* the penitential form of the retreat demands assimilation by any reader wishing to come to a full sense of Stephen's nature.

This imperative to understand Stephen's background becomes that much stronger when one recalls that, although he ultimately rebels against the institutions that surround him, Stephen can never dismiss or ignore them. When he explains his aesthetics to Lynch in chapter V, the central tenet of his belief is a determination to position himself in opposition to his environment. This projects an attitude that does not simply represent an abandonment of beliefs. Rather it asserts personal independence despite the potency of the system confronted. Even as he declares his intention of escaping the constricting atmosphere of the Irish intellectual environment, he asserts his intention of re-forming the Irish consciousness. "Welcome, O Life! I go to encounter for the millionth time the reality of experience and to forge in the smithy of my soul the uncreated conscience of my race" (*P,* 253). Stephen does not make the statement lightly or without cognizance of its possible consequences. If he is to become the artist who will forge the uncreated consciousness of his race, he must be willing to incorporate the tradition of its beliefs into his art.

Throughout its narrative, *Portrait* indicates the lasting impact that these attitudes have on Stephen's personality, and the reader wishing to give Stephen's nature the dimensions it deserves must elaborate upon the emotional content of the retreat to understand the powerful competitive force of the Catholic Church, and by extension of other Irish institutions, on Stephen's development. In a similar manner, the form of the sermons, with their very straightforward, didactic account of the material, stands in opposition to the reader's efforts to exert creative control over the text. As such they remind us of the literary tradition we oppose by the act of reading *Portrait.* In his acceptance and then in his rejection of the tenets of the retreat sermons, Stephen still has reached only the intermediary stage of his maturation. The reader must complete the process only suggested to Stephen by delineating the contradictory forces within his nature and by using that impression to outline Stephen's potential for attaining his artistic goals.

In contrast to the socially intrusive genre of the retreat sermon, chapter V incorporates two forms demonstrating Stephen's incipient artistic talent and aesthetic values—the villanelle and the diary section. Although neither shows the power of a mature artist, each passage in *Portrait* provides the reader with the raw material necessary to create an image of the artist that Stephen will become. The villanelle acts as a transition piece. Stephen writes it in a highly agitated condition, but its completion, in accordance with his aesthetic theory, brings calm. It appears piecemeal, only gradually forming itself before the reader. Its retention of much of the symbolic baggage of the decadent period makes it a flawed poem; still it demonstrates Stephen's creative ability and intellectual discipline. The diary section, appearing on the final pages of the work reflects Stephen's kinetic concerns transcribed to produce stasis. It affirms Stephen's artistic potential by presenting the raw material of his imagination, and it implicitly invites the reader to complete the gesture through the creation of an aesthetically satisfying text.

Portrait begins with the repetition of a fairy tale—a set piece. It ends with Stephen's own creation, but a creation that is left to the reader to form into a whole. All of the intervening interpolated genres highlight material that will become an integral part of Stephen's consciousness and art: the matter of Ireland—social, cultural, and religious. Further, each shows Stephen in various creative roles—listener, faltering poet, unselfconscious diarist—marking his intellectual and artistic development. Context links the genres and the roles explicitly to Stephen, but all derive an additional significance from their direct, formal manipulation of the reader, an effect which we must self-consciously apprehend in order to appreciate fully its impact.

Much of the stimulus for the reader's creative intervention comes directly from the proliferation of diverse constructions within the novel. In addition to the broad application of free indirect discourse, the formal variance of the patterns of narrative language and the introduction of incorporated genres set the rhythm for the unfolding action of the text in the opening selection, cited above, and in subsequent passages throughout the book. Though not always precisely delineated or presented with equal force, these elements contribute diverse perspectives influencing but not determining the reader's response to the emerging consciousness of Stephen. Each offers its own approach to the completion of meaning based on standards shaped by its own perspective, and each strives ultimately for the reader's approbation by justifying itself at the expense of other alternatives. Together they reflect what Mikhail Bakhtin might have labeled the heteroglossia of the work.

> [A] diversity of social speech types (sometimes even diversity of languages) and a diversity of individual voices, artistically organized. . . . Authorial speech, the speeches of narrators, inserted genres, the speech of characters are merely those fundamental compositional unities with whose help heteroglossia can enter the novel; each of them permits a multiplicity of social voices and a wide variety of their links and interrelationships (always more or less dialogized).[16]

Despite implications that one might be tempted to draw from the preceding lines, Bakhtin does not find this diversity as an inevitable source of chaos. Rather he sees within such competing demands the potential for greatly expanded reader perception brought about through the dialogical tension of voices within the work.

> Heteroglossia, once incorporated into the novel (whatever the forms for its incorporation), is *another's speech in another's language*, serving to express authorial intentions but in a refracted way. Such speech constitutes a special type of *double-voiced discourse*. It serves two speakers at the same time and expresses simultaneously two different intentions: the direct intention of the character who is speaking, and the refracted intention of the author (emphasis Bakhtin's).[17]

In *Portrait* these discourses occur on different levels, and they function without the weighted (and in my view misplaced) significance ascribed by Bakhtin to authorial intentionality. They reflect stylistic rather than contextual aims, for *Portrait* impels the reader to assume the dialogic function that Bakhtin assigns to the author. In effect the novel consciously shifts the terms of engagement from the subject-centered consciousness to the language-centered discourse described by Roland Barthes and by Michel Foucault.[18]

As I will show below, in the narrative of *Portrait* Joyce avoids the didactic impulse of opposing, even obliquely, his own refracted aims to the direct intentions of his characters. Rather he projects a range of perceptions and leaves it to the reader to resolve the dialogic confrontation by producing provisional, idiosyncratic meanings. Through this approach *Portrait* foregrounds the subjectivity inherent in all interpretation, and it accentuates the role of the reader who must form some resolution of apparent dialogic contradictions within an evolving work.

Up to this point, I have suggested in only a general way methods or strategies for the reader to follow in responding to Joyce's challenge to participate in the creation of a text for *Portrait*. For the remainder of the chapter, I would like to elaborate an approach for creating meaning through an accommodation of the implicit ambiguities of the work. I have already noted the inherent tension between the narrator's position and Stephen's consciousness, juxtaposed through free indirect discourse. The ambivalence produced by their interaction displaces any notion of the existence of a putative objective reality dispensed through a voice representing the overriding authorial position. A range of views, often conflicting or even contradictory, receive equal weight, frustrating attempts to interpret the work in terms of cause-and-effect logic. Instead, competing consciousnesses within the narrative all contribute to the formation of an unassimilated repertoire. As a consequence, one achieves a sense of the unity of the work only through what Kenneth Burke has termed a "compensation for disunity," an acceptance of the paradoxes intrinsic to the unresolved/unresolvable dialectic condition.[19]

Michael McCanles, in applying Burkean logic to analyses of Renaissance literature, has demonstrated concretely the ability of this approach to produce a balanced interpretation that still accommodates apparently contradictory artistic positions. In a contrast that foregrounds the central concerns of his method, McCanles offers the following description of the frustration inevitable in an epistemology that depends entirely upon linear responses to conditions.

> Dialectic occurs, whether within literature or out of it, when men attempt to put an either-or question to a both-and reality. The ultimate source of the question is the radical structure of human thinking insofar as it is governed by the principle of non-contradiction. Enforced with rigid and tyrannical urgency, this principle continually generates antinomies when it comes face-to-face with a world characterized by diversity and change.[20]

Although McCanles chooses to describe the relationship in terms of antagonisms, within his statement lies the assumption that dialectic sophistication involves a movement towards a compensation for the disunities producing conflicts between elements rather than towards a complete amalgamation of those elements to create a totally new entity. Dialectic confrontation in *Portrait* stands as an important feature in the process of interpretation. Although its application does not require the complex exploitation demanded by *Ulysses* or by *Finnegans Wake*, its employment serves to illuminate important stages of Stephen's (and Joyce's) growth.

As with other narrative features already noted—free indirect discourse, temporal gaps, and incorporated genres—dialectical manipulations within *Portrait* engage the reader in the act of forming meaning. Dialectics, however, differs from the other techniques in that it operates both within and outside the act of creating a particular text. Its function originates within the structure of the novel in both dialogue and narration. At the same time, its impact extends from efforts to affect the reader through manipulation of plot, setting, and characterization to the point of confronting directly the act of reading. It fulfills a mediating function by explicitly moving between the fictional and the metafictional level, providing readers with the nexus between *Portrait*'s paradigm and a personal text. In other words, the dialectic subverts the impulse to reify a particular interpretation. Instead, it encourages a process of continuing revision while maintaining stability within one's overall response to the work.

The striking difference between reader engagement in *Dubliners* and in *Portrait* derives in part from this development, and the dialectic process reciprocally gains its legitimacy from the habituating impact of free indirect discourse on the mind of the reader. As I have observed earlier, through the growing stylistic sophistication with which Joyce employed free indirect discourse, one can trace the emergence of his creative fluency. This developing artistic power also places demands upon readers extending beyond the response that one conventionally makes to prose fiction. If implemented progressively, however, this process increases one's ability to comprehend Joyce's art, and this, in turn, makes possible even greater experimentation in successive writings.

The incipient features of dialectical confrontation appear irregularly in *Dubliners*, but it manifests itself with sufficient clarity to allow one to form a clear sense of the advances that Joyce made in the composition of *Portrait*. In various stories, characters in *Dubliners* struggle with the ambiguities of their environment, and they fail to reach a resolution because of their efforts to impose either/or questions on both/and realities. Most suffer from a stagnation that to some degree follows inevitably from the form of the work. We see them only in a moment in time, and we have no other moments to use as standards for measuring their growth or degradation. Generic form enforces a rough consistency within each story, directing our impressions toward a single, unified interpretation. Stylistic experimentation, as it appears in the stories, underscores the views of the central character. When dialectic confrontation occurs, the ambiguity it generates cannot lead the reader to sustained creative development of a text since the story ends with the character on the verge of realizing the ambivalence of his or her position.

In *Portrait* Joyce has the space to expose Stephen to what Mikhail Bakhtin has called "the world of other equal consciousnesses."[21] A series of episodes—the Christmas dinner, Father Conmee's recollections of the events surrounding Stephen's pandying, the retreat-master's sermon, Cranly's response to Stephen's apostasy—confront Stephen and the reader with characters espousing alternative points of view of the world in which Stephen exists. Such passages do not receive full development and consequently cannot displace the views of Stephen from central consideration, but they do remind him and readers of the necessary circumscription of his way of seeing the world.

Not only do other characters question the primacy of a single way of perceiving, Stephen himself continually shifts positions to accommodate his evolving connection to the society he alternately embraces and scorns. The dialectic confrontation produced by Stephen's divergent attitudes does not come to an abrupt halt at the end of each chapter; rather it moves toward a unification without synthesis that sets the boundaries for the struggle that will begin with the next chapter. Stephen's process of character evolution, tracing a spiral development, derives from his dialectic revolution between self and society. Each chapter produces a tentative resolution looking toward continued conflict at the next stage. At each point Stephen reaches an accommodation that subsequent events will overturn. Nonetheless the development underscoring the process moves Stephen beyond the frustrated endings that characters in the *Dubliners* stories must face.

Interpretation hinges on a creative resolution within a text of the tension formed by dialectical situations throughout the novel. Indeed one could trace the action of each chapter as evolving from nodes of dialectical conflict. Chapter I grows out of a form paralleling the immature consciousness trying to comprehend its environment. It ends with Stephen enjoying the success of his challenge of Father Dolan's authority, but Stephen gains his victory by appealing to a higher level within the institution not by stepping outside it. Chapter II articulates the perspective of the pre-adolescent and adolescent Stephen. It opens with an abrupt shift in the routine of Stephen's life that he initially views with equanimity; he will not be returning to Clongowes Wood. As the chapter unfolds and a series of episodes gradually makes Stephen aware of the declining economic position of his family, events come to undermine his confidence in social institutions that he had earlier assumed would protect him. In his encounter with the prostitute—the physical and metaphysical climax of the chapter—he moves, temporarily, away from the controlling influence of those institutions. Stephen, however, cannot as yet maintain a position independent of social support. Chapter III begins with the adolescent Stephen in the equivocal position of a hypocrite. Nighttown has lost its mystery but not its attraction, and Stephen finds himself caught between the wish to maintain the appearance of respectability and the physical needs he longs to satisfy. His return to the Church at the end of the chapter represents his inability at that point to sustain the complexity of a both/and reality. Consistent with the dialectic process, however, conflicting forces continue to assert themselves, and chapter IV opens with the spiritual regime that Stephen had imposed upon himself degenerating into a rote performance that fails to sustain the satisfaction he had hoped to attain. Later, by rejecting the formal support that would have been given to him as a Jesuit novice, Stephen again steps beyond the boundaries of social institutions, and in the chapter's lyrical finale, the birdgirl episode, he establishes art as the moral center of his universe. The shabby surroundings of the Dedalus household, described in the first few pages of chapter V, emphasize the limits of his art: it cannot insulate one from mundane, physical reality. As the aesthetic discussion with Lynch and the religious debate with Cranly show, Stephen has come to realize that he cannot accommodate the either/or choices that his life in Dublin imposes upon him. The chapter ends with Stephen articulating his commitment to art, but he does not sever all connection with the society from which he has come. In the novel's final pages Stephen declares that he will fly the nets of family, church, and state, but he also affirms his intention of forging "the uncreated consciousness" of his race, a goal that aims back at the society from which he has claimed he wishes to escape.

One's inability to see Stephen as a completely genuine or as a completely ironic hero does not derive from aspects of individual taste but from *Portrait*'s depiction of the ambiguity of Stephen's, or for that matter of any character's, choices. The dialectic condition emphatically refuses to tolerate either/or choices, and it repeatedly confronts the reader with the inevitable ambiguity of both/and conditions. While defining the paradigm within which one can complete the action introduced within the novel, it refuses to prescribe the direction that one must follow to create a text.

As the fluctuations of the fictional repertoire cause Stephen to struggle throughout *Portrait* with conflicting impulses to conform to the society in which he exists or to defy it, the novel produces parallel tensions at the metafictional level between the incipient text and the reader generating it. When our efforts to create meaning out of narrative events confront the polyphonic assertions of *Portrait*, we vacillate between ironic and straightforward perceptions of Stephen and his world, never settling on one or the other. Our attitudes shift, and (consciously or not) we experience a disorientation similar to Stephen's, as structure reinforces content. On the formal level the dialectic process continually asserts its literary nature(s) through disruptions—most evident in the opening and the closing passages but prominent throughout the novel—analogous to those occurring at the thematic level. Each chapter reflects a stylistic maturation analogous but not coincidental with Stephen's growth. As *Portrait* unfolds the reader must hold these forms in suspension, balancing one against another to achieve a hypostatic comprehension of content, structure, and style.

Acknowledging the multiplicity of interpretations inherent in free indirect discourse and in dialectic conflict may seem to frustrate actual interpretative efforts. Shifts in style and in characterization make inevitable the parallactic nature of any interpretation of *Portrait*: a reader sees not the whole work but that portion of it revealed from a particular intellectual perspective. Again this does not mean that *Portrait* gives itself over to any idiosyncratic meaning that one chooses to assign to it. Disruptive forms fix the range and limits of those possible perspectives. They establish the paradigm of creative possibilities from which Joyce constructed the text and from which readers derive interpretations.

VI | *Exiles*: The Development of Multiple Characterizations

Up to this point in my study, I have been emphasizing the formal achievement that Joyce attained through the innovative styles employed in *Dubliners* and in *Portrait*. Naturally enough, the introduction of these methods also had a marked impact on the contextual development of his fiction. One can specifically see a self-reflexive duality in the discourses of *Dubliners* and of *Portrait*. This duality allows them to reject the interpretive limitations inherent in a narration relying exclusively upon either a first-person or a third-person point of view to explain the perceptions and the motivations that frame the action. Instead the narrative voice and central character implicitly comment upon one another's perspectives, underscoring for the reader the provisional nature of any single point of view.

At the same time, certain broad attitudes—the narrator's and the central character's—achieve a privileged status. As a result, the reader's ability to exploit the multiplicity of the discourse always remains circumscribed. The narrative voice unfolds a version of the action that stands in tension with that construed by the consciousness of the main character, and the reader can comprehend the discourse only through the amalgamation of their essentially binary relationship. Despite the broader sense of the discourse derived from the introduction of additional perspectives, however, the commanding narrative feature in each story of *Dubliners* remains the interplay between the consciousness of the narrative voice and that of a single personality. A similar condition obtains in *Portrait* where Stephen Dedalus's nature exerts pervasive influence in shaping our comprehension of the descriptive structure. In effect, in Joyce's early prose fiction free indirect discourse, despite its intimation of a fluctuating point of view, concentrates our attention on a single feature: the primacy of the bond between the narrative voice and the consciousness of a central character.

Characterization further limits the thematic boundaries of the paradigms of *Dubliners* and of *Portrait*. Most of the central figures, from the boy of "The Sisters" to Stephen Dedalus, derive their natures from a common social repertoire, and they respond to it with the same basic pattern of beliefs and attitudes. While the protagonists in *Dubliners* do not represent carbon copies of Stephen Dedalus, even those who appear least in sympathy with his attitudes—Maria, Eveline, Lenehan, Farrington, for example—confront the same types of frustrations and feel the same categories of repression against which Stephen rebels. As a result, the development of the discourse follows a fairly restrictive pattern. In each work the dominant character dictates the course of events, and other individuals enter the narration only to reflect (through support or opposition) the attitudes of the protagonist.

Surviving evidence relating to the composition of *Ulysses*—notes, drafts, personal recollections—indicates that from its inception Joyce planned a work developed along radically different lines: one with expansive contextual concerns and multifarious characterizations that would completely dispel any inclination in the reader to give precedence to a particular social disposition by bringing into play a range of diverse attitudes, a multiplicity of responses, functioning within the same situation. With such goals in mind it must have been obvious to Joyce that a narrative strategy analogous to the ones employed in *Dubliners* and in *Portrait* could not anchor the complex plot line that he envisioned for *Ulysses*.

Of course, one finds aspects of *Dubliners* and *Portrait* echoed in particular perspectives and themes presented in *Ulysses*, but the amplification of its characterizations and the diversification of its narrational incursions show a marked departure from the narrower conceptions of his earlier fiction. Joyce wished to juxtapose different personalities without a single dominant nature stifling the depictions of the others or narrowing the alternatives for the elaboration of the plot. (In fact several years after he had begun composing *Ulysses*, Joyce acknowledged to his friend Frank Budgen that Stephen no longer interested him. "He has a shape that can't be changed."[1]) *Ulysses* develops its action not through the perspective of one individual with views analogous to Joyce's own but through the eyes of three diverse central figures whose attitudes are supplemented or contrasted by those of numerous supporting characters. As a consequence its plot progresses along distinctive but converging lines determined by the disposition and the actions of a variety of people. To synthesize these divergent attitudes into a coherent overview, Burke's unification of disunities, Joyce needed to extend his techniques for framing a story beyond the contextual boundaries established in *Dubliners* and in *Portrait*. *Exiles* became the vehicle for this stylistic and thematic reordering.

While still working on the final draft of *Portrait*, Joyce began making notes for the play and roughing out a version of act one during the fall of 1913.[2] For the first seven months of 1914, he seems to have given himself over to the completion of his novel, but in August of that year he returned to work on his play, composing additional fragments and drafts of acts two and three. On 17 March 1915, at around the same time that he was beginning work on *Ulysses*, Joyce wrote to Ezra Pound to say that he had completed *Exiles* (*Letters*, III.508), but this announcement of closure seems to have been premature. Textual evidence, uncovered by John MacNicholas, shows that, as work on *Ulysses* heightened his awareness of the need to balance the emphasis of competing consciousnesses, Joyce continued to refine elements of the drama.[3]

This chronology suggests an overlapping similar to the process occurring during the final revisions of *Dubliners* and the crucial stages of the composition of *Portrait*, and from this simultaneous writing one can infer a reciprocal influence between *Exiles* and the early stages of *Ulysses*. Additional evidence of creative continuity, as MacNicholas has observed, comes from the pattern of notes, fragments of dialogue, and evidence of revision that clearly replicate the procedure for composition followed by Joyce in writing other works.[4] While the fragments and the revisions outline the direction of Joyce's development, specific motivations for undertaking such a project in the midst of ostensibly more pressing concerns remain difficult to ascertain. It does seem clear that the revisions had broad contextual aims, echoing the process that was evolving simultaneously through work on the early stages of *Ulysses*. Specifically in their efforts to strengthen portrayals of individuals, the changes highlight approaches to rendition marking the final stage of the development of characterization in *Exiles*: a method that alternately emphasizes and undercuts each of the central figures, achieving through this fluctuation a roughly balanced distribution of perspectives.[5] (A closer examination of a fragment of dialogue and an analogous portion of the final version appears later in this chapter.)

Joyce's previous habits of composition underscore his inclination towards incremental development: his ability to amplify character and action beyond the provenance of a narrator and a focal individual emerged only after a period of experimentation provided the transition. In this instance, however, the evolution proceeded more rapidly than had previous creative advances because he had a very precise sense of the abilities that he intended to cultivate. In writing *Exiles* Joyce wished to explore methods for articulating a variety of responses to a specific condition, giving approximately equal weight to each. To do so, he focused his attention on the sexual appetites manifesting themselves in the relations of the three central characters in the play.

Because of the powerful descriptive detail of his earlier prose compositions, one might question whether, at this point, Joyce needed further refinement of his technical skills or whether the result—a deft portrayal in *Ulysses* of the gritty side of human sexuality—stands as a particularly noteworthy development in his artistic maturation. As early as 1906, Joyce himself, in a letter to his putative publisher Grant Richards, commented on the harshness of certain passages in *Dubliners*, acknowledging "that the odour of ashpits and old weeds and offal hangs round my stories" (*Letters*, I.64). Similarly, H. G. Wells found this same sort of earthiness evident in *Portrait*, for, in an otherwise laudatory review (reprinted in *P,* 329–33), he felt it necessary to call attention to the novel's "cloacal obsession." These views, however, can be misleading. Depictions of basic biological functions are not, for most readers, analogous to descriptions of erotic pleasure, and accounts of coarse self-indulgence do not evoke a sense of the dynamics of shared human experience.

In fact, the ability to amplify the metaphoric potential inherent in descriptions of sexual activity—especially for conveying a sense of his characters' psychological needs—evolved slowly in Joyce's canon. His earlier compositions emphasized solitary experience and circumscribed attitudes to the point of delineating protagonists as little more than self-absorbed individuals with a perception of sensuality that hardly extended beyond narcissism. The poems of *Chamber Music* present a mystical view of love, sensuous without being overtly sensual, articulating the drives within the mind of the lover without dwelling upon the moment of their satisfaction. In *Giacomo Joyce* the devotee of *Chamber Music* has grown older (and in fact is troubled by the process of aging), but his basic concern remains the same: solipsistic sexual reverie. Joyce sketches erotic moments, noting more specifically the details of physical attraction, but the mental turmoil of Giacomo receives much greater attention.

In Joyce's more mature works, the sexuality remains incipient and self-centered. The boy of "Araby," Eveline, Farrington, and others never go beyond themselves. Only in Gabriel Conroy does Joyce present the possibility, clouded by ambivalence, of a major character acquiring the ability to experience conjunctive love. Even this tentative move, however, proves to be only a transitory gesture. *Portrait* draws back from the evocative power of sexuality implied in "The Dead," ultimately suggesting that aesthetic pleasure has replaced physical gratification as the focal point of sustained individual interest. Chapter I is dominated by the childish *amour-propre* of the young Stephen. Although chapter II climaxes with Stephen's initial encounter with a prostitute, his passivity and detachment belie the sense of engagement. As chapter III begins, he has already lapsed into a jaded condition of self-centered satiety. At the close of chapter IV, in the best-known erotic passage of the novel, the beauty of the birdgirl mutes Stephen's drive for physical fulfillment. Sexual desire cannot hold his full attention, and sensuous satisfaction, through artistic rather than biological creativity, supplants it. Chapter V extends this impulse, confirming Stephen's secular vocation as "priest of eternal imagination" (*P,* 221). Thus only with the composition of *Exiles*—explicit in its concern for the relations between couples and not simply with individual lust—does Joyce finally begin to expand the figurative range of his carnal imagery to accommodate extensions in his thematic interests.

Exiles, of course, does not represent for Joyce a complete break with his earlier habits of composition, but it does throw into relief specific aspects of his creative process that have taken on new significance for him. It underscores particularly his efforts to reconcile the impulse to expand his contextual range with the desire to explore the artistic possibilities inherent in the formative experiences of his youth. With the completion of *Portrait,* certain dominant features of the Dublin ambiance had already become fixtures in his work, but, at the same time, the constraints of realism had begun to inhibit continuing growth. While he showed himself remarkably adept at exploiting the rich and varied texture of lower-middle-class life in his native city, Joyce realized that too strict an adherence to the traditional naturalistic limits imposed by straightforward chronicles of Dublin would lead to an intellectual stagnation similar to that which he already depicted in his fiction.

In writing *Exiles* Joyce demonstrated a commitment to reconciling important features of his intellectual and cultural development with the demands of creative innovation. He made a concerted effort to retain the thematic issues and the typological boundaries of urban life established in *Dubliners* and in *Portrait,* but he also attempted to enrich and to diversify the play's content through a greater attentiveness to the dynamics of interactions between individuals within this milieu. The shift in genre allowed him to reexamine the contextual as well as the stylistic assumptions that had conditioned his previous writing and to expand further his concept of the reader's role in this creative activity.

Piety, superstition, provinciality, hypocrisy, and, of course, paralysis provide the emotional boundaries for the action in *Dubliners* and *Portrait*. These features also intrude upon the characterization of *Exiles*, allowing Joyce the latitude of thematic experimentation within the secure parameters of well-known material. Consequently, although its setting and atmosphere evolve out of what at this point in his writing has become for Joyce an artistic commonplace, the sexual interplay by which *Exiles* unfolds its plot defamiliarizes the signature presentations of these attitudes through the multiple points of view of the play's three central figures.

In the stories of *Dubliners* and in *Portrait*, solipsism inevitably dominates the consciousness of every central character, even in moments of greatest physical, emotional, or spiritual intimacy (cf. Mr. Duffy's thoughts in the closing pages of "A Painful Case," or Stephen's attitude towards Emma Clery, or his efforts to compose his villanelle). This concentrates the reader's interest on a relatively narrow band of feelings. In contrast, the sexual interaction of *Exiles* and the perspectives of it that Joyce chooses to present disperse the focus of attention over a number of figures. While individual characterization within the play remains uneven, the energy generated by sexual tension enriches the depictions of human interactions and prefigures the complex relations that will be presented in *Ulysses*.

This conjunction of familiar and innovative forms marks *Exiles* as a watershed in Joyce's canon. For the first time in his career as a writer, he compiles an interpretation of the familiar Dublin setting from the consciousnesses of several prominent personalities of variegated sentiments. Diverse attitudes create open conflict, and the concept of an integral perspective guiding the development of the discourse weakens.

The play's central features intentionally turn upon an ambiguity that serves as an implicit demand for the participation of the audience. The indeterminacies that fill its scenes invert the conventions of free indirect discourse. They invite us to form our own commentary upon the conflicting views and unresolved conflicts presented in the dialogue to complete the discourse of the play. One can always distinguish the voices of individual characters, but, unlike the dramas of Ibsen or of other contemporary playwrights, no figure provides the reassurance of a definite narrative voice, articulating the standards for judging perceptions.[6] Because of the absence of a unifying perspective, the audience must assume that role and integrate its own views into the action.

Consequently, the play's organizing propositions unfold with less certainty but with more polemic vigor—diffused among the central characters—than those Joyce introduced in *Dubliners* or in *Portrait*.

These efforts produce some distortion and artificiality, but the play goes much further than any of Joyce's previous works in its attempt to offer a balanced view of the complex interactions of heterogeneous consciousnesses. In writing *Exiles* Joyce did not attain the mastery of diversification and of multiple contexts that would become the hallmark of later works. His efforts to present a range of personalities fully integrated into the action of the drama did, however, stimulate its development, and information relating to the composition of *Exiles* reinforces one's perception of the timely, meliorative role it played in forwarding Joyce's facility for employing the tension of sexual interaction to enhance the thematic elements of *Ulysses*.

At the most basic level, the existing notes for the play give one some sense of the details that Joyce initially wished to work into his drama, and they set up interesting contrasts with what actually appeared. Despite the dispassionate tone of the play itself, Joyce gave a great deal of thought to the physical aspect of sexuality: He extrapolated on the aspects of an extramarital affair to consider it in terms of a ménage à trois; he speculated on Bertha's probable willingness to participate in diverse forms of intercourse; and he touched upon various aspects of sadomasochism (*JJA*, XI.39–48). Bluntly described in his notes, these topics appear in the play only through insinuation. Limitations on the degree to which one could depict explicit sexuality in the theater explain some of the disparity between the open descriptions in his notes and their muted portrayal on stage. But the languid and apparently pleasureless exchanges between his characters suggest another reason. Joyce did not yet feel confident in his ability to present or even to suggest erotic behavior, without distracting attention from other elements in the drama. Perhaps more precisely, in *Exiles* Joyce honed his ability to convey the motivations behind the behavior of a range of characters. As he worked to develop techniques to present these attitudes faithfully, he did not want to give undue emphasis to sexuality.

Consequently, the oscillation of desire within the central characters foregrounds a variety of conflicting attitudes, yet much remains implicit, leaving the task of resolution to the audience. *Exiles*, in a departure from the pattern set in Joyce's earlier work, places emphasis on the implications surrounding the mutual consent that leads to fulfillment rather than on the stress inherent in individual exigency that precedes it. This emphasis directs our attention to the alternating impact of power and of appetite in shaping or reshaping the nature of relations between characters. Sexuality emerges as a necessary but complex feature of one's nature rather than as a shameful adjunct, and it assumes a representative involvement by serving as a mediative element for suggesting, without defining, aspects of individual development. A variety of predilections—Bertha's willingness to elope with Richard, Robert's wish to supplant Richard by seducing Bertha, Richard's determination that Bertha should act according to her own will—all depend for their coherence upon the complementary features of one consciousness developing in conjunction with that of another, yet no instance offers a prescriptive delineation of character.

From the following examples, one can derive a sense of the dramatic force that Joyce's play acquired through the stylistic insinuation of ambiguous sexual motivation. They offer contrasting renditions of a portion of the scene in act three in which Bertha and Richard encounter one another for the first time after having separated at Robert's cottage on the preceding night. The first is one of the dialogue fragments composed by Joyce fairly early in the process of writing *Exiles*. The second passage is drawn from the final version of the interchange.[7]

BERTHA: I wish I had never met you.

RICHARD: You would like to be freer now than you are.

BERTHA: Yes.

RICHARD, *pained*:   So that you could go to that house at night more freely to meet your lover.

BERTHA, *putting her arms about his neck*:   Yes, dear. I wish I had never met you. I wish you were my lover waiting for me there.

RICHARD: Or he?

BERTHA, *shaking her head*:   You, dear. I want to love you over again. I want to forget you. *Kissing him.* Love me, Dick. Forget me and love me.

RICHARD: Have you forgotten me for him?

BERTHA: No. I remember you. You have a different way of giving yourself to a woman—a more beautiful way than he has. *She smooths back his hair.* Dick, never embrace her the way men do.

RICHARD: Her? Who?

BERTHA: Beatrice. Never do. Let her remember you always as I can see you now.

RICHARD: And if she does will you envy her?

BERTHA: No. I want her to remember you always and to think of you. But not like others. Because she is a fine kind of person too. (*JJA*, pp. 70–71)

This sketch of the couple's confrontation lays bare a variety of attitudes, and the audience faces only the task of sorting them out and giving to each the proper emphasis. In its final form, the scene blurs the delineations of both Richard and Bertha by truncating and concentrating their dialogue. The transitions joining segments within the original passage have disappeared, and innuendo has deflected the strict, linear associations.

> BERTHA, *clasping her hands*:   O, how I wish I had never met you! How I curse that day!
>
> RICHARD, *bitterly*:   I am in the way, is it? You would like to be free now. You have only to say the word.
>
> BERTHA, *proudly*:   Whenever you like I am ready.
>
> RICHARD: So that you could meet your lover—freely?
>
> BERTHA: Yes.
>
> RICHARD: Night after night?
>
> BERTHA, *gazing before her and speaking with intense passion*:   To meet my lover! *Holding out her arms before her.* My lover! Yes! My lover!
>
> *She bursts suddenly into tears and sinks down on a chair, covering her face with her hands.* RICHARD *approaches her slowly and touches her on the shoulder.*
>
> RICHARD: Bertha! *She does not answer.* Bertha, you are free.
>
> BERTHA, *pushes his hand aside and starts to her feet*:   Don't touch me! You are a stranger to me. You do not understand anything in me—not one thing in my heart or soul. A stranger! I am living with a stranger! (*E,* 103–4)

In the initial portrayal Bertha's frank assertions of desire had weakened the sexual tension of the exchange. In the subsequent version of the scene ambiguity prevents either character from fully expressing his or her feelings, conferring potential legitimacy on any of a range of possible attitudes behind the conflicting feelings. This revised form compels each viewer to assume the responsibility for assigning motivations for the behavior of Richard and of Bertha, but, as with analogously structured episodes in *Portrait*, all interpretations remain provisional. Functioning in this way, these emendations underscore Joyce's determination to give greater depth to his depictions of individual figures by involving the reader in the scripting of the discourse. The changes place situations and motivations in an amorphous state, and they suggest the sophisticated sense for multiple characterization and the overt dependence upon reader participation that will become consistent features in *Ulysses*.

Despite the ambitious project for reader involvement operating in

Exiles, at this transitional stage between Joyce's early fiction and his mature work the implementation of innovations in characterization necessarily progresses haltingly. This fluctuation between experimentation and reliance upon proven forms manifests itself strikingly in the depiction of Richard Rowan. The central aspects of Richard's personality expand upon and distort the model provided by Stephen Dedalus. Richard's nature overrides Stephen's passive idealism and determination to be free of societal control, and replaces these attitudes with an aggressive cynicism and an obsession to control.

Actions rather than feelings, however, most strikingly establish the differences between the nature of Richard and that of Stephen. Both characters set themselves outside the conventional bounds of society, but they differ in the manner by which they assert their independence. Richard aggressively pushes his ideas, actively implementing patterns of behavior either absent in Stephen or represented in his consciousness only as latent tendencies. Richard has reached the point where his dedication to his own beliefs has undermined his ability to respond to the humanity of those around him. Manipulation, often tinged with sadism and voyeurism, dominates his relations with others, and the reader, in forming a sense of Richard's character from composite impressions, must reconcile this behavior with Richard's legitimate demands for artistic freedom. In the passage below, for example, Richard, speaking with Beatrice Justice ostensibly about his work, orchestrates the interchange, forcing her to reveal her own feelings while aloofly withholding his own.

> RICHARD: If I were a painter and told you I had a book of sketches of you you would not think it so strange, would you?
>
> BEATRICE: It is not quite the same case, is it?
>
> RICHARD, *smiles slightly*: Not quite. I told you also that I would not show you what I had written unless you asked to see it. Well?
>
> BEATRICE: I will not ask you.
>
> RICHARD, *leans forward, resting his elbows on his knees, his hands joined*: Would you like to see it?
>
> BEATRICE: Very much.
>
> RICHARD: Because it is about yourself?
>
> BEATRICE: Yes. But not only that.
>
> RICHARD: Because it is written by me? Yes? Even if what you would find there is sometimes cruel?

BEATRICE, *shyly*: That is part of your mind, too.

RICHARD: Then it is my mind that attracts you? Is that it?

BEATRICE, *hesitating, glances at him for an instant*: Why do you think I come here? (*E*, 18)

Both the strengths and the flaws of Joyce's characterization of Richard lie precisely in the depiction of this ability to strip the corporeal nature from moments of intimacy between two individuals, retaining only the resonance of sexual tension. One can see this by contrasting the passage above with Stephen's experience on Dollymount Strand with the birdgirl. Stephen, while not denying the girl's humanity, finds aesthetic pleasure without any effort to intrude upon the scene. He makes an open response to the girl's physical beauty, yet he has no wish to interpose himself by speaking to her. Richard, on the other hand, articulates a much more complex attitude. While aware of Beatrice's vulnerability, he dispassionately makes her the vehicle for his art, manipulating the course of events from the start of the action. Sensuality hovers around the edges of the dialogue quoted above, but convention and Richard's disingenuousness keep it implicit rather than explicit. The situation develops as a controlled experiment with Rowan taking the role of an aloof observer, gathering more raw material for further artistic endeavors.

Stephen's attitude toward the girl on the beach conveys a humaneness absent in Richard's treatment of Beatrice in part because Stephen's youth allows him to experience an isolated, idealizing reverence toward women that Richard can no longer feel. Life with Bertha and the experience of middle age make it impossible for Richard to indulge in the same sort of physical solipsism that insulates Stephen. He does, however, manage to preserve a certain asexual aura by shifting his concern from intercourse as an act unto itself to the idea of intercourse as a concrete manifestation of power. In the notes for the play Joyce clarifies the motivation for such sexual displacement in a description, blunter than any articulation within the play, of what features he wished to present as the central traits of Richard's character. "Richard must not appear as a champion of woman's rights. His language at times must be nearer to that of Schopenhauer against women and he must show at times a deep contempt for the long-haired, short-legged sex. He is in fact fighting for his own hand, for his own emotional dignity and liberation in which Bertha, no less and no more than Beatrice or any other woman is coinvolved" (*JJA*, XI.29). *Exiles* mutes these sentiments somewhat, but dislocation still conditions Richard's relations with women. Both publicly and privately, physical intimacy stands less as an expression of his love for another person than his means for defining self. When Richard declines to repudiate the circumstances of Archie's birth out of wedlock or to hide his continuing refusal to legitimize his union with Bertha through marriage, he does so because he has made sexual intercourse the emblematic manifestation of his moral vision.

Near the end of the play a scene takes place between Richard and Bertha that has strong ironic parallels to the one between himself and Beatrice quoted above. Action revolves around the question of Bertha's possible infidelity the previous evening, but Richard, like Beatrice in the earlier scene, rejects the possibility of linear resolution. Unlike Bertha, however, Richard cannot embrace the dialectic condition standing as an alternative.

> BERTHA: Dick!
>
> RICHARD, *stopping*: Well?
>
> BERTHA: You have not spoken to me.
>
> RICHARD: I have nothing to say. Have you?
>
> BERTHA: Do you not wish to know—about what happened last night?
>
> RICHARD: That I will never know.
>
> BERTHA: I will tell you if you ask me.
>
> RICHARD: You will tell me. But I will never know. Never in this world.
> (*E*, 102)

Events reveal this position as untenable, for Richard finds that, although he has spent his life rebelling against the conventionality dominated by either/or thinking, he cannot live with the ambiguity of a both/and reality. He wishes to maintain the concept of free choice, but he recoils from the pain produced by pursuing such a philosophy to its logical end. As he tells Bertha at the close of the play, "I have wounded my soul for you—a deep wound of doubt which can never be healed" (*E*, 112).[8]

His artless conception of personal liberty (the ability to act without the curb of any external restraints) inevitably gives rise to conflicting impulses within Richard and impedes the reader's consistent interpretation of his actions. Richard's dogmatic adherence to his views makes inevitable the sort of struggle suggested in the notes quoted above, but his beliefs do not provide him with the detachment necessary to achieve a satisfactory resolution. In separate confrontations with Bertha at the close of act one and with Robert at the beginning of act two he defends his own position, implicitly acknowledges the possibility of being cuck-olded, and takes the pose of a man unwilling to compromise his stan-dards of freedom by intervening in conformity to the conventional expectations of society. These declarations, however, reflect how im-perfectly he is reconciled to his own theory. He refuses to put an end to Robert's efforts to seduce Bertha, but at the same time he interposes himself at every stage of the evolving events. Through these gestures Richard acknowledges that he holds the possibility of sexual congress between Bertha and Robert Hand to be a condition intolerable to him. For the audience they demonstrate the limitations of his values not sim-ply as drawbacks inherent in any system but as inconsistencies within his characterization.

In a fashion similar to the creation of Richard Rowan, Joyce derives a significant portion of the nature of Robert Hand from the reflexive patterns of composition which he established for forming minor char-acters in his earlier works. In *Portrait*, for example, the reader's sense of secondary figures like Cranly and Davin grows out of their reactions to ideas or to situations defined by Stephen. In a similar fashion in *Exiles* our impressions of Robert grow out of our evolving sense of Richard Rowan's consciousness. Like the supporting characters of *Dubliners* and of *Portrait*, Robert stands in a reciprocal relationship to Richard as a pal-pable embodiment of the social norms that individuals like Stephen and Richard inevitably oppose. Robert's personality, however, also reflects Joyce's efforts to endow other figures within the play besides Richard with self-reliant forms of expression, extending Robert's role beyond that of a foil for Richard and expanding the reader's options for inter-preting his nature.

Robert's characterization does not easily achieve independence from Richard's, and it appears most natural and convincing only in the por-tions of the play in which he struggles against Richard to establish the legitimacy of his own views. In fact, as the following passage illustrates, it is Richard's priggishness and detachment that most effectively bring out the fullness of Robert's nature.[9]

> ROBERT: For me it is quite natural to kiss a woman whom I like. Why not? She is beautiful for me.
>
> RICHARD, *toying with the lounge cushion*: Do you kiss everything that is beautiful?
>
> ROBERT: Everything—if it can be kissed. *He takes up a flat stone which lies on the table.* This stone, for instance. It is so cool, so polished, so delicate, like a woman's temple. It is silent, it suffers our passion; and it is beautiful.

He places it against his lips. And so I kiss it because it is beautiful. And what is a woman? A work of nature, too, like a stone or a flower or a bird. A kiss is an act of homage.

RICHARD: It is an act of union between man and woman. Even if we are often led to desire through the sense of beauty can you say that the beautiful is what we desire?

ROBERT, *pressing the stone to his forehead*:   You will give me a headache if you make me think today. I cannot think today. I feel too natural, too common. After all, what is most attractive in even the most beautiful woman?

RICHARD: What?

ROBERT: Not those qualities which she has and other women have not but the qualities which she has in common with them. I mean . . . the commonest. *Turning over the stone, he presses the other side to his forehead.* I mean how her body develops heat when it is pressed, the movement of her blood, how quickly she changes by digestion what she eats into—what shall be nameless. *Laughing.* I am very common today. Perhaps the idea never struck you?

RICHARD, *drily*:   Many ideas strike a man who has lived nine years with a woman. (*E*, 42)

Joyce's notes indicate precisely this intention to exploit the disparity in the attitudes of the two men to create for the audience distinct personalities:

> Richard has fallen from a higher world and is indignant when he discovers baseness in men and women. Robert has risen from a lower world and so far is he from indignation that it surprises him that men and women are not baser and more ignoble. (*JJA*, XI.13–14)

Joyce here implicitly articulates his aim to vivify the impression he hopes to create of Robert by underscoring an engaging nature with a compelling, if cynical, world view and by juxtaposing Robert's attitudes with the perspectives of Richard. The contrast clarifies our sense of their opposing positions although, as the passage above illustrates, it also tends to point up the rigidity of Richard's character.

Robert, however, despite his pivotal function of creating a dialogic perspective through his scenes with Richard, remains hampered by inconsistent development, particularly through associations with the stereotypical figure of the seducer that crop up in his scenes with Bertha. There his behavior conforms to Richard's expectations, taking on an artificial, shallow pose verging on a comical rather than a dangerous depiction. As act two opens, for example, his movements, his props, his attitude, outlined in the stage directions quoted below, combine to convey an impression of superficiality and of triviality.

> Robert Hand, in evening dress, is seated at the piano. The candles are not lit but the lamp on the table is lit. He plays softly in the bass the first bars of Wolfram's song in the last act of "Tannhäuser." Then he breaks off and, resting an elbow on the ledge of the keyboard, meditates. Then he rises and, pulling out a pump from behind the piano, walks here and there in the room ejecting from it into the air sprays of perfume. He inhales the air slowly and then puts the pump back behind the piano. He sits down on a chair near the table and, smoothing his hair carefully, sighs once or twice. (*E*, 57–58)

Robert is clearly playing a part familiar to him, but in it he looks slightly ridiculous because, unlike his encounters with Richard, here no one gives a legitimacy to his pose by a willingness to engage him or his ideas. Joyce continues to emphasize the ludicrous elements of Robert's portrayal in the subsequent seduction scenes when Bertha does not assume a stylized role complementary to Robert's own. She behaves neither as a woman whose virtue has been offended nor as one eager to indulge her senses. Rather in her open approach to whatever she encounters she heightens the foolish appearance of Robert's machinations while her response to his advances, tolerance without warmth, overlays her nature with an ambiguity never completely clarified in the dialogue of the play.

Bertha's personality, hovering between the extremes of the consciousnesses of the two men, alternately reflects confusion, vulnerability, strength, and insight, but the very range of her feelings serves to betray the elements of insubstantiality within her own character.[10] She slips easily from one attitude to another. She retains a commitment to Richard, and to a lesser degree to Robert, rather than to any particular intellectual position of her own. The ambivalence that a reader might naturally feel toward her range of emotional responses comes not so much from Bertha's complexity as from Joyce's conscious decision (as explained in his notes) to use her as a figure mirroring the natures of others. "Bertha wishes for the spiritual union of Richard and Robert and *believes* (?) that union will be effected only through her body, and perpetuated thereby" ([Joyce's question mark] *JJA*, XI.39). Like her body, her personality acts as a conduit for ideas and perspectives by which Richard and Robert reveal themselves, but, although she attempts to conjoin them, she never fully understands the attitudes of either man.

These points, however, should not diminish one's view of her larger importance, for Bertha's characterization highlights a significant point in Joyce's artistic development. She represents his first extended effort to sketch a woman's character, and like any initial attempt her portrayal bears the marks of his learning process. As in the depiction of Robert, the presentation of Bertha alternates between delineations of an ineffectual and a powerful individual.

In the first two acts she appears as a type, barely distinguishable from the rest of the stage property. Her character develops through a definition she draws of herself from the clash of male wills going on around her. *Exiles* initially appears to encourage this impression of a derivative nature by fostering little sense of her except in terms of Robert's and Richard's struggles. Their conflict gives the audience a sense of Bertha's nature to the degree that she reflects/refracts the attitudes of the men struggling around her. It is only when the struggle apparently ceases with Richard's spiritual abandonment that Bertha's character begins to develop independently, and the figure who comes to dominate the action of the final scenes emerges. In his notes for the play, Joyce charts this transformation by comparing Bertha's response to Richard's desertion to "that of Jesus in the garden of olives. It is the soul of woman left naked and alone that it may come to an understanding of its own nature. . . . Through these experiences she will suffuse her own reborn temperament with the wonder of her soul at its own solitude and at her beauty, formed and dissolving itself eternally amid the clouds of mortality" (*JJA*, XI.7–8). This shift causes her to appear in the third act as a sharply defined, independent individual, so that in her curtain speech she ends the play with a resolve not apparent earlier in the drama. "Forget me, Dick. Forget me and love me again as you did the first time. I want my lover. To meet him, to go to him, to give myself to him. You, Dick. O, my strange wild lover, come back to me again" (*E*, 112).

The frank discussions of sexuality and its relation to power that inform many of the speeches within *Exiles* suggest Joyce's awareness of the potential for exposition that could be realized by playing off alternating perspectives of equal force within exchanges between individuals. His dialogue, however, also reveals a still-evolving grasp of the means of controlling characterization and of moving the action forward through the interplay of markedly different personalities. The discourse attempts with varying success to set off each figure with strong distinguishing traits, but, measured in terms of the characterization of *Ulysses*, none is finished. Individuals bluntly articulate their personal beliefs, yet physical detachment and emotional aloofness belie their openness. They remain only tangentially connected to events unfolding around them, and consequently the action advances in awkward, jerky bursts that often make motivation ambiguous. In essence these figures, imperfectly fitted to the demands of the plot, mark the midway point in Joyce's movement from a concern for the actions of an individual to a concern for the interaction between characters.

As the play progresses, this tension between previous methods and evolving techniques exerts a cumulative, disruptive influence. Richard Rowan's single-minded determination to confront Bertha with the choice of taking another lover suppresses development of any of the sub-plots—the relationship between Richard and Beatrice, the struggle between Richard and Bertha for the affection of their son, the position of the unconventional artist in Ireland. As Richard's idée fixe comes to dominate the action, it blurs distinctions between individual and archetypal identities, and it closes down alternative possibilities for character development. Gradually, it even comes to limit the play's original concerns. The question of personal freedom displaces consideration of the bonds created by the act of intercourse as the pivotal concept of the play. Everyone's behavior becomes circumscribed by this topic, and only the consummation of the action remains ambiguous. By emphasizing attitude over action, the center of attention contracts, and a monologic perspective, Richard's, reasserts its hegemony.

While not completely successful in terms of the play, Joyce's efforts in *Exiles* to incorporate fully developed personalities into a dialogic framework provided him with the experience necessary to resolve the question of unifying disunities when he came to write *Ulysses*. A growing sense of empathy undermines previous impulses towards solipsism. It fosters an interest in the array of motives and of interactions influencing human behavior, and establishes a powerful conjunctive force in *Ulysses*. *Exiles* struggles to present protagonists both self-reflective and sensitive to the attitudes of others. It strives to broaden individual representation and to allow a wider range of personalities to come to the fore, providing readers with a sense of openness to the vagaries of the work. The play itself fails to achieve these ends, but the efforts that it brought forth realigned Joyce's paradigmatic view of characterization. In *Ulysses* the Stephen Dedalus type recedes, and Leopold Bloom steps forward to meet a sexual situation similar to the one encountered in *Exiles* by Richard Rowan.

Analogous characters and thematic parallels in *Exiles*—specifically established in the love triangle of Bertha, Richard Rowan, and Robert Hand—rehearse aspects of action and of character development that would in *Ulysses* surround the cuckolding of Leopold Bloom by his wife, Molly, and her lover, Hugh "Blazes" Boylan. Two men desire the same woman. The men are friends, but there is an indication (more overt in *Ulysses* than in *Exiles*) that the friendship rests largely on the attraction that each feels for the woman.

> The secondary and lower phase of Robert's position is the suspicion that Richard is a cunning adventurer using Bertha's body as a bait to gain Robert's friendship and support. The corresponding phase in Richard's attitude is the suspicion that Robert's admiration and friendship for him is simulated in order to lull and stupefy the vigilance of his mind. Both these suspicions are borne in upon the characters from purely external evidence and do not in either case spring into existence spontaneously from the soils of their natures. (*JJA*, XI.8–9)

Both Leopold Bloom and Richard Rowan are aware of the possibility of being cuckolded, yet each chooses to do nothing to prevent it. In neither case, however, does inaction reflect weakness. Although their personalities sharply diverge, each man retains control of the situation and in that respect escapes the stigma of being deceived. Both act out of love for their wives, yet neither finds complete satisfaction in the experience. The infidelity (real or imagined) wounds both husbands and both wives, but it does not destroy either marriage.

A number of critics have already commented on the obvious similarities.[11] Draft material, however, underscores more precisely the evolution of dialogic characterization between the play and the novel. Sharp contrasts inevitably emerge, and these variances permit one to form a sense of the artistic ambitions motivating this expansion and to trace the maturation of craftsmanship between the completion of *Exiles* and the composition of *Ulysses*.

The notes from *Exiles*, though small in comparison to the surviving raw material that contributed to the composition of *Ulysses*, continued to exert an influence on Joyce's writing after the completion of the play. He copied directly or paraphrased a significant amount of the material relating to parallels between the character of Bertha and his own wife, Nora, from the *Exiles* notebook into sections of his *Ulysses* notesheets dealing with the development of Molly Bloom's character. In the examples presented below, selections from the notes for *Exiles* are matched to references to analogous passages drawn from the Penelope section of Phillip Herring's edition of Joyce's note-sheets for *Ulysses*.

Exiles	*Ulysses*
"for nearly two thousand years the women of Christendom have prayed to and kissed the naked image of one who had neither wife nor mistress nor sister" (*JJA*, XI.30)	Jesus no wife ?or sister or mistress ("Penelope" 7.25)
"Emily Lyons" (32)	Emily Lyons ?emigrant (3:18)
"buttoned boots" (33)	present of buttoned boots (7:28)
"visual"	visual (3:26)
"currant cake"	currant cake (3:28)
"tactual"	tactual (3:27)
"A persistent and delicate vanity also, even in her grief"	vanity in grief (3:17)
"buttoned boots" (34)	present of buttoned boots (7:28)
"feels vaguely the forgotten cares and affection"	feels vaguely forgotten cares (3:37 & 7:29)
"not because they were kind to her but because they were kind to her girlself" (35)	Kind to her as she was then (3:38) her girlself is more (7:30)
"tears which fill her eyes as she sees her friend go"	Emily Lyons goes: she cries (7:26)
"can travel alone, braver" (36)	brave to travel alone (3:43); brave to go alone (7:26)
"that extinction of personality which is death in life" (38)	distinction of personality & ?dents (3:39)
"For this reason she would like more a child of his by another woman than a child of him by her" (45)	Prefer child of his by other woman (not risk her womb) (3:47) prefer child of Boylan other woman (7:31)
"secret flesh" (47)	fuck—secrets of flesh (7:32)
"Richard . . . the organ of his friend" (51)	LB couldn't adulter go gets BB to do it (3:50); Cdn't he go & fuck Mrs Breen? (7:34)[12]

Despite the crude parallels that the notes establish between the sexual interactions within *Exiles* and within *Ulysses*, refinements in characterization in the novel radically alter the disposition of events. The essence of Leopold Bloom's nature, the quality which allows Joyce to make him the focal point of the action without causing his personality to overshadow others' in the work, lies in Bloom's willingness to relinquish control, in his ability to accept events.[13] As with Richard Rowan, the central features of Bloom's character emerge through his response to his imminent cuckolding, but important distinctions between the two men obtain. Resigned by temperament to the inevitable, Bloom recoils from pleading his own case or from manipulating the actions of others. Bloom does not confront Boylan in the way Richard Rowan faces down Robert Hand because Bloom knows what Richard does not (as the Joyce of *Ulysses* has learned what the Joyce of *Exiles* was unaware of).

Bloom in conversation or in thought does not need to dissect his behavior as does Richard. Because he sends his daughter off to Mullingar or announces to his wife that he will be away from home for all of June 16th, one need not assume that he is pushing Molly toward adultery. Rather he is tidying up details that, typical of her nature, she has forgotten. He sets matters straight so that if she does choose to betray him it will do the least possible emotional harm to others. Bloom faces his impending cuckolding with no less resolution than does Richard Rowan, but his method for dealing with the situation reflects his deep understanding of Molly's independent humanity. His resignation to the inevitability of her betrayal shows not an indifference but a comprehension of the forces that shape her actions as well as of those which shape his own.

The effectiveness of Bloom's characterization in *Ulysses* comes, in part at least, from the full and balanced depiction of his sensual environment. Sexual activity can become a more graphic element of the narrative than it could be in previous works because Joyce better understands his material and has better control of his techniques. It never degenerates into the mechanical descriptions of pornography because Joyce never allows us to forget the human beings that participate in the affairs.

Ulysses frees the spirit of Richard Rowan. It turns from single-minded insistence on an individual code to a compassionate examination of individuals' foibles. Gross descriptions of Bloom's whorehouse fantasies do not shoulder aside subtler aspects of his characterization because Joyce does not introduce the lurid details of the hallucinations as ends in themselves. Rather, they evoke in readers a sense of the emotional turmoil that underscores Bloom's humanity. Moreover, the comprehensiveness of his feelings directly supports his tolerance/respect for Molly's nature: his impulse towards depravity allows him to understand depravity in others, and his humanity allows him to accept it. Consequently Joyce presents fuller depictions of human emotions and attitudes in Bloom's fantasies than he does in Richard's expostulations, for even in the frankest articulations of his beliefs Richard remains distant, obsessed with his personal concerns but unable to comprehend completely Bertha's attitudes. Richard seeks to experiment in freedom while keeping control over the events around him. Bloom does not wish to order and then to analyze life; rather he seeks only to accommodate and to unify. The flaws of characterization that emerged in the composition of *Exiles* allowed Joyce to understand more precisely the implications of sexual manifestations, and so in *Ulysses* he could present examples of it more explicitly.

The distinctions between the two works remain as important as their similarities. Although Padraic Colum in his introduction to the play rightly points to Bertha as a prototype of Molly Bloom (*E*, 9), one must not, through such an association, elide the sophisticated growth of Joyce's ability to depict a woman's consciousness. Like Bertha, Molly's independent nature emerges late in the work in the Penelope chapter, but in her characterization Joyce combines elaboration and control to achieve a much more fully articulated figure than that of Bertha. Molly's moods fluctuate with a rapidity that seems if anything to exceed Bertha's shifting temperament, but her soliloquy never abnegates a clear sense of the self behind the oscillating temperaments. The vacillation between remorse, satisfaction, anger, and compassion comes from Joyce's own clearer perception of the emotional dynamics of the situation. Her affair becomes more than a dirty joke or a leering reference made in an offhand way in a Dublin pub. We come to see it as an act precipitated by her needs and fears, and from this perspective we have a much broader range for interpreting those needs and fears. *Ulysses* demonstrates that Joyce has acquired the capacity to understand and to convey both male and female perspectives without prejudicing his readers in favor of one character or the other. In *Exiles* he could only articulate fully the feelings and the motivations of the husband. Bertha acts predominantly in response to Richard, Molly (mis)behaves independently.

This expansion in characterization enlarges in turn the thematic scope of the novel. In *Ulysses* no single concern dominates the action, as the Bertha/Richard/Robert triangle does in *Exiles*. Personal freedom remains a prominent constitutive feature of the plot, but Joyce no longer presents it in terms of binary oppositions or from relatively fixed perspectives. The significance given to attitude and to action in *Exiles* has been reversed. Ambivalence rather than assurance informs a character's consciousness, and only the consummation of action in adultery stands as a certainty. Extrapolating beyond the drama's either/or conditions, Joyce blurs Bloom's motivations and makes his complicity in Molly's infidelity much more problematic for the reader. Likewise, Molly's rambling soliloquy careens between various attractions and repulsions, continually reforming our suppositions about her character and about her relations with Bloom. Her ambivalence fixes attention on the dynamics of their family life, expanding rather than limiting the interpretation one could give to her behavior.

The distinctly different conclusions in the two pieces also reflect a development of Joyce's consciousness. In the final act of *Exiles*, Bertha and Richard confront the problem of fidelity and independence without bringing the matter to a clear resolution. As the play ends, neither Richard nor the audience knows what has happened, although both inevitably create texts reflecting their presumptions about the ambiguities. At the close of *Ulysses* Bloom and Molly have a clear sense of their situation, and each understands what the other knows. Discussion could only lead to guilt, a solution that Joyce eschews. Instead the closing episodes move toward accommodation and through accommodation to reunification. Here, too, readers create texts based on their assumptions, but their focus goes beyond concern for specific events to a more general assessment of conditions.

The similarities and the differences in these two works summarize Joyce's artistic advancement. Using a plot in *Ulysses* similar to the one that governs *Exiles*, he drew on the insights that he had acquired in composing his play to articulate the feelings that dominate love situations. This greater comprehension of a range of alternative human perspectives allowed him to depict relations between characters more precisely in *Ulysses*, and this in turn gave him greater freedom in his approach to sexual activity. *Exiles* conveys the force of desire through dialogue and action limited by the moral conventions of early twentieth-century theater. *Ulysses* introduces unvoiced longings and fantasies, using frank depictions of physical drives as keys to understanding the human feelings which guided a character's actions, enhancing readers' comprehension of the central ideas and of subtleties in characterization.

Exiles attempts to create a sensitive rendition of the physical, emotional, and intellectual ties conjoining contrasting personalities, and it manipulates this depiction to advance the action of the drama. This achievement required a fuller projection of a range of consciousnesses than had any of Joyce's previous works, and the scope of the efforts necessary to satisfy such a demand impressed Joyce with the need to devise a convincing method for presenting, in subsequent writing, alternating or fluctuating points of view. Because of these endeavors this metastatic stage in the evolution of Joyce's artistic development signals an emerging ability to manipulate character and action that will be masterfully brought into play in the text of *Ulysses*: the polyvocal perspectives that, to an even greater degree than the interior monologue, throw into relief the individuality of figures within the structure of the novel. *Exiles* highlights Joyce's inchoate efforts to shift his approach to characterization from a monologically dominated format to a polyphonically diffusive structure and through this amplification of views to articulate a more diverse range of topics.

VII | The Shift in Stylistic Imperatives

The preceding chapter focused on Joyce's decision to introduce into his paradigm polyphonic voices, greatly expanding the range of texts that one can derive from a fixed social repertoire. *Exiles* highlights this movement. It provides a bridge between the fiction in Joyce's canon distinguished by discourses built upon homogeneous perspectives and that given over to pluralistic combinations.

The very concept of reading a work as a transitional piece, of course, confers upon it heuristic properties, and in the case of *Exiles* these meta-contextual factors assume particular significance that exceeds interpretations strictly limited to the play. The constitution of several central characters frankly committed to different systems for giving value to experience introduces an approach heretofore absent in Joyce's canon. It signals a shift in creative emphasis going beyond the simple elaboration of one aspect of the process of composition, and it establishes a pattern of multiple perspectives, both for the writer and for the reader, that will come to dominate perception of the narratives of *Ulysses* and of *Finnegans Wake*.

Formal changes in Joyce's approach to characterization in *Exiles* go beyond stylistic and thematic refinement. They mark a realignment signaling aesthetic and artistic revaluation. By foregrounding multiple perspectives and by attempting to deny primacy to a single point of view, *Exiles* concomitantly extends and intensifies the parameters of the discourse, a gesture that encourages one to make connections that reconstitute the thematic delineations of *Exiles* beyond previously articulated limits. The change in the depiction of the play's central characters brought a concurrent revaluation in the models to which Joyce turned for inspiration. It led him to shift the emphasis of his compositional approach from the evocation of elements of literary works that he respected to the incorporation of strategic recapitulations and modifications of techniques from works generally dismissed as hackneyed.

Exiles marks the beginning of Joyce's efforts to capitalize on the features of presumably trite material through a process of defamiliarization rather than through straightforward parody. It consistently presents individuals who initially appear to behave in apparent conformity to clichéd genres, and then it overturns the habitual, predictable patterns of their behavior by introducing more complex capabilities. As a result, the discourse evolves through parallel dictions that overlap and even interfuse. The one dominated by cliché exists simultaneously with its antithetical representation. Together they challenge the reader not to suppress one while amplifying the other but instead to reconcile the two into a re-formed perception of the character or the situation. The impetus to re-view overly familiar forms, by extension, exerts a pronounced impact upon the perception of the play's topical elements, inevitably disrupting many of the expectations, established in the reader's mind by Joyce's earlier writings, regarding the development of the play's broader thematic concerns.

While the work itself provides immediate indication of the interpretive alternatives implicit in this expansion, a reader wishing to exploit all of the available options for forming a text for the play cannot simply rely upon elements within *Exiles* to comprehend the full creative potential that this change in characterization endows upon it. The basic traits delineating the central figures, for example, generally suggest stock types. That is to say, they rely upon convention to establish, at least initially, a reader's sense of the meaning of the play. In examining representative works as sources of the conventions paraphrased in *Exiles*, however, one begins to comprehend the varying degrees to which aspects of the literary tradition influence the reader. This experience is by no means static or consistently replicated in subsequent encounters with the work, so a comprehension of the allusive alternatives open to the reader becomes the first stage of any conscientious interpretation.

As I have noted already in my examinations of *Dubliners* and of *Portrait*, perception of the concatenation of stylistic influences acting on the form of a particular passage gives one a greater immediate understanding of the paradigm of the work. This awareness also allows the reader to develop a greater sensitivity to the stylistic decorum governing other portions of the canon. *Exiles* introduces compositional features that call for the same approach to specific meta-contextual resonances in the play and that encourage its application in the examination of subsequent writings. The play goes even further, however, in its foregrounding of elements conditioning a reader's response. Specifically, attentiveness to the materials informing Joyce's inversion of the central dramatic issue—the conventional depiction of marital infidelity—illuminates his new approach to the thematic exposition evident in both *Exiles* and *Ulys-*

ses, and it heightens one's awareness of the formative impact of diverse sources contributing to our comprehension of both works.

Joyce's notes for *Exiles* indicate a wide-ranging interest in the alternative modes for portraying marital infidelity. While clearly favoring the redefined concepts of the cuckold that he saw emerging in relatively recent fiction, Joyce did not cut himself off from the tradition from which they had evolved. He cultivated a sense of the historical perspective characterizing the nature of the betrayed husband, demonstrating in his comments a precise awareness of the artistic impact that one could hope to achieve by the conventional portrayal. At the same time, he balanced this perspective against the changing social and literary attitudes towards the subject.

> Since the publication of the lost pages of *Madame Bovary* the centre of sympathy appears to have been esthetically shifted from the lover or fancy-man to the husband or cuckold. This displacement is also rendered more stable by the gradual growth of a collective practical realism due to changed economic conditions in the mass of people who are called to hear and feel a work of art relating to their lives. This change is utilized in *Exiles* although the union of Richard and Bertha is irregular to the extent that the spiritual revolt of Richard which would be strange and ill-welcomed otherwise can enter into combat with Robert's decrepit prudence with some chance of fighting before the public a drawn battle. Prage in *La Crisi* and Giacosa in *Tristi Amori* have understood and profited by this change but have not used it, as is done here, as a technical shield for the protection of a delicate, strange, and highly sensitive conscience. (*JJA*, XI.9–11)[1]

The entry quoted above deftly sketches Joyce's views both on the works of his literary antecedents and on trends in public receptiveness to the topic that he had chosen. It also evinces a highly attuned sensitivity to the response that his own characterizations might be expected to receive depending upon the narrative strategy that he chose. Most significantly, it indicates Joyce's clear perception of the evocative power of the both/and conditions inherent in the gradual change of attitudes of middle-class readers towards fictional depictions of adultery. As the composition of *Exiles* progressed, exploitation of the paradoxically meliorative force created by these dialectical confrontations became an increasingly significant factor in determining the contextual formation of the play and of Joyce's subsequent writing.

As noted in chapter four, Joyce had a strong sense of the broad allusive value of *Madame Bovary*, and material drawn from the novel influenced both the fabrication of plot and the refinement of characterization in *Exiles*. To some degree Joyce exploited the renown of emblematic representations made familiar by Flaubert to highlight patterns of behavior and to give a sense of ambiguity to the drama's thematic dimensions.[2] Generally, however, in the construction of *Exiles* as in all his previous writings, Joyce showed little inclination for referring explicitly to the work of others or for maintaining the integrity of received ideas. Instead he used oblique allusions as points of departure, drawing upon salient, recognizable features while manipulating elements of characterization to suit the artistic demands of his play.

Through a comparison of the natures of Emma Bovary and of Bertha one can see how this tendency diffuses much of the overt impact of *Madame Bovary* on the final version of *Exiles* and, at the same time, how a sense of the parallels enhances one's understanding of Bertha's character. Like Emma Bovary, Bertha is a woman shaped/constricted by the men around her. Each woman, in her own fashion, seeks romantic happiness outside of marriage, yet striking differences separate their personalities. Emma, in Tony Tanner's words, tries to be both *épouse* and *courtisane*, ultimately conflating the two and making them "indistinguishable and thus meaningless."[3] Joyce, who wished to center attention on the struggles of Richard, ultimately gave Bertha such a keen sense of the separation of identities within herself and within others that her closing references to "her lover" initially mystify Richard. Emma instinctively resists the coercive force of bourgeois morality. Bertha, while showing no regard for its judgment of her own behavior, fights to protect her son from its disapprobation. This bifurcation in Bertha can occur because the discourse of *Exiles* has pushed her self-awareness and self-control appreciably beyond that of Emma Bovary. Since she understands her position much more clearly than does Emma, she struggles with the individuals who threaten the equilibrium that she has established—specifically with Richard, but to lesser degrees with Robert and Beatrice as well—rather than with herself and with the abstractions of social mores.

Madame Bovary, of all of Joyce's literary antecedents, probably produced the strongest single impact on the composition of *Exiles* in terms of stylistic innovations, apposite thematic interests, and characterization, and it still exerts a strong influence on the play's readers. Certain less obvious works, however, draw attention to a broader shift in Joyce's approach to writing and in turn to the coinciding realignment of reader expectations. One such book, Charles Paul de Kock's novel *Le Cocu*, appeared nearly two decades before *Madame Bovary*, and its literary connections to *Exiles* demonstrate the range of evocative material that Joyce could find in apparently banal works.

Joyce acquired his copy of *Le Cocu* sometime after he arrived in Trieste, and he probably read or reread it shortly before beginning work on *Exiles*. The novel recounts the events surrounding the marriage of a Parisian couple, Henri and Eugenie Blemont, following the relationship, from courtship through cuckolding, to the end of their union. Henri, who has lived as a rake before meeting the chaste Eugenie, completely reforms after his marriage and remains steadfastly faithful to his wife. Eugenie, at first happy with her marriage, becomes jealous of Henri's past and restless after the birth of their second child. She embarks on an affair which leads to the dissolution of her marriage and ultimately to her death.

The title and the subject matter of *Le Cocu* in themselves account for Joyce's initial motivation for taking up the work. The notes that Joyce made during the process of composing *Exiles* supply explanations for his sustained interest. As he read through this apparently programmatic morality tale, Joyce became engaged by its deviation from the usual pattern followed in the rendition of infidelity.

> A striking instance of the changed point of view of literature towards this subject [the cuckold] is Paul de Kock—a descendant surely of Rabelais, Molière and the old *Souche Galoise*. Yet compare *George Dandin* or *Le Cocu Imaginaire* of Molière with *Le Cocu* of the later writer. Salacity, humour, indecency, liveliness, were certainly not wanting in the writer yet he produced a long, hesitating, painful story—written also in the first person. Evidently that spring is broken somewhere. (*JJA*, XI.58–59)

Joyce's allusion to a broken spring might seem, at first glance, to relegate de Kock to the position of an incomplete, derivative author and to debar him from any position of influence, but de Kock's willingness to write against the comic tradition of cuckoldry foregrounded for Joyce subtleties of characterization absent in otherwise superior works. *Le Cocu* functions as more than simply a moral tale, a prudish alternative to the salacious thrust of French comedy, because de Kock acknowledges the variety of often conflicting attitudes engendered by instances of infidelity.

This trait of overturning the expectations of traditional depictions of cuckolding runs through the various subplots of the novel. One example of this can be found in a passage from *Le Cocu*, marked off in pencil in

Joyce's copy of the work. It appears to project a predictable response to a stock situation.

> Cependant . . . il parait que, quand une fois ces maudites idées vous viennent à l'esprit, elles ne s'en vont pas si vite . . . J'ai rêvé toute la nuit aux pièces de Molière, à *George Dandin* au *Cocu imaginaire*. J'ai rapproché certaines circonstances . . . [author's ellipses].[5]

> [Nonetheless . . . it appears that, once these evil thoughts have entered one's mind, they do not quickly pass away . . . All night I dreamed of the plays of Molière, of *George Dandin* and of *Le Cocu Imaginaire*. I have established parallels between certain events.]

The words are those of Ferdinand de Belan, a minor character whose cuckolding follows the satirical lines that one finds in contemporaneous comedies of infidelity. Here he stands as a ludicrous figure, struggling against incontrovertible evidence of his wife's betrayal. Recollections of Molière's comedies add to his immediate discomfort, but after some vacillation, Belan ignores the evidence and continues to assert his wife's fidelity.

The literary allusions tie Belan to the traditional portrayal of the cuckold, but this subplot, as it unfolds in de Kock's presentation, strays from the conventional depiction. While Belan takes on the stock characteristics of a buffoon, neither his wife nor her lover displays the admirable traits commonly used in the literature of this genre to win the reader's sympathy. Instead they embody a tawdry and degraded version of the unfaithful couple, and their characterizations subvert the connotations suggested by the reference to Molière. Belan's allusion subtly reminds us that the very popularity of the tradition in which Molière wrote has turned such cuckolds into clichés, debasing their evocative power in contemporary works. Further, the passage lays down a foundation for the antinomy that will confront the reader when Blemont, whose behavior sets him off as the antithesis of Belan, suffers the same fate as his friend. The scene retrospectively warns one against making quick assumptions about the nature of the deceived husband, and this divergence between Molière's satirical perspective and de Kock's more humane views graphically illustrates a dialectic tension similar to that suggested by the notebook entry quoted above.[6]

While the subplots of *Le Cocu* underscore features of the main plot, they do not always do so through irony. The narrative counterpoint to the Blemont marriage traces events surrounding the life of a young couple, Ernest and Margarite, who resist the pressure of public opinion to marry, yet at the same time remain devoted to each other. Joyce seems to have been particularly taken by such material, for marked passages in his copy of *Le Cocu* offer insights into the formation of his own concepts regarding the depiction of interactions between men and women. Specifically, they suggest that he drew upon selections from *Le Cocu* reshaped to fit into his dramatic setting, to structure several exchanges underscoring one of the conflicts nagging at Richard throughout the play: public opinion versus personal morality.

Scenes which elaborated details of the socially unorthodox existence of Ernest and Margarite took on a particular significance for Joyce. In one passage that he marked, for example, Blemont's young friend Ernest acknowledges the small concessions that the couple have made to public opinion.

> Je dis ma femme . . . quoique nous ne soyons pas mariés: mais pour des portiers, pour des étrangers, il faut bien dire ma femme: c'est un sacrifice aux convenances. Après tout, quelle différence y a-t-il entre nous et des gens mariés? Rien qu'une signature sur un gros registre! . . . et ce n'est point cette signature, le serment, et tous les engagements pris devant les hommes, qui font que l'on se conduit mieux [author's ellipses]. (II.93)

> [I say my wife . . . even though we are not married: for doormen, for strangers, I must say my wife: it's an accommodation to propriety. After all what is the difference between us and married couples? Only a signature in a big book! . . . and it's not that signature, the solemn declaration, and all the commitments made before men, which mean that people behave any better.]

Ernest's regard for appearances calls to mind Robert Hand's words to Richard on the same topic in act one of *Exiles*, but the play maintains an important distinction. By shifting the impulse toward accommodation from the man living with a woman to a supposedly concerned friend, Joyce upholds the integrity of his central character and underscores Robert's willingness to submit to deception to avoid public pressure. "I am thinking of your future life—here. I understand your pride and your sense of liberty. I understand their point of view also. However, there is a way out; it is simply this. Refrain from contradicting any rumours you may hear concerning what happened . . . or did not happen after you went away. Leave the rest to me" (*E,* 39). De Kock does not allow Ernest and Margarite to escape the condemnation of others, however, as the following exchange between Blemont and his wife, marked by Joyce, indicates.

—Mon Dieu! monsieur, comme vous prenez feu!—C'est que je ne puis souffrir les injustices, et que celle-là se renouvelle souvent dans la société. Quant à moi, je vous déclare que je me mettrai toujours au dessus des préjugés, et que je recevrais très volontiers Ernest et sa femme chez moi.—Je vous remercie, monsieur; j'espère cependant que cela ne sera pas. (II.101)

[Good God, sir, how angry you are!—It's because I cannot endure the injustices, and those are often revived in society. As for me, I tell you that I always put myself above prejudices, and that I shall most willingly receive Ernest and his wife at my house.—I thank you, sir; I hope, however, that that will not happen.]

Joyce works the same sort of middle-class abhorrence of unmarried couples into a conversation between Richard and Beatrice regarding the attitude of Richard's mother toward her son's elopement, but he reverses the emphasis controlling the tone of the passage from *Le Cocu*. By reporting rather than enacting the rejection, attention remains fixed on Richard's integrity rather than on his mother's reaction.

RICHARD: While [my mother] lived she turned aside from me and from mine. That is certain.

BEATRICE: From you and from . . . ?

RICHARD: From Bertha and from me and from our child. And so I waited for the end as you say; and it came. (*E*, 23)

The muted inflection, characteristic of Richard, underscores the central difference between Joyce's approach and that of de Kock. Ultimately, *Le Cocu*, like all of de Kock's books, cannot escape conveying an overbearing moral tone, and Joyce's antipathy toward such strident didacticism necessarily led him to prefer to respond to it refractively rather than reflectively. The novel did, however, reinforce his own attitudes on depicting the nature of the cuckold, and it also foregrounded in his artistic consciousness the value of material singularly available in otherwise banal works.

Joyce marked a number of other passages in the de Kock novel. Some of the highlighted selections contain contextual features that closely parallel the central concerns of scenes appearing in the final version of *Exiles*. Other passages singled out by Joyce go beyond the thematic parameters set down by his play and draw attention to his engagement with the wider range of attitudes and perspectives relating to infidelity. Taken together, this material assumes a paradigmatic significance in terms of Joyce's sources. It reiterates the interest demonstrated in the composition of earlier works for models that assist in giving shape to his writing, and it also marks a growing concern for the expectations of readers. In terms of an appreciation of Joyce's aesthetic and artistic development, it provides evidence of a movement in Joyce's writing away from sources that developed his technical skills and toward those that provided imaginative inspiration.

Thus, while Joyce's notes for *Exiles* provide certain strong indications of how the novel contributed to specific perspectives on extramarital sexuality that he introduced into the play, the thematic scope of the markings in his copy of de Kock's book point out its impact on even broader interests. The play's structure precluded the development of ambiguities not relating to the immediate issues being considered. Concerns touched on in many of the passages of *Le Cocu* that attracted Joyce's attention, however, provided ample material for characterization in the project he was just beginning: the composition of *Ulysses*.

At several points in de Kock's novel, for example, Joyce marked off segments relating the sardonic observations made by the yet unmarried Blemont and by his friends on the hypocritical attitudes of society towards marriage and fidelity:

Il fallait donc qu'Hélène allât retrouver son *Ménélas*. . . . Ah! ah! c'est très-drôle, *Ménélas*! . . .—Vous êtes Pâris, vous . . .—C'est cela même . . . je suis *Pâris* . . . Ah! quel dommage que je ne puis pas rire maintenant! . . . Hélène devait donc aller retrouver son mari son chez Giraud, qui donne une soirée . . . Vous connaissez Giraud . . . une bavard! . . . qui croit qu'il a un cabinet d'affaires parce qu'il a trois cartons rangés sur son bureau . . . et qui a la manie de louloir marier tout le monde; . . . le tout, pour que sa femme et lui aillent à la noce? [author's emphasis and ellipses] (I.40)

[So Helen had to join her *Menelaus* . . . O, my it's very droll, *Menelaus* . . . — You are *Paris*, you . . .—It's just so . . . I am Paris . . . Ah, what a pity that I cannot laugh now! . . . Helen was to join her husband at home where they were giving a soiree . . . You know Giraud . . . a babbler! . . . who thinks that he has a business because he has three cartons arranged on his desk . . . and who has a mania for seeing everyone married; . . . all, so that he and his wife may go to the wedding?]

*   *   *   *

Armide est tombée décemment, et n'a rien montré à la société; ce qui eût été fort désagréable pour le marié, qui espère être le premier à voir cela, et qui sans doute aurait fait pousser des sanglots à sa belle-mère. (II.76)

[Armide fell with propriety, and never showed anything in public; that was very disagreeable for her husband, who hoped to be the first to see what doubtless would have caused his mother-in-law to sob.]

They articulate perspectives of married life far more cynical than any held by the characters in the play, including those of Robert Hand. Their tone more closely parallels the misogyny of the Dublin males whose salacious gossip contributes to our ambiguous impression of Molly, as in the passage in which the sardonic wit Simon Dedalus deftly turns a reference to the time that the Blooms dealt in secondhand apparel into slanderous innuendo: "Mrs Marion Bloom has left off clothes of all descriptions" (U, 11.496–97).

Elsewhere, Joyce noted passages, such as those quoted below, emphasizing the willful naiveté of the foolish cuckold Belan and highlighting his determination to ignore the warnings of others. Here the aura of cynicism intensifies as the reader listens with Belan's friends to the cuckold's adamant refusal to accept the fact of his wife's betrayal.

> J'ai engagé le marquis à venir nous voir; il est venu, il est même venu très-souvent. C'est sur cela que les Giraud ont lancé des quolibets. Quand ma femme a su cela, elle, qui est très-sévère, voulait sur-le-champ que je priasse le marquis de cesser ses visites; mais moi j'ai montré du caractère. J'ai dit au marquis: «Vous venez tous les jours, tâchez de venir deux fois par jour, et ca me fera plus de plaisir. Il le fait. . . . Et cette fois, du moins, ma belle-mère a trouvé que j'avais très-bien agi» [author's ellipses]. (II.128)

> [I invited the marquis to come to see us; he came, he now comes very often. The Girauds jeer at that. When my wife learned of it, she, who is very critical, wished that I immediately ask the marquis to stop visiting; but I showed some resolve. I said to the marquis: "Come everyday, try to come twice a day, and that would give me great pleasure. He did it. . . . And that time, at least, my mother-in-law found that I behaved well.]

*　*　*　*

> J'ai couru au boudoir, j'ai frappé comme un sourd; ma femme m'a ouvert et m'a fait une scène. . . . Le marquis a paru choqué de mon air soupconneux, je me suis cru dans mon tort [author's ellipses]. (III.45)

> [I ran to the boudoir, I knocked softly; my wife opened the door and made a scene. . . . The marquis appeared shocked at my suspicions. I realized my mistake.]

Both formally and contextually, the material appears to fall outside the tenor of elements in Exiles. At the same time, Belan's complicity in his own cuckolding and his willful denial of the obvious call to mind examples of Bloom's efforts to deny the sexual precocity of his daughter Milly and the impending infidelity of his wife Molly. The passage below begins with thoughts of Milly that lead almost inevitably to a consideration of Molly, and in each instance, even in his own mind, Bloom stops short of articulating his dilemma:

> O, well: she knows how to mind herself. But if not? No, nothing has happened. Of course it might. Wait in any case till it does.

> * * * *

> A soft qualm, regret, flowed down his backbone, increasing. Will happen, yes. Prevent. Useless: can't move. Girl's sweet light lips. Will happen too. He felt the flowing qualm spread over him. Useless to move now. Lips kissed, kissing, kissed. Full gluey woman's lips. (*U*, 4.428–30 and 4.447–50)

Just as modification characterizes the transmutations of borrowing from *Le Cocu* integrated into *Exiles*, elaboration becomes the hallmark of the borrowings from *Le Cocu* evident in *Ulysses*. The most extreme example appears in the reformation of the scene on the threshold of the boudoir of Madame Belan (quoted above) into the more baroque encounter that Bloom imagines during his whorehouse reveries in the Circe chapter:

BOYLAN

(jumps surely from the car and calls loudly for all to hear) Hello, Bloom! Mrs. Bloom dressed yet?

BLOOM

(in flunkey's prune plush coat and kneebreeches, buff stockings and powdered wig) I'm afraid not, sir. The last articles . . .

BOYLAN

(tosses him sixpence) Here, to buy yourself a gin and splash. (he hangs his hat smartly on a peg on Bloom's antlered head) Show me in. I have a little private business with your wife, understand?

BLOOM

Thank you, sir. Yes, sir. Madam Tweedy is in her bath, sir.

* * * *

BOYLAN

(to Bloom, over his shoulder) You can apply your eye to the keyhole and play with yourself while I just go through her a few times.

BLOOM

Thank you, sir, I will, sir. May I bring two men chums to witness the deed

and take a snapshot? (he holds out an ointment jar) Vaseline, sir? Orange-
flower . . . ? Lukewarm water . . . ? (*U*, 15.3756–67 and 15.3787–92)

Belan's stubborn denials of self-evident infidelity give way to Bloom's
aggressively masochistic distortion of Molly's betrayal. In both instances the cuckolds struggle to distort the circumstances confronting
them, but different emphases in the scenes graphically mark the extent
of Joyce's development. The ridiculousness of Belan's willful ignorance
gives the reader little latitude for interpreting his behavior. Bloom's determination to exacerbate his own humiliation, however, presents a
broad range of possible responses—from complete abhorrence to un-
mitigated sympathy.

Of course, given the variety of influences actively shaping Joyce's
perceptions during the time he was writing *Exiles* and *Ulysses*, it becomes
a moot point as to whether de Kock's work inspired Joyce or whether
it reinforced parallel views which he always meant to incorportate into
his play.[7] Convergences, for example, exist between the characterizations of Henri Blemont and Richard Rowan, yet, given the obvious projection of Richard Rowan's character as an older version of Stephen
Dedalus's, it would seem precipitous to label such affinities as strictly
derivative of a single source. As with the influence of other works, however, the primary value of a literary work like *Le Cocu* rests on its ability
to highlight trends in Joyce's thinking: in this case an interest in offering to the reader a range of alternative interpretations of the victim of
infidelity. While the passage in the notes for *Exiles* dealing with Flaubert
gives some sense of the broad thematic perspectives that Joyce wished
to introduce into both *Exiles* and *Ulysses*, his interest in de Kock's writing
shows a more concrete contextual concern. Joyce did not simply wish
to emulate *Madame Bovary* by shifting "the centre of sympathy" to the
husband. Rather than put any character at the apex of the love triangle
that he outlined, Joyce turned to works like *Le Cocu* to survey the detail
and the variety of the points of view informing the nature of the cuckold.

Paradoxically, however, for Joyce the significance of *Le Cocu* and
works like it lay not in their stylistic innovation but in their tendency
both to enforce and to subvert traditional and even hackneyed literary
conventions. Grant Allen's novel *The Woman Who Did*, another book in
Joyce's personal library bearing bibliographical and biographical traces
linking it with the composition of *Exiles*, offers further evidence of
Joyce's growing inclination to derive inspiration from mediocre sources.[8]
Like *Le Cocu*, Allen's book deals with the social and emotional problems

of sexuality outside of marriage, and it carries markings, similar to those found in de Kock's novel, highlighting points in the work of particular interest to Joyce.

The Woman Who Did follows the conventional story line of a social melodrama. An Englishwoman, Herminia Barton, conceives a child out of wedlock. Shortly after Herminia learns that she is pregnant the child's father dies, and Herminia finds herself without resources and with the responsibility of caring for her baby. To ensure the child's proper rearing, Herminia sacrifices her life to her daughter, Dolores, but as the girl grows up she embraces conventional morality and deserts her mother when she learns of her illegitimacy. The novel concludes with Herminia, alone and heartbroken, dying of grief.

The Woman Who Did, like *Madame Bovary* before it, draws its evocative power from ambivalence within the discourse. The novel's unconventional choice for its central character clashes with its perfectly predictable middle-class morality, leaving the reader to determine the credibility to assign to each. Furthermore, *The Woman Who Did,* like *Le Cocu,* eschews the strict linearity of a morality tale, so that an arch-hedonist (and arch-hypocrite) like Frank Harris would find little to recommend in the novel—calling it "a ridiculous book as a life's message."⁹ Joyce, on the other hand, took a more inclusive approach. In particular he cultivated an interest in elements that fostered a sense of the ambiguous relationship between the dominant ethos of the social repertoire and the values shaping the central character.

In his copy of the work Joyce took note of passages like the ones quoted below that underscore the struggles of Herminia to uphold her principles as she copes with the problems of being an unwed mother.

> Woe unto you, scribes and hypocrites; in all Christian London, *Miss Barton* [author's emphasis] and her baby could never have found a "respectable" room in which to lay their heads.¹⁰

> * * * *

> Herminia was far removed indeed from that blatant and decadent sect of "advanced women" who talk as though motherhood were a disgrace and a burden, instead of being, as it is, the full realization of man's faculties, the natural outlet for woman's wealth of emotion. . . . (165)

Although Herminia's sexual and social independence affirms a commitment to standards distinct from those held by society in general, the clear delineation of her personal morality and her rigorous adherence to its tenets convey a legitimacy rivaling those found in any conventional middle-class household. These values present the same sort of dialectic tension that appeared in portions of *Le Cocu*, and, despite the novel's maudlin tone, such attitudes raise interesting interpretive cruxes. Herminia's characterization resists easy identification through analogue to social types, for she projects neither the temperament of a rebel nor the attitude of a conformist. Her idiosyncratic views place her apart from any group, and the narrative forces the reader to resolve the antinomies within her nature before judging the merit of her actions.

This problem, with its similarities to the dramatic situation of *Exiles*, clearly fascinated Joyce, and many of the passages in the book that he highlighted emphasize Herminia's determination to retain self-respect and to free Dolores from the prescriptive demands of society. A series of marginal markings traces a path toward the long section describing the ultimate failure of Herminia's efforts, when Dolores learns of her illegitimacy and castigates her mother for it. Here Joyce gave special attention to the histrionic closing lines of their interchange. "When she rose to go to bed, Herminia, very wistful, held out her white face to be kissed as usual. She held it out tentatively. Worlds trembled in the balance. But Dolly drew herself back with a look of offended dignity. 'Never!' she answered in a firm voice. 'Never again while I live. You are not fit to receive a pure girl's kisses'" (253).

Despite Allen's rococo style, entries in Joyce's notes relating to the development of various characters in *Exiles* suggest an awareness of the evocative potential of such narrative elements. In sketching the distinguishing features of Bertha's nature, Joyce outlined traits seemingly inspired by his impressions of Herminia's situation. Like Herminia, Bertha has a deep affection for her illegitimate offspring. "[T]he love of Bertha for her child must be brought out as strongly as simply and as early as possible in the third act. It must, of course, be accentuated by the position of sadness in which she finds herself" (*JJA*, XI.55–56). Just as Herminia's daughter Dolores develops a set of values strikingly different from those of her mother, the nature of Bertha's son Archie, as Joyce's notes for the play reveal, is conditioned by values far different from those of his father. "Problem: Archie, Richard's son, is brought up on Robert's principles" (*JJA*, XI.16).

The notes for *Exiles* often provide a useful commentary on the action of the drama. Even an apparently disassociated musing on Bertha's moral nature contains thematic echoes of *The Woman Who Did* suggesting that its aspects were inspired by Herminia Barton's sexual awakening. "Richard having first understood the nature of innocence when it had been lost by him fears to believe that Bertha, to understand the chastity of her nature, must first lose it in adultery" (*JJA*, 11.22–23). The point, of course, is not that Joyce needed to turn to a mediocre novel to find inspiration for creating melodramatic scenes but rather that in seeing the clash of conventions in Grant Allen's work, Joyce derived a clearer sense of how the manipulation of literary conventions can lead to a greater reader engagement.

The examples already cited show that Joyce approached *The Woman Who Did* in much the same way as *Le Cocu*, with the intention of gathering material useful for conveying the social consequences of acts that defy convention, especially in terms of the perspectives and the attitudes of those who live unconventionally. As he immersed himself in these sources, however, a more salient aspect of this writing emerged. Having taken direct application of his personal experiences about as far as he could in *Dubliners* and in *Portrait*, Joyce began to face the need to expand his formal and thematic sources. He had always displayed an interest in artistically marginal figures (his youthful enthusiasm for the Irish poet James Clarence Mangan being perhaps the most notable, though not the only, example), but up to this point Joyce generally had centered his creative borrowings on material drawn from a range of established artistic forebears. His research for *Exiles* turned his attention to the literary periphery, the panoply of mundane or flawed models offering him the possibilities within apparently predictable forms for the recuperation of alternative meaning.

Didactic, melodramatic overtones aesthetically disable both *The Woman Who Did* and *Le Cocu*, yet these flaws did not in themselves inhibit their initial popularity or the popularity of similar contemporary works. In fact the two novels stand as representative of a form well known to readers of the time. Joyce saw that these hackneyed forms generated a predictable repertoire of expectations, and he realized the advantage of invoking their features in his own writing. Through selective imitation and negation of certain distinctive traits of popular fiction, the discourse could set up a dialectic between a reader's protentions/retentions and the inversions of the conventions upon which they are based, underscoring the novel's polyvocal nature and broadening the paradigm.

As intimated by the examples that I have already presented, some of the most familiar writing upon which Joyce drew, and hence the most evocative, centered on aspects of physical and romantic love. As Steven Marcus has discovered, by the turn of the century the conventions governing the presentation of various aspects of sexuality in nineteenth-century literature had calcified into familiar prescriptive forms, so Joyce could allude to such works with the assurance that they would be easily recognized.[11] He followed this procedure for foregrounding in *Ulysses* and in *Finnegans Wake* the stylistic and contextual signatures of a range of literary conventions. For now, however, I will confine myself to his descriptions of sexuality to exemplify his method and to illustrate the compositional connection between the models for *Exiles* and the sources shaping the structure of *Ulysses*.

The intertextual resonances appearing in *Ulysses*, evoked with much more sophistication than the instances of integrated genres employed in *Portrait*, proceed accretively. Fragmentary elements of this approach occur throughout the narrative discourse, but the most sustained resonances, and therefore the most effective, appear relatively late in the work, after readers have become conditioned to apprehending a range of Joyce's styles. The following passage from the Sirens episode illustrates this method of foregrounding, adumbrating the subtler manifestations that would follow in subsequent chapters:

> Miss Douce's brave eyes, unregarded, turned from the crossblind, smitten by sunlight. Gone. Pensive (who knows?), smitten (the smiting light), she lowered the drop-blind with a sliding cord. She drew down pensive (why did he go so quick when I?) about her bronze over the bar where bald stood by sister gold, inexquisite contrast, contrast inexquisite nonexquisite, slow cool dim seagreen sliding depth of shadow, *eau de Nil*. (*U*, 11.460–65)

The selection characterizes Lydia Douce as an older version of Gerty MacDowell, by integrating into the discourse the same sort of over-romantic effusion that characterizes depictions in Nausikaa of Gerty. Although the allusions are not elaborated in Sirens, the parentheses draw the reader's immediate attention to the dialectic of sentimentality and irony. Nausikaa can omit the parentheses because the reader, conditioned by previous chapters, approaches the episode already with the inclination to insert them.

As part of this narrative strategy, instances of popular fiction permeate the discourse from the moment Bloom appears. Overt stylistic echoes of pornography are scattered throughout the early chapters from Calypso onward. Cyclops mixes allusion and parody as a style reminiscent of the nineteenth-century sentimental novel, within several of the interpolated passages of the chapter, comments formally and contextually on the narrative discourse (*U*, 12.635–78). It also, over the course of the chapter, evokes a number of sub-genres of popular journalism on topics relating to sports, travel, politics, science, and social events. And the Nausikaa chapter gives over the entire first half of the narration to a voice filled with the same sort of clichés and euphemisms that readers would link to the popular romance novels of the time.[12]

Joyce scholars have long been aware of these borrowings, but until now no one has explored the implications of the responses that such forms invite readers to make. The depictions in each chapter call to one's mind specific reactions conditioned by the identificative traits of the genre that they reflect, yet throughout the work the discourse dexterously balances these impressions with the overriding concerns of the narrative. We are continually reminded of these stock conventions, yet never permitted to take them completely seriously or to dismiss them altogether.

Integrated genres, of course, do not function without the support of other formal techniques, yet without doubt they significantly accelerate and diversify the process of textual formation within narrative discourse. This becomes evident when one contrasts the impact of an analogous technique, free indirect discourse, as it functions in a chapter like Nausikaa, with its effect in *Portrait*. In each instance free indirect discourse fosters impressions of both irony and sympathy for a particular individual. In *Portrait*, however, several chapters elapse before one comes to a firm understanding of Joyce's treatment of Stephen's character. In Nausikaa, while free indirect discourse conveys the outlines of Gerty's consciousness, one reaches a similar sense in just a few pages because the reader's association of its descriptive tone with that of melodramatic novels foregrounds transparent contradictions in her nature.

> Gerty MacDowell who was seated near her companions, lost in thought, gazing far away into the distance was, in very truth, as fair a specimen of winsome Irish girlhood as one could wish to see. She was pronounced beautiful by all who knew her though, as folks often said, she was more a Giltrap than a MacDowell. Her figure was slight and graceful, inclining even to fragility but those iron jelloids she had been taking of late had done her a world of good much better than the Widow Welch's female pills and she was much better of those discharges she used to get and that tired feeling. (*U*, 13.79–87)

In mimicking the romance novel style, the narrative encourages the reader to measure Gerty against the expectations for a typical heroine of such a work, a simple comparison that inevitably heightens her normal human flaws to the level of ludicrous affectations. At the same time, the narrative moves to neutralize any impulse towards stereotyping. By following a digressive path analogous to that which will become the dominant linguistic feature of Molly's monologue in the final chapter, the discourse also introduces a subtle link between Gerty's nature and Molly's that will only be realized at the conclusion of the work. Consequently, while the scene unfolds graphically, climaxing in Gerty's exhibitionism, the impressions it creates operate to overturn any easy assumptions regarding the characterization of women. The dialectic tension between actions and anticipation and the narrative defamiliarization of the commonplace romance novel form deflect attention from the erotic and toward the banal way that Gerty's mind reshapes perceptions of the world to suit her emotional needs. At the same time, the analogue between Gerty and Molly, although only an insinuation at this point, sets up a counterforce, for even in this inchoate form it encourages the reader to distrust assumptions based upon types by drawing attention to the sensual impulses in all women.

Even when the descriptions of sexuality employ the traditional lexicon of erotic literature, the narrative, in a gesture closely allied to the replicative stylistic allusions employed in *Portrait*, insinuates the possibility for reinterpretation. The account in the Circe chapter of Bloom's meeting with Bella Cohen, for example, stands as one of the more obvious evocations of the conventions of pornographic novels, yet, at the same time, the characterizing features of that genre never completely dominate the reader's impression of the scene. Instead, parody offsets allusiveness, producing a temporary equilibrium through dialectic tension that prevents any single perspective from achieving ascendancy.

The section begins with more or less direct emulation, through a description that very neatly conforms to the characteristics typically given a female flagellant.[13]

> Bella Cohen, a massive whoremistress, enters. She is dressed in a three-quarter ivory gown, fringed round the hem with tasselled selvedge, and cools herself flirting a black horn fan like Minnie Hauck in Carmen. On her left hand are wedding and keeper rings. Her eyes are deeply carboned. She has a sprouting moustache. Her olive face is heavy, slightly sweated and fullnosed, with orangetainted nostrils. She has large pendant beryl eardrops.[14] (*U*, 15.2742–49)

As the scene progresses, however, the modification of the genre by the discourse becomes increasingly apparent. The narrative veers slightly but significantly from the physical concerns usually featured in sadomasochistic literature toward an exploration of Bloom's psychological milieu. Images of physical degradation continue to appear, but they are now punctuated with allusions to the mental anxiety producing Bloom's hallucinations—the despair, the frustration, and the guilt. By overlaying each new indignity with a reference to Bloom's past (Bakhtin's heteroglossia), the discourse shifts the emphasis from fantasies of sexual deviation to the emotional upheaval that stimulated them. As Bloom laces Bella's boots, for example, he calls to mind the night Boylan and Molly met while assiduously avoiding naming the man who would become his wife's lover: "Not to lace the wrong eyelet as I did the night of the bazaar dance. Bad luck. Hook in wrong tache of her . . . person you mentioned. That night she met . . . Now" (*U*, 15.2829–31). Finally, intertextual citations within the narrative turn from replication back to generic distortion. Instead of the extravagant depravity that one would expect to conclude a pornographic episode, the sins of the past offer a comic summation of Bloom's own venal perversions. (Although the exchange between Bloom and Bella/Bello continues for several more pages, the passage subsequently drops all erotic pretensions and instead focuses on an elaboration of Bloom's psychosexual guilt.)

> He went through a form of clandestine marriage with at least one woman in the shadow of the Black church. Unspeakable messages he telephoned mentally to Miss Dunn at an address in d'Olier street while he presented himself indecently to the instrument in the callbox. By word and deed he frankly encouraged a nocturnal strumpet to deposit fecal and other matter in an unsanitary outhouse attached to empty premises. In five public conveniences he wrote pencilled messages offering his nuptial partner to all strongmembered males. And by the offensively smelling vitriol works did he not pass night after night by loving courting couples to see if and what and how much he could see? Did he not lie in bed, the gross boar, gloating over a nauseous fragment of well-used toilet paper presented to him by a nasty harlot, stimulated by gingerbread and a postal order? (*U*, 15.3028–40)

Through a subtle shift in emphasis the discourse has gone beyond exclusive consideration of sensual indulgence to a display of Bloom's comic frailties and insecurities. At the same time the reader cannot simply assign to Bloom the role of either burlesque comic or stripper, for more complex elements of Bloom's psyche remain in the forefront of our consciousness, both encouraging and diffusing associations with pornography. The narrative initially can take advantage of the evocative force of pornography and, at the same time, develop in a manner uninhibited by the limitations of that form.

By the time he came to write *Ulysses*, Joyce's sensitivity towards the characterizing elements of a particular genre allowed him to go beyond simple imitation or parody. Instead the novel presents the reader with a potently ambiguous contextual allusiveness. In the specific instance of references to sexuality, the discourse underscores the particular vulnerability of conventional literary assumptions to (mis)direction. Throughout *Ulysses* innuendo heightens the sexual overtones of works which in fact were quite innocuous, and the inherent conflict between assumption and actuality in turn increases the dialectic tension, the multiplicities, at the heart of the narrative.

Naturally enough, these implications expand the opportunities for interpretation well beyond the alternatives open to the reader in the actual works from which they were drawn. In one application of this approach, for example, by dropping the first name in references to the author Charles Paul de Kock and by playing on his surname's suggestiveness, Joyce encourages (without prescribing) analogies between Bloom and sexual depravity (Paul de/Poldy), and he fosters the assumption that the books have a salacious rather than a humane intent.[15] At the same time, the narrative reveals, to readers familiar with de Kock's real aims, an irony in the evocation of an allusion that bases its effect on the distortions conditioning our own assumptions about the range of Bloom's behavior.

The same exploitive pattern obtains for allusions appearing throughout *Ulysses* to the putatively pornographic *Ruby: Pride of the Ring*. Joyce adapted his title from that of the actual work, *Ruby: a Novel of Circus Life*, to heighten the sexual overtones of his references. Both Mary Power and Bernard Benstock have already examined Joyce's use of this fictitious title as a device for directing reader response, but it would be useful in terms of the thesis of this chapter to add a postscript to their findings.[16] After planting the initial impression of the book's lascivious nature, the discourse exploits reader reactions which would naturally grow out of these assumptions. (As Benstock points out, in one instance Bloom describes an illustration from the actual work in such a way as to give a disingenuous impression of the book's prurience.) In fact, according to Power's synopsis, *Ruby*, like *Le Cocu*, is a rather moral story, and this tone, in its own way celebrating the humanity of individuals rather than their bestiality, fits precisely the pattern of exploiting assumptions towards popular fiction that I have been outlining. In a gesture paralleling the references to the works of de Kock, by suggesting the salacious, the discourse heightens our sensitivity to the physical and emotional implications of Bloom's own situation. By developing this reference from a work with an antithetical moral perspective, the paradigm reminds us of the necessary provisionality of all interpretations that presume a single, overriding motivation governing Bloom's thoughts or actions.

The range of contradictory feelings evoked within a reader by erotic innuendo complements a variety of other dialectic perspectives articulated by the central characters of *Ulysses*. Juxtaposed antithetical attitudes reflect the contextual changes brought about by Joyce's work on *Exiles*, and they demonstrate his growing inclination to exploit the literal echoes of particular genres to enhance the creative potential within his own work. Obviously such a move demands of the reader an analogous revaluation of aesthetic standards, for it signals not simply a discrete technical change in Joyce's writing but a significant shift in perspective that goes beyond any newfound enthusiasm for a particular style or genre.

In a gesture similar to Stephen Dedalus's simultaneous efforts to confront and to evade the tension that exists between the permanence and the mutability of his self, when we contemplate the evolving intellectual features of the author of *Ulysses*, we must face the paradox of contiguity within change.

> —As we, or mother Dana, weave and unweave our bodies, Stephen said, from day to day, their molecules shuttled to and fro, so does the artist weave and unweave his image. And as the mole on my right breast is where it was when I was born, though all my body has been woven of new stuff time after time, so through the ghost of the unquiet father the image of the unliving son looks forth. (*U*, 9.376–81)

The James Joyce who published *Ulysses* in 1922 certainly differed markedly from the one who began it in late 1914 or early 1915, and he was strikingly different from the one who in 1904 initiated the process of writing that would eventually constitute his canon. As the author approaching the project of composing *Ulysses* differed from the author(s) of the earlier works in the canon, so too does the (ideal? common?) reader about to constitute a text for *Ulysses* differ from the reader(s) who had composed texts from the earlier works. In similar fashion the individual who composes a text for Ulysses during his or her second, third, fourth, or hundredth reading is not the same reader as the one who composed a text on the first reading. Intervening external experiences and thematic and formal elements within the work have conditioned and reconditioned our disposition toward the novel.

At the same time, artistic and intellectual similarities link each author and each piece of writing to the others. (Just as our own intellectual contiguity binds us to the readers responsible for all preceding texts generated by our consciousness.) Indeed, these similarities act as a raison d'être for any consideration of the works as a related body. We cannot ignore the stylistic, generic, and thematic differences that obtain between *Dubliners, Portrait, Exiles,* and *Ulysses,* nor can we divorce any from an overriding consciousness joining them all. Consequently, any study of the forces shaping the composition of *Ulysses* faces the challenge of integrating our perception of the new influences directing the creative process into an interpretation acknowledging the impact of previous experience.

With a premeditation attesting to Joyce's full confidence in the creative powers of his readers, *Ulysses* formally and contextually exudes an intrusive and diverse referentiality. By this statement I do not intend to deny the cumulative effect of discursive elements on the thematic and stylistic constitution of any of his previous writing. In each of the earlier works, however, Joyce always overlaid his borrowings with his own material so that readers recuperate traces of influence with the greatest difficulty and often only after recourse to collateral writings. *Ulysses* foregrounds the act of Joyce's borrowing, giving readers unequivocal encouragement to do the same in forming their texts. The heteroglossia implicitly conditioning our readings of all Joyce's works prior to *Ulysses* now becomes explicit.

Paradoxically, the most overt thematic instances of this technique—introduction of arcane facts, presentation of details impinging upon the Dublin ambiance, catalogues of little-known persons, places, or things—provide the lesser impact with respect to long-term reader response, but they do assert a strong, immediate influence upon one's perceptions. The allusive impulse, reiterated in every chapter, underscores an interest in a wealth of material extending well beyond the range of topics delimited by Joyce's earlier writing, and the offhand introduction of so many facts confronts the reader, conditioned by the muted acknowledgments of influence buried in *Dubliners* and in *Portrait,* with the task of discovering a new method for integrating the information into any coherent text. On a subtler level the assault, initiated in *Portrait,* on the impulse to interpret characterization through cause-and-effect thinking now expands to cover the entire discourse. Dialectical tension appears in a number of instances, so that even as the reader becomes accustomed to masses of unfamiliar facts, the often contradictory tendencies that arise through the juxtaposition of the material remains unresolved. At the same time, despite the narrative's insistence upon legitimizing the ubiquitousness of a both/and reality, the volume of information does not receive uniform emphasis, and so it does not eliminate the necessity for some form of stratification.

Consequently, the influence of dialectical tension obtains even more forcefully in the formal structure of *Ulysses* than it does in Joyce's earlier works. Researching background material for *Exiles* gave Joyce the opportunity to consider the impact of popular literature on the consciousness of the reader. In *Ulysses* the narrative begins to exploit a number of the traits associated with distinctive, if marginally considered, forms of writing for mass consumption. This maneuver presents an array of perspectives, fluctuating between imitation and parody, enforcing a series of intentionally contradicting impressions and effectively blocking the emergence of a single point of view as dominant.

Since the central intention of applying such techniques lies in the cultivation of an aura of ambiguity, the challenge facing the reader wishing to harmonize the diverse allusive elements of *Ulysses* within a coherent text does not lie in a painstaking explication of every reference or in the precise identification of every style contained in the work. Rather, a reconciliation of disunities comes about through a reordering of the basic assumptions underlying how one goes about perceiving. The increasing emphasis on details and on alternatives within *Ulysses* does not point toward a more complex linear structure still supported by cause-and-effect thinking. Instead, this technique seeks to turn attention toward multiple meanings and toward both/and realities. To comprehend this, one must come to a broad sense of the connecting framework of aesthetic and artistic standards governing the application of intertextuality and of dialectical tension and not to a necessary awareness of the sources for specific details. Perceiving the patterns emerging from such associations enables one to discern the paradigm of the novel, and following that emergence standards for framing meaning and interpretation become manifestly evident.

An important relationship obtains between this shift in thematic and stylistic emphasis and the protocol governing the reader's formation of a text. Beyond testifying to a virtuoso's command of a range of diverse facts, this gesture of evoking a mass of seemingly disconnected information pushes readers to consider the meta-textual ambiance of the novel. It illustrates the provisional nature of every effort to relate the mass of data contained within the social environment to specific interpretations of individual events and consciousnesses. This in turn emphasizes the challenge faced by an artist who wishes to assert the presence of a particular aesthetic experience in the midst of so much competing matter. Through the paratactic gesture of linking these elements without an effort to place emphasis or stress on particular parts, the narrative discourse of *Ulysses* refuses to enforce a dominant reading. Instead it introduces the notion of a reader's responsibility for weighing the significance of diverse elements in the process of forming a text.

Far from renouncing creative control, this strategy of allusiveness, by exploring some of the elemental questions of creative identity that first surfaced in *Exiles*, draws attention to significant aspects of the creative reciprocity of reader and writer, and it reminds one of the provisionality of all interpretation. Initially, the process can prove to be quite unnerving, for it runs against the impulse to impose order and by extension to derive meaning through the consistent application of a clearly articulated mode of perception. As the condition asserts itself, however, one comes to see in this approach the denial of certitude—a gesture essential not simply to the Modernist novel but to any artistically satisfying experience. The play of the imagination instinctively resists the imposition of closure while it simultaneously calls for the articulation of boundaries to guide its efforts. Through underscoring multiplicity while not embracing infinity, the narrative fosters possibilities without succumbing to anarchy. The very wealth of references introduced into the discourse establishes finite limits for meaning without giving prominence to a single, dominant response.

Such an approach rests on the premise that commonplace writing, even that which has become clichéd, has the potential to evoke a particular set of responses as effectively as any other form. By manipulating the expectations inspired by a style associated with a particular context or theme, Joyce could exploit the tendencies of readers to project such expectations, at least in part, onto texts derived from his own writing. At the same time through the incorporation of antithetical styles and discordant contexts into the narrative discourse, Bakhtin's heteroglossia, he could prevent the clichéd form from establishing a predominant version. This maneuver heightens the subtlety of the narration and expands the range of texts that one can educe from the work. It creates a dialectical tension based on what experience had taught readers to anticipate from a particular style working against what they perceived the discourse as actually presenting.

For decades critics have concerned themselves with analogues between various styles in *Ulysses* and those associated with other writers, both well known and obscure,[17] but until now the common connection between this formal diversity and the overriding plan for the composition of *Ulysses* has remained obscure. Now, with a clearer knowledge of Joyce's habits of reading and of his application of sources, one can discern the impulse to create a formal texture matching the social diversity of the environment of the novel.

VIII | *Ulysses*: From Respondent to Creator

The approaches to characterizations that developed out of the composition of *Exiles* exerted a continuing and pronounced impact on Joyce's approach to his later writing, but the play's internal flaws limit its impact upon Joyce's readers. Conversely, the stylistic developments first manifested in *Portrait*, while only a starting point for Joyce, signal to us the advent of ways of reading that will shape our responses to all of his subsequent artistic achievements and, retrospectively, to his entire canon. The constitution of *Portrait* establishes Joyce's masterful creative ability to manipulate a variety of sophisticated formal techniques. The methods employed in the novel, however, do not simply highlight the imaginative force of its author. They also foreground the (re)creative power bestowed upon the reader by the novel's structure. As I emphasize in chapter five, *Portrait* does not simply involve one in the intellectual transcription of its images. It increases one's direct involvement in the full articulation of a text by presenting the reader with ambiguities, gaps in the narrative, and apparent contradictions that must be resolved to bring unity to the discourse.

Specifically, the intellectual proximity of the consciousnesses of Stephen Dedalus and of the narrative voice poses interpretive cruxes which one must resolve in order to determine the nature of our experience in reading *Portrait*. Over the course of the work, the diction and the stature of the narrative voice mature in a fashion paralleling Stephen's own development. For the reader creating a text from the novel, it establishes itself as a separate character who reflects, without duplicating, many of the elements in the nature of Stephen. In fact, a reciprocity develops. We find our perceptions of the nature of the narrative voice directed by our impressions of aspects of the character of Stephen and vice versa. At the same time, the varying emphases that one can assign to their distinct voices endow the discourse with a mutability that conditions and reconditions the meaning(s) we give to subsequent encounters with the work. Neither can achieve a position of hegemony because neither can completely separate himself from the other character, and so in tan-

dem the consciousnesses of Stephen and of the narrator shape our efforts at reading and respond to our attempts at interpretation.[1]

The antinomies of *Portrait*, of course, do not originate with the
reader, but they do grow out of one's impulse to shift attention between
the expressions of the two central personalities whose natures dominate
the development of the narrative discourse. Taken together the impressions created by these figures define for the reader the limits of the psychological ambiance within which events and ideas develop in the
novel, but they do not impose a prescriptive response to it. As one's own
sense of the significance of the narrative presence and of Stephen fluctuates, the range of potential texts and of possible interpretations—all
equally valid—increases.

The bifurcation of attention demanded by such a confrontation of
strong voices goes against common habits of reading by which one rou-
tinely assigns of privileged position to the voice narrating events of the
work. Even in a novel unfolding through first-person narrative (*Heart of
Darkness* or *David Copperfield* comes immediately to mind) the individual
whose voice relates the events of the work assumes a privileged status
when acting as narrator that he or she does not enjoy when participating
dialogically with other characters in the book.[2] *Portrait* allies the narrator's voice closely with that of Stephen while maintaining the uniqueness of each, and thus it undermines the assumption that a single
perspective will dominate the discourse. I have already alluded to this
process for overturning the conventional expectations of the reader,
identifying it with Mikhail Bakhtin's polyphony: the presentation in the
narrative of a voice or voices "standing as if *alongside* the author's word
and in a peculiar way combining with it."[3] Strictly speaking, however,
the term only applies analogously, because Bakhtin was not prepared
to call upon the reader to suppress completely one's concern for the primacy of authorial intention. Since the polyphonic pronouncements in
Portrait never achieve unification in a single, composite voice, they endow the novel with an ambiguity supporting a range of alternative readings. Nonetheless, for those readers familiar with Bakhtin, his comments on polyphony clarify the functions of the central elements of the
discourse of *Portrait*.[4]

A precise sense of polyphony becomes an integral part of any sophisticated reading of *Portrait*. The voices of Stephen and of the narrator
neither articulate independent, competing perspectives, nor do they
blend together to form a strictly unified point of view. Instead, they affirm separate but complementary attitudes so similar that for countless
lines in the novel the case can be made for selecting either voice as the

intelligent source behind the narrative discourse. The controversy over the irony in the novel, noted with displeasure by Wayne Booth, reflects the effectiveness of such subtle distinctions. Most of us would resist readings that either completely ignored irony or that used it to invert the meaning of every statement, yet the consensus that one can draw from a range of interpretations is that the emphasis given to irony will vary from reader to reader and even from reading to reading. As a consequence, the tones of Stephen and of the narrator become implicit commentaries on one another, each modifying the reader's impressions without establishing the self-sufficient dominance of the speaker.

As noted in chapter five, this condition in the characterization leads to disjunctions in the narrative that press the reader to go beyond reconciling diversities and towards elaborating upon the structure of existing discourse. These gestures towards extension contribute to our sense of alternative forms of perceiving, leaving us with a growing awareness of the possibility for intervention. *Portrait*, in fact, does not simply call for an amalgamation of elements already present in the work. It demands a creative extension of that material from which one can derive the basis for forming a unified, though provisional, text.

In a manner important to the development of the text in the mind of the reader, polyphony in *Portrait* evolves through Stephen's growing awareness of the fragmented aspects of his environment. While the intrusions of Stephen's voice into the narrative through free indirect discourse present the most forceful instances of a specific character challenging the limits imposed by the position of the narrative consciousness, secondary figures in the novel express less sustained but equally emphatic ways of seeing. The behavior of individuals like Simon Dedalus and his Cork cronies in chapter II, the retreat master in chapter III, and Stephen's friends at the university in chapter V offer samples of the multiplicity of views that Stephen encounters. Their diverse convictions refute the assumption that a monolithic social, religious, familial order surrounds Stephen. They show rather the existence of a series of shifting positions that, at any particular moment, he only imperfectly understands. Further, this polyphony enforces in the mind of the reader the realization that Stephen's impression of Clongowes is not the same as Wells's, and that neither boy sees the school in the same way that Father Dolan does. Likewise, Stephen's perception of Parnell differs from his father's and Mr. Casey's, and theirs in turn differ from Dante's. No objective view exists. Rather the events of Stephen's life, described by an independent persona or derived directly or indirectly from the consciousness of Stephen, stand as fragmentary alternative perspectives of the discourse, necessarily completed and unified by anyone seeking to interpret the action.

I have recapitulated these aspects of *Portrait* as a prelude to emphasizing distinctions between the voices of *Ulysses* and those of *Portrait*. These differences highlight the changes in Joyce's artistic abilities and in his aesthetic aims. The new creative demands placed upon the reader by *Ulysses* require a sensitivity to these changes. As I have established earlier in this study, one can already detect in the narrative discourse of *Portrait* evidence of the multiplicity of voices that will constitute the structures of Joyce's later works. *Portrait*, however, only begins the process. Most figures remain relegated to minor roles, and no voice except the narrator's seriously challenges the hegemony of Stephen's views.

The format of *Ulysses*, on the other hand, refines and expands the formal methods inaugurated in *Portrait*, drawing the reader into a deeper commitment to the creative process involved in the production of a text. As disjunctions and logical inconsistencies become essential components of the work's structure, one must face the growing need not only to interpose oneself more fully in the process of creation but to acknowledge the degree to which ambiguities within the novel shape the creation of texts. Necessarily, the function of the reader evolves to embrace this more intense and expanded concept of creativity. Paradoxically, by foregrounding the role of the reader, the virtuosity of the writer assumes an even greater significance. The author provides a broad range of alternatives, but he must insure that the ambiguities retain a plausible relationship to the discourse that perpetuates the reader's desire for engagement with the novel.

This approach advances *Ulysses* beyond both the model of dialogic imagining proposed by Bakhtin and the formal structure of *Portrait*. The individual voices of characters do not contribute to an overall point of view distilled through the consciousness of the narrator. Nor do two dominant figures vie to assert a particular perspective that will control the reader's perception of the discourse of the novel. Instead, Joyce resigns even the appearance of hegemony, and the figures in *Ulysses* voice a multiplicity of perspectives, all bidding for the attention of the reader struggling to create a text from the printed page.

In *Portrait* the reader can, with some degree of confidence, choose to rely upon a single consciousness—Stephen, the narrator, or an incorporated version of the two—to articulate norms from which a specific text for the novel can be derived. *Ulysses* disbars even that provisional gesture towards primacy, impelling one to a more multifaceted response. No character possesses the preeminence to lay uncontested claim to the role of protagonist. No one stands as the dominant force reflecting the complexities of the entire work, for the attention demanded by a variety of characters does not allow a reader to derive a single, continuous perspective that encompasses the formal and thematic virtuosity of *Ulysses*. Instead the focus that we give to individual natures, even if only for a short time, dissipates one's sense of a controlling central consciousness. The narrative voice remains a continuous presence, but its metamorphoses throughout the work go far beyond the changes that informed the discourse of *Portrait*. As it mimics a range of literary conventions, it resists any permanent characterization or any long-term association with one of the characters. Consequently, the novel fosters the impulse to embrace a method of reading analogous to the work's cacophonous polyphony. Just as the number of printed pages becomes the ultimate arbiter of the physical make-up of *Ulysses*, the imagination of the individual reader becomes the ultimate arbiter of any text for the novel. Thus the reader becomes the dominant consciousness of the work, reconciling its multitude of voices by amplifying or muting elements of the discourse in an effort to achieve a balanced impression of the aesthetic experience.

This process of reconciliation requires a complete revision of undifferentiated linear thinking. The effort must go beyond the associative modifications accomplished through the experience of reading *Portrait*, for the structure of *Ulysses* repeatedly and overtly subverts efforts to create a text that retains a nostalgia for cause-and-effect logic. As a result one will not be able to reconcile an evolving text with the array of contradicting perspectives that continually assault its integrity merely by acknowledging the provisionality of a particular reading. Instead, as one proceeds through *Ulysses*, it becomes increasingly apparent that no single perspective achieves a position which allows one to derive a consistent and logical meaning from the diverse elements of the discourse and that no discrete creative pattern proves sufficient to encompass all of the vagaries of the work. Rather, as the reader proceeds through *Ulysses*, a variety of successive perspectives moves to the foreground, and one struggles to balance them against the points of view that the discourse has already established.[5] In such an atmosphere, then, the obvious interpretive challenge to outline the paradigm—the limits laid down by the structure of the work within which one can create a range of texts—takes on imperative force.

The fluctuations present a paradox analogous to the image of the hermeneutical circle—the whole receives its definition from the parts, and reciprocally, the parts can only be understood in reference to the whole. *Ulysses*, however, expands the implications of this trope. Although the perspective that forges the circle creates a provisional interpretation upon which all of the elements are centered, the elements themselves undermine the authority of a single point of view. Irreconcilable antinomies continually call for a recentering and continually question the legitimacy of any reordering. The both/and dialectic that stands as the best response to the experience of reading *Portrait* becomes the only tenable position in an encounter with *Ulysses* as protensions crumble and retensions become eroded by conflicting retrospections.[6]

It is because of this multiplicity within the discourse that, despite his assumptions regarding the significance of authorial intentionality, Bakhtin's concept of polyphonic discourse remains a useful starting point for any effort to sort out the initial narrative dispositions of *Ulysses*. Although he does not address himself directly to the application of free indirect discourse or of interior monologue, Bakhtin's views on the impact of competing voices very neatly describe effects created by these techniques in Telemachus, Nestor, and Proteus. Like the importunate voices that Bakhtin finds in Dostoevsky, the contrasting and often conflicting impressions articulated by the discourse opening *Ulysses* deny hegemonic primacy to any character, yet they contribute to a single, consistent, definable perspective governing the narrative of the first part of the novel.

Telemachus, Nestor, and Proteus delineate Stephen's position within the narrative discourse as initially similar to the one that he held in *Portrait*. The nature of the narrative voice also initially appears analogous to the one appearing in the previous novel. As in *Portrait*, the two stand at the center of the discourse. Their views bound back and forth, with gestures providing evidence of the broad applicability of Bakhtin's views on polyphony, blurring but not eliminating distinctions in the narrative.

Ulysses opens without overtly linking its narrative voice with the consciousness of any specific individual, but its own implicit and explicit evocations of *Portrait* might lead one toward the assumption that the first five lines originate from a consciousness closely associated with the nature of Stephen Dedalus. "Stately, plump Buck Mulligan came from the stairhead, bearing a bowl of lather on which a mirror and a razor lay crossed. A yellow dressinggown, ungirdled, was sustained gently behind him on the mild morning air" (*U*, 1.1–5). As demonstrated by the ironic apposition of adjectives—the portentous "stately" under the subversive threat of the images associated with "plump"—the narrative begins by announcing a presence as attuned to antinomies as that of the consciousness dominating the descriptions of *Portrait*. Like the preceding novel, it evolves through ambiguities that disrupt any sense of certitude within the reader regarding the identity of initial sources. The first few lines engender a conflicting sense of its derivation with a tone suggesting not one but several possible sources, and the diction of succeeding passages continues to develop a range of possibilities. As a result one may feel disposed to extend to *Ulysses* the protocol for reading that characterized the previous novel.

Almost immediately, however, elements in the discourse imply a mutability that promises a more persistent extension of the limits of the narrative than similar efforts outlined in *Portrait*. The initial description, with its mordant wit generally absent from the discourse of the earlier novel, is followed by the monologue of Buck Mulligan.

> [Mulligan] held the bowl aloft and intoned:
> —*Introibo ad altare Dei*—
> Halted, he peered down the dark winding stairs and called out coarsely:
> —Come up Kinch! Come up, you fearful jesuit! (*U*, 1.5–8)

These lines identify the pattern of Mulligan's irreverent clowning, and they imply a conjunction of the voices of Mulligan and of the narrator analogous to the impulse in *Portrait* to connect the voice of Simon Dedalus with that of the narrator of the Baby Tuckoo tale. Yet, while the association of Simon Dedalus and the narrative voice of *Portrait* quickly subsides, *Ulysses* sustains, for a time at least, affinities between Mulligan and the narrator. His gentle self-mockery continues to surface, reminding us of the diction of the opening sentences. "My name is absurd too: Malachi Mulligan, two dactyls. But it has a Hellenic ring, hasn't it? Tripping and sunny like the buck himself. We must go to Athens. Will you come if I can get the aunt to fork out twenty quid?" (*U*, 1.41–44). More overtly, time after time in the first chapter, through free indirect discourse, elements of Mulligan's nature assert alternative perspectives by insinuating themselves into the narrative.

> And putting on his stiff collar and rebellious tie he spoke to them, chiding them, and to his dangling watchchain. His hands plunged and rummaged in his trunk while he called for a clean handkerchief. God, we'll simply have to dress the character. I want puce gloves and green boots. Contradiction. Do I contradict myself? Very well then, I contradict myself. Mercurial Malachi. A limp black missile flew out of his talking hands. (*U*, 1.513–18)

As the novel unfolds, of course, the narrative of *Ulysses* frustrates any effort by the reader to assign to Mulligan's consciousness the position of the force sustaining the book's descriptive voice, just as the discourse of *Portrait* suppresses voices competing with Stephen Dedalus. The gesture toward the consciousness of Mulligan, however, has not been superfluous. The intrusion of Mulligan's viewpoint into the discourse heightens the reader's sensitivity to the presence of Stephen's perspective in much the same way that Mulligan's competing performances underscore our awareness of Stephen's efforts to gain recognition. It establishes in readers an awareness of the polyphonic tones that will shape the content and the form of the remainder of the novel.

In addition to its effect upon the response of readers, this intensification of vocality within the discourse has a pronounced impact on the formal arrangement of the narrative. The conflation of free indirect discourse and interior monologue reaffirms one's sense of the bitter irony that has come to typify Stephen's view of Ireland. The tone of *Portrait* that frequently undercuts Stephen's sententiousness now spills over into Stephen's self-reflexive thoughts. The selection below presents his resentment of the old milkwoman's obsequities to Mulligan, and it hints at his own desire for her approval.

> Stephen listened in scornful silence. She bows her old head to a voice that speaks to her loudly, her bonesetter, her medicineman: me she slights. To the voice that will shrive and oil for the grave all there is of her but her woman's unclean loins, of man's flesh made not in God's likeness, the serpent's prey. And to the loud voice that now bids her be silent with wondering unsteady eyes. (*U*, 1.418–24)

Characterization changes here because Stephen is resisting replication of his role in *Portrait*. He has progressed beyond his detached youthful bitterness, and so the discourse now makes readers aware of his new capacity for self-parody. Perhaps taking his cue from Mulligan, Stephen has developed the knack of drawing from his idiosyncrasies whatever humor they will yield. When Mulligan chafes him about his aversion to bathing, he responds that "[a]ll Ireland is washed by the gulfstream" (*U*, 1.475). Stephen has also shed the sense of self-righteousness that made many of his earlier views, expressed in *Portrait*, seem supercilious. When Haines presses him on his religious views, for example, he maintains the integrity of his beliefs but diffuses any traces of sententiousness by confessing with resigned self-deprecation that "[y]ou behold in me . . . a horrible example of free thought" (*U*, 1.624–25). (The exchange recalls Stephen's deft deflection of the youthful Vincent Heron's efforts to interrogate him at Belvedere [*P*, 78]. In *Ulysses*, however, the ironic humor has become a more consistent feature of his personality.)

In subsequent chapters modifications in the discourse and in the nature of Stephen continue to erode the solipsistic pose that had dominated his consciousness in *Portrait*. While Stephen maintains the habit of viewing everything from a predominantly self-centered perspective, he cultivates an awareness of the significance of social context surrounding him. In essence he is moving toward the realization that, to a large degree, the success of his artistic endeavors depends upon the cultivation of an empathy for polyvocality—attentiveness to the voices of the intellectual, social, and moral heritage of the world surrounding him.

Responding to this concern, he begins to commingle his sense of himself with his sense of the natures of others. In Nestor this impulse moves Stephen to amalgamate images of the contest taking place on Mr. Deasy's playing field with recollections of similar games which he witnessed during his own boyhood at Clongowes Wood. Not content with this simple association, Stephen then extrapolates to produce—out of the clichéd metaphor that games prepare one for later adult struggles—an impression both ironic and sincere of a medieval Irish battlefield of the sort that might have provided the initial impetus for field hockey.

> Shouts rang shrill from the boys' playfield and a whirring whistle.
> Again: a goal. I am among them, among their battling bodies in a medley, the joust of life. You mean that knock-kneed mother's darling who seems to be slightly crawsick? Jousts. Time shocked rebounds, shock by shock. Jousts, slush and uproar of battles, the frozen deathspew of the slain, a shout of spearspikes baited with men's bloodied guts. (*U*, 2.313–18)

In Proteus the cultural interdependency becomes even more explicit. Stephen, in a reverie of racial consciousness, recreates a series of scenes from the Irish past until he finally succeeds in integrating his own presence into the midst of his forebears.

> Galleys of the Lochlanns ran here to beach, in quest of prey, their blood-beaked prows riding low on a molten pewter surf. Dane vikings, torcs of tomahawks aglitter on their breasts when Malachi wore the collar of gold. A school of turlehide whales stranded in hot noon, spouting, hobbling in the shallows. Then from the starving cagework city a horde of jerkined dwarfs, my people, with flayers' knives, running, scaling, hacking in green blubbery whalemeat. Famine, plague and slaughters. Their blood is in me, their lusts my waves. I moved among them on the frozen Liffey, that I, a changeling, among the spluttering resin fires. I spoke to no-one: none to me. (*U*, 3.300–09)

Stephen's sense of heritage becomes a force of artistic inspiration, and, reciprocally, the images that he creates preserve the past in his artistic present.

In terms of interpretive strategies, Proteus also serves to summarize for the reader the movement away from the linear thinking that had been developing in Telemachus and Nestor. The chapter begins with a confident assertion of the objective elements in perception—"Ineluctable modality of the visible . . . Ineluctable modality of the audible" (*U*, 3.1 and 13). Its narration, however, consistently undermines this confidence by foregrounding examples of alternative perception: Bishop Berkeley in conflict with the senses, Patrice Egan in conflict with his father, and Stephen's initial mistaken identification of two gypsies as midwives. It ends with a backward glance—"rere regardant" (*U*, 3.503)—emphasizing the impulse for reconsideration.

Stephen's ambivalence toward his impressions of self and of the world he inhabits underscores an important divergence in the plan of *Ulysses* from that followed in *Portrait*. The ambiguous nature of the novel's narrative form sharply restrains the impulse to allow any particular set of values to inform exclusively the interpretations. Changes in Stephen's views and a chorus of competing voices, often expressing contradictory attitudes, all impinge upon the discourse, discouraging reliance on a similar, single set of perspectives. They overtly signal to us polyphony's coming into maturity out of the blurred binary tension of *Portrait*.

Part of the difficulty in fixing Stephen's position comes from the prominence that he must share over the first half of the work with another character, Leopold Bloom. After Stephen's sinuous self-reflection in the Proteus chapter, the novel formally and temporally begins again in Calypso. It shifts from Stephen standing on Sandymount Strand at 11:00 A.M. to Leopold Bloom preparing breakfast at 8:00 A.M. in the kitchen of his house at number 7 Eccles Street. There the discourse initiates realignment of the structural lines characterizing the first three chapters.

The intimate and detailed account of Bloom's routine that unfolds becomes an essential feature of the narrative strategy. The disjunction between the third and the fourth chapters proceeding from the unheralded appearance of Bloom urges a revaluation of accumulated expectations, and it begins the process of conditioning the reader to accept subsequent formal and contextual disruptions. Bloom is introduced by a narrative voice that has adopted the same irreverent tone that first presented Mulligan—"Mr Leopold Bloom ate with relish the inner organs of beasts and fowls" (*U*, 4.1–2)—but within a relatively short space, its descriptions clearly begin to reflect the influence of the consciousness of Bloom. (In Lestrygonians Bloom, with a similar pun, demonstrates how close the narrative voice comes to his own—"Ham and his descendants mustered and bred there" [*U*, 8.748].) Three paragraphs after the passage quoted above, a blend of stream of consciousness and free indirect discourse associate the narrative persona with what will become the familiar mental idiosyncrasies of Bloom's personality: "Another slice of bread and butter: three, four: right. She didn't like her plate full. Right. He turned from the tray, lifted the kettle off the hob and set it sideways on the fire" (*U*, 4.11–13). In a format paralleling the Telemachia, for the next three chapters—Calypso, Lotus Eaters, and Hades—Bloom stands both as a figure at the center of the action and as a presence imbedded in the narration as we follow his morning movements down to the most quotidian detail with the same close scrutiny allowed to Stephen's.

A situation such as this initially appears to confront the reader with a binary decision. By foregrounding diverse formal and thematic elements associated with Stephen and with Bloom, the discourse may seem to be tempting us to abandon multiplicity in favor of adopting the perspective of one character or the other and of following the development of the narrative discourse from that point of view. By singling out either individual and by adopting his ethos as a yardstick against which to measure the unfolding action, one establishes a clear basis for examining any provisional narrative discourse discerned through an examination of the relation between the work and the reader. Neither figure, however, can sustain such a role.

After the Proteus chapter Stephen's centrality quickly recedes, and the focus of the narrative becomes dispersed over a range of other concerns. Stephen remains an important feature of the action, but the degree to which his consciousness influences one's perception of events in the novel has become circumscribed. In subsequent appearances, he must struggle to make his ideas heard and to draw from others some acknowledgment of their worth. He spends much of the remainder of the day striving to earn the regard of his fellow Dubliners, and he must also pass the remainder of the novel competing for the attention of the reader. In chapter seven, Aeolus, Stephen tells his "Parable of the Plums," trying to hold the interest of Myles Crawford and Prof. MacHugh while fighting against the noise of newspaper presses and the bustle of O'Connell Street. At the National Library, in the Scylla and Charybdis episode, Buck Mulligan's competition for attention disrupts

Stephen's disquisition on Shakespeare. In much the same manner Mulligan's appearance at the Holles Street Maternity Hospital in Oxen of the Sun interrupts Stephen's rambling thoughts on the mysteries of birth. In Circe, Stephen's free spending gives him some measure of the attention that he so much desires, but his drunkenness and the disorder of Bella Cohen's brothel cause a great deal of what he says to pass uncomprehended. Finally in Eumaeus his own exhaustion renders him barely articulate.

Diminished but not banished, Stephen stands as an enigmatic figure for the reader who recalls his prominence in Joyce's earlier novel, and he requires some reconciliation to determine his function in this subsequent work.[7] Here Bakhtin's methods seem to me to be particularly useful, for he foregrounds the necessity of understanding the social context that shapes the comprehension of a figure like Stephen.

> For Dostoevsky the important thing is not how the hero appears to the world, but, most importantly, how the world appears to the hero and how the hero appears to himself.
>
> * * * *
>
> Thus, the *function* of the hero's self-consciousness becomes the subject of the author's vision and representation. While self-consciousness is usually only an element of the hero's reality, merely one aspect of his integrated image, here all reality becomes an element of the hero's self-consciousness.
>
> * * * *
>
> The functions that were performed by the author are now performed by the hero as he elucidates himself from all possible points of view; the author no longer elucidates the reality of the hero, but rather his self-consciousness as reality of the second order.[8]

At the same time, Bakhtin's emphasis on the centrality of a "hero" by implication affirms a much narrower range of readings than those offered by *Ulysses*.

While Stephen's intermittent appearances after the first three chapters inhibit a resumption of the privileged status that he enjoyed in *Portrait*, one can find ample justification for the inclination to follow such a course in Bloom's case. At first glance Bloom appears to dominate the work. When one thinks of the novel in general terms, Bloom often comes to mind as its focal character, with all of the events of the story summed up in a single word: Bloomsday. Because of this ubiquitousness, Bloom's nature assumes a much more assertive position in the narrative scheme than does Stephen's. Although less concerned with recognition than Stephen, Bloom still strives for a share of esteem. With oppressive regularity, however, his psyche is undercut or suppressed with even greater frequency than is Stephen's: At Glasnevin Cemetery the solicitor Menton snubs him. In the newspaper office he is thrust aside by Myles Crawford and aped by newsboys. At the National Library and at Barney Kiernan's pub Irish bullies slander his ethnic character. At the Holles Street Maternity Hospital drunken medical students patronize him. And in Nighttown whores make him confront his sexual inadequacies. Only in isolated instances—in the bath, over dinner at the Ormond Hotel, in the cabman's shelter, and later in his own kitchen—does he feel unthreatened confidence.

Further, an assumption of Bloom's prominence ignores how closely his role in the discourse parallels Stephen's and too easily elides the functions of others in the narrative and their impact upon readers. In fact, while Bloom figures directly or indirectly in much of the action around which the work unfolds, others often occupy significant portions of its depiction. Even after his introduction in Calypso, whole chapters unfold with Bloom playing a relatively minor part. In Molly's soliloquy in the Penelope episode, Bloom appears simply as part of the bedclothes. Aeolus, Scylla and Charybdis, and Wandering Rocks give us only fleeting glimpses of him. Even where his presence is felt—in Sirens, Cyclops, Nausikaa, Oxen of the Sun, Eumaeus, and Ithaca—the narrative persona or other characters do much to overshadow him. Bloom remains prominent in the minds of many readers because he serves as an obvious figure for empathy and an easy reference point from which to measure the action, but he is no more successful at achieving ascendancy in the narrative than he is at gaining it in his own household.

This diminution cannot simply be explained by casting Bloom in the role of antihero, for that would imply a centering of attention every bit as pronounced as one would expect for a hero. What does occur instead is a reiteration of the pattern developed in the opening segment of *Ulysses*. Despite Bloom's presence throughout the work, over the course of the novel his nature has an increasingly nominal impact on the discourse. The narrative continually displaces Bloom's consciousness with a variety of other voices that all present alternative perspectives through temporary dominance of the discourse. After the Proteus chapter and again after the Hades chapter the horizons of the novel, in Wolfgang Iser's sense of the term, shift.

As one strays from a perspective congruent with Bloom's or with Stephen's, cruxes suddenly begin to appear. One can, however, as legitimately consider this a strength as a weakness in any alternative text. With cruxes comes a variety of possibilities easily overlooked when one reads everything from the either/or perspective of Stephen or of Bloom. In fact, the voices of the work's various narrators sound a rich counterpoint equal in weight to Bloom's, and the consciousnesses of Stephen and of Molly make important contributions to the possibilities of the novel.

This displacement of emphasis occurs in an accretive fashion, and one's ability to perceive it hinges on a clear sense of the privileges and responsibilities inherent in the creation of an intellectually valid text. Unfortunately, the subjectivity that this entails remains a hobgoblin for many critics. Stanley Fish, in his review essay of *The Act of Reading*, for example, articulates the concern among some who pursue methods of reader response (including himself) for staking out an intellectual middle ground.[9] Nonetheless, while inspiration and anarchy can appear perilously similar in a work like *Ulysses*, one cannot rely upon a false sense of detachment to resolve the dilemma. Both Iser and Fish, each in his own fashion, while striving for a balanced view, fail to relinquish a sense of the primacy of certain privileged readings. I intend to propose an approach that acknowledges *Ulysses* as a work that limits the range of valid idiosyncratic experiences but that does not oppose all readings that deviate from a single privileged interpretation. As with *Portrait*, no definitive meaning exists for *Ulysses*, and any response providing aesthetic pleasure within the novel's paradigm stands as convincing. A clear illustration of this method appears in tracing the evolution of our response to the diversity of voice within the discourse.

Beginning with the Aeolus episode, the reader experiences an expansion of attention beyond the world as seen by either Stephen Dedalus or Leopold Bloom. As the action of *Ulysses* unfolds, one comes increasingly to sense what Stephen struggles against and what Bloom suppresses: their marginal social position in Dublin and the relatively minor part that they play in the affairs in which they are involved. To give formal balance to this realignment of contextual emphasis, the narrative discourse shifts to other modes (which will be explored in the next chapter) to guide the constitution of descriptions.

In the first six chapters a single voice, influenced by the consciousness of either Stephen or of Bloom, has represented the central concerns of the work. The relationship changes in Aeolus with the narrator assuming the role of an evolving central character susceptible to a variety of influences. A number of separate, disembodied forces begin to counterpoint the discourse even as the narrative voice itself undergoes a continuing metamorphosis.

In Aeolus the headings subdividing the episode counterpoint the voice of the discourse that presents a direct depiction of the action. In addition, representations of rhetorical forms within the body of the episode, like instances of chiasmus, intrude upon the naturalistic presentation of the features of any individual consciousness characterizing the narrative. "Grossbooted draymen rolled barrels dullthudding out of Prince's stores and bumped them up on the brewery float. On the brewery float bumped dullthudding barrels rolled by grossbooted draymen out of Prince's stores" (*U*, 8.21–24).

In Wandering Rocks, the narrative voice again asserts itself. Still attuned to sardonic wordplay (sometimes at the expense of the individual described), it evokes a tenor similar to Telemachus and to Calypso. At the same time it appears to have lost its powers of concentration, interrupting itself throughout the episode with interpolations disrupting the spatial consistency of the discourse.

Sirens, with its opening overture (*U*, 11.1–63), replicates the independent gesture of Aeolus. The musical undertone running through the work integrates the tempo and the diction of song into the unfolding discourse, and the interruptions that surfaced in Wandering Rocks become more insistent.[10] "Cowley, he stuns himself with it: kind of drunkenness. Better give way only half the way of a man with a maid. Instance enthusiasts. All ears. Not lose a demisemiquaver. Eyes shut. Head nodding in time. Dotty. You daren't budge. Thinking strictly prohibited. Always talking shop. Fiddlefaddle about notes" (*U*, 11.1191–95).

In Cyclops a new narrator—the dun—temporarily takes control of the discourse. His jaundiced perspective of events and characters offers yet another reminder of the novel's protean ambiance. Further, the repeated interpolations of parodic episodes introduce a series of dialogues running counter to any of the forms previously introduced. (As David Hayman has noted, those gestures have meta-textual implications that contribute significantly to our sense of displacement.[11])

Nausikaa marks the return of the original narrative voice. Its timbre has changed, however, for it is now highly attuned to the diverse consciousnesses and rhetorical strategies that it encounters. The episode contrasts an initial discourse derived from Gerty MacDowell's corrupted romance-novel perspective with a second narrative based on the more familiar attitude of Bloom.

Oxen of the Sun follows with the densest narrational representation of the novel. There the discourse surveys the principal forms of English literature through the narrative voice's mimicry of conventional literary styles from Anglo-Saxon to the contemporary period. (In chapter nine I will examine these formal variations and their impact on the reader's expectations in greater detail. At this point, I allude to them to draw attention to their influence on the shifting diction of the narrative voice.)

In Circe, the prominence of the narrative voice subsides as Stephen and Bloom conjointly attain dominant positions in shaping the descriptive elements of the discourse, but their impact differs markedly from their earlier influence on the discourse. Each man figures prominently in the action, and each man, through his fantasies, directs but does not prescribe the reader's interpretations. Their hallucinations contradict without denying a naturalized perception of the action. At the same time, their views clearly reflect distortions unperceived by others. Consequently, both of these points of view must be maintained and reconciled in any reading.

The tone is set in the opening paragraph when those described initially as "stunted men and women" resolve themselves in a few sentences into "children," and throughout the episode descriptions derived from the hallucinations of either Stephen or Bloom clash against the reader's sense of the actual scenes surrounding them.

BLOOM

Who? (he ducks and wards off a blow clumsily) At your service.
(He looks up. Beside her mirage of datepalms a handsome woman in Turkish costume stands before him. Opulent curves fill out her scarlet trousers and jacket, slashed with gold. A wide yellow cummerbund girdles her. A white yashmak, violet in the night, covers her face, leaving free only her large dark eyes and raven hair.)

BLOOM

MOLLY! (*U*, 15.295–304)

* * * *

STEPHEN

Ho!
(Stephen's mother, emaciated, rises stark through the floor, in leper grey with a wreath of faded orangeblossoms and a torn bridal veil, her face worn and noseless, green with gravemould. Her hair is scant and lank. She fixes her bluecircled hollow eyesockets on Ste-

phen and opens her toothless mouth uttering a silent word. A choir
of virgins and confessors sing voicelessly.) (*U,* 15.4155–62)

Such extravagant descriptions dominate the discourse throughout
Circe, free of the temporizing effect exerted elsewhere by the narrative
voice. They are derived from the perceptions of Bloom and of Stephen,
distorted by drink, fatigue, and sexual desire. As a consequence they
reflect only one aspect of the repertoire in which the action unfolds. No
one takes these descriptions as complete or sufficient renderings of the
chapter's ambiance. Rather the structure solicits from the reader the
same sort of elaboration suggested by *Exiles,* foregrounding a process of
recuperation that has been taking place less explicitly since Aeolus.

As in drama, the typology of the discourse of Circe confronts one
with a literal script, inviting the individualizing and the elaboration of
the act of interpretation. In seeking to bring breadth and consistency
into the formation of a particular text, one more or less automatically
settles upon a provisional perspective, determining the limits of overt
distortions in relation to what one assumes to be the physical consistency of elements making up the more prosaic settings of the episode.
The gap of six hundred and five lines intervening between Zoe's "Go
on. Make a stump speech out of it" (*U,* 15.1353) and the continuation
of her remarks "Talk away till you're black in the face" (*U,* 15.1958)
stands as only one example of how elements within the discourse suggest this parallel world, tangential to the consciousnesses of either
Bloom or of Stephen, that must be incorporated into any text. What
makes the effort significant in my eyes is that the breadth of this naturalistic backdrop is not always so clear. Often it must be projected by the
reader, for the ethos of disorder and of misrule dominating the atmosphere of the whorehouse undermines the independent integrity of detail that would normally obtain.

The problem confronting readers, of course, is how to reconcile such
diverse features within a consistent (though provisional) text. While the
identification of polyphony in *Portrait* has suggested general strategies
for assigning significance to the fluctuation in perspective between Stephen and Bloom, the format of *Ulysses* more specifically encourages multiplicity in interpretations of the shifts in the action. The nature of the
descriptive segments in Circe exemplifies a tendency in evidence
throughout the work, and in every instance it serves to advance the
breakdown within the reader of habits of hegemonic interpretation. Different points of view do not simply compete with one another; they emphasize the range of equally valid and equally provisional perceptions.

Thus the parallax quality of the narrative obtains as a motif throughout the book.

As instances of parallax recur, it comes to suggest that both the object perceived and also the perceiver have a range of qualities not apparent in a single viewing. All of our observations are synecdochical since we extrapolate from the incomplete discourse confronting us on the printed pages to create a representation of the whole. In *Ulysses* we must face the continual reminder of the imperfection of such a mode of perception.

> Parallax. I never exactly understood. There's a priest. Could ask him. Par it's Greek: parallel, parallax. (*U*, 8.110–12)

> * * * *

> Parallax stalks behind and goads them, the lancinating lightnings of whose brow are scorpions. (*U*, 14.1089–90)

> * * * *

> Never put on you tomorrow what can wear today. Parallax! (*U*, 15.2334–35)

At the same time, as the novel repeatedly demonstrates, the parallax phenomena can as easily liberate as constrain. By complementing the work's formal organization and by reinforcing the reader's awareness of diversifying impressions, parallactic views become an important technique for emphasizing the significance of polyphonic vocalization and of both/and thinking. This sense extends not only to figures in the action but also to the consciousness(es) behind the narrative voices. Although parallax itself has been Bloom's fixation throughout the day, his inquisitive gesture reinforces the concern for the modalities of the visible and the audible introduced by Stephen in the Proteus chapter. Recognition of its function in *Ulysses* strips away any vestiges of realistic expectations that a reader might entertain in texts derived from the work.

The very acknowledgment that the form of *Ulysses* diverges from the realistic mode would seem nothing more than a painful demonstration of a keen grasp of the obvious, if the impulse within us all to seek a form of closure through a realistic interpretation were not so strong. (The pull seems to me to be analogous to the attraction we feel for linear thinking.) Certainly, throughout the work one senses that the limits imposed by a realistic reading from a fixed point of view simply do not obtain, but in Circe they all break down completely. There a view from a single perspective or from a discrete consciousness simply will not work.

Not only do individuals in Circe echo the phrases and develop the ideas that originated in other consciousnesses throughout the novel, but, by the time the hallucinations begin in the whorehouse, characters in the episode draw freely on the experiences of other figures in the novel and even in other works in Joyce's canon: Zoe uses the same expression—"Hoopsa" (*U*, 15.2025)—that opens the narrative of the Oxen of the Sun chapter. Buck Mulligan's inventions—Philip Drunk and Philip Sober—invade Bloom's hallucinations and tell the same story about the Virgin Mary (*U*, 15.2583–85) that ran through Stephen's mind in the Proteus episode (*U*, 3.161–62). Bloom's image of Lipoti Virag expressing concern for a moth circling perilously close to a flame—"O, I much fear that he shall be most badly burned" (*U*, 15.2463)—echoes Stephen's reply, in *Portrait*, to Father Ghezzi's criticism of Giordano Bruno. "He said Bruno was a terrible heretic. I said he was terribly burned" (*P*, 249). One might introduce additional examples, but the point, I believe, is quite clear. The reader's recognition of the paradigm of *Ulysses* keeps shifting, at least in terms of social environment, and the relatively easy association of central character and narrative consciousness established by *Portrait* no longer holds sway. The linear integrity of the milieu does not break down completely (as it does subsequently in the paradigm of *Finnegans Wake*), but *Ulysses* pushes it towards its limits as the stylistic ambiance begins to challenge the social environment for paradigmatic control.

Eumaeus, with an opening reminiscent of Telemachus and Calypso, returns to the narrative voice familiar features now made somewhat ambiguous by repeated instances of diffusion. Its tautology and inflated language lampoon the events in the cabman's shelter with a sardonically detached perspective analogous to Bloom's attitude. At the same time, despite its understatement, it presents perhaps the harshest views yet expressed of Bloom.

> The elder man, though not by any manner of means an old maid or a prude, said it was nothing short of a crying scandal that ought to be put a stop to *instanter* to say that women of that stamp (quite apart from any oldmaidish squeamishness on the subject), a necessary evil, were not licensed and medically inspected by the proper authorities, a thing, he could truthfully state, he, as a *paterfamilias*, was a stalwart advocate of from the very first start. (*U*, 16.739–45)

The reader, conditioned by previous episodes to reconstitute or at least to reinterpret the discourse, must decide whether to continue to revise his or her text to suit this modified impression of Bloom or to maintain a text that resists the depiction in Eumaeus.

The structure of Ithaca, with its question-and-answer format, continues to encourage the reader to consider revaluing impressions of the discourse. In a voice as near a monotone as possible, the narrative omits many of the subjective markers that usually guide one's response.

> What satisfied him?

> To have sustained no positive loss. To have brought a positive gain to others. Light to the gentiles. (*U*, 17.351–53)

The narrative of Ithaca strips its voice of any previously articulated style of expression through an overtly mechanical articulation. This puts pressure upon the reader to enhance the discourse by supplying descriptive transitions appropriate to the text that he or she is creating.

Penelope, the final episode of *Ulysses*, appears to concentrate on retrogression instead of on the expansion of the range of the narrative voice. The chapter's structure overtly imitates stylistic patterns of the opening sections by representing the stream of consciousness technique in a form more concentrated than in any episode since Proteus. In representing Molly Bloom, it (re)introduces a character who has previously appeared only briefly and who has until now been relegated to the role of objective correlative for Bloom's torment. Yet, even with this apparent reversion to what has become by this point in the work a commonplace method and even with the exposition of familiar material, Penelope continues to place new demands upon the reader seeking to form a text. Molly's monologue presents a new consciousness directly confronting many of the facts, the pseudofacts, and the misrepresentations that we already have in our possession with a series of facts, pseudofacts, and misrepresentations of its own. It impels the reader to continue to take into account the impact of polyphony and parallax in order to create meaning.

Powered by the sheer force of Molly's personality, the soliloquy overwhelms us, and we find opinions which we had earlier considered commonplaces now overturned. Molly sees flaws in many of the characters in the novel that other voices have not commented on. She presents a different view of family life with Bloom and their daughter Milly. But most importantly, she reveals much about her own complex and contradictory personality that other Dubliners miss.

In essence, Molly recapitulates events of the story, so that even while we read the final chapter we are continually revising the impressions that we have brought to it. The Penelope chapter demands not only that we make sense of Molly's disquisition, but the episode also requires us to fit it into the context of the entire work that we have evolved. As she thinks of Bloom's request for breakfast in bed, a gamut of emotions runs through her speech characteristic of the tone of the entire episode.

> I know what Ill do Ill go about rather gay not too much singing a bit now and then mi fa pieta Masetto then Ill start dressing myself to go out presto non son piu forte Ill put on my best shift and drawers let him have a good eyeful out of that to make his micky stand for him Ill let him know if thats what he wanted that his wife is fucked yes and damn well fucked too up to my neck nearly not by him 5 or 6 times handrunning theres the mark of his spunk on the clean sheet I wouldnt bother to even iron it out that ought to satisfy him if you dont believe me feel my belly unless I made him stand there and put him into me Ive a mind to tell him every scrap and make him do it out in front of me serve him right its all his own fault if I am an adulteress as the thing in the gallery said O much about it if thats all the harm ever we did in this vale of tears God knows its not much doesnt everybody only they hide it I suppose thats what a woman is supposed to be there for or He wouldnt have made us the way He did . . . (*U*, 18.1506–20)

The coarseness of Molly's recollections seems at first glance to substantiate the salacious descriptions applied to her by Simon Dedalus and by the sponge Lenehan, and her frank use of the word fuck seems to contradict the romantic and sentimental view of adultery that she has earlier articulated. On close examination, however, the contradictions of the passage invite us to form an impression of consistency within the intricacies of Molly's consciousness and in conformity to the formal structure of the novel. By the end of the episode we have seen the full range of Molly's personality jarring with our sense of her formed over the first seventeen chapters, and we necessarily feel confused by the antinomies it reveals. As we resolve them into a text, we arrive at a counter-image of Molly's character that no single segment of the work has overtly described and that remains open to continual re-vision.

Critics have come to see Bloom, Molly, and Stephen as forming a Trinity around which the action of *Ulysses* revolves, and to some degree that image gives a fine account of their roles in the work. The apparent catholicity of the metaphor, however, can lead one to oversimplification. Each offers a solipsistic response to the ambiance of turn-of-the-century Dublin, and through the alternate perspectives of a young, Irish Catholic (lapsed) proto-artist, a middle-aged Jewish advertising canvasser, and his adulterous, Spanish-Irish (and possibly Jewish) wife, the reader finds ample material to weave into a wide-ranging text. But, as the Protean narrative voice reminds us, *Ulysses* contains much more. Joyce told Arthur Power that

[i]n *Ulysses* I tried to express the multiple variations which make up the social life of a city—its degradations and its exaltations. In other words what we want to avoid is the classical, with its rigid structure and its emotional limitations. The mediaeval, in my opinion, had greater emotional fecundity than classicism, which is the art of the gentleman, and is now as out-of-date as gentlemen are, classicism in which the scents are only sweet, he added, but I have preferred other smells.[12]

While pungent, the odors surrounding Bloom, Molly, and Stephen do not encapsulate Dublin, and that was what Joyce aimed to do. In striving toward the universal, Joyce felt the attraction of a narrative strategy that would step over the bounds of individual consciousnesses while retaining the personal view. To achieve this goal, he eschewed a narrative discourse acting solely under the influence of his central characters and introduced into half of the work a narrative persona deriving the shape of its features from the forces of a range of more abstract influences. No reader can ignore the range of odors and hope to form a coherent text. At the same time each reading gives us the freedom to (re)create from our impressions the aesthetic experience which best satisfies us.

IX | *Ulysses*: Narrative Metamorphoses

In the preceding chapter, I emphasized the emergence in *Ulysses* of a truly polyphonic discourse evolving out of characterizations established in *Portrait* and in *Exiles*. In this chapter I intend to extend my analysis to trace its paradigmatic influence. As I have noted earlier in this study, to frame the imaginative boundaries of works by Joyce written prior to *Ulysses* one must turn to intellectual forces outside the canon to discern the full range of the sensibilities brought to bear on his writing. In *Ulysses* creative debts do not lie submerged within the narrative but emerge from allusive echoes articulated by various discourses. One no longer cites specific literary figures as analogous to stages in Joyce's artistic evolution, for with the overt evocation of multiple forms the paradigm and the novel become coincidental. In short, with the composition of *Ulysses* Joyce moves his aesthetic and artistic allegiances from Modernism to Postmodernism.

Although I have, up to this point in my study, relied only fleetingly on terms that attempt to delineate various literary movements, I feel that they become particularly relevant for *Ulysses*, a novel often used to measure the high point of Modernism. Since individual conceptions of Modernism and Postmodernism have their own idiosyncratic elements, I would like to digress briefly to explain some of the suppositions influencing my approach. As I see it, at the center of Modernism stands the rejection of the moral codes imposed by the pressure of contemporary social institutions in favor of those derived from the artist's personal experience. A work that gives primacy to the values of an individual, like *A Portrait of the Artist as a Young Man*, embodies this impulse. Postmodernism, on the other hand, reacts to this condition. It undermines such views by questioning any authority, even that situated within the self. This gesture assaults the perspective of discourse, essentially linear and stratified, that Modernism condones, for it asserts that no single viewpoint occupies a privileged position within a narrative. While the thematic implications of such an approach appear obvious—evoking a Bakhtin-like attentiveness to polyvocality—such considerations also exert a strong influence on the work's stylistic constitution.

This gesture of foregrounding manifests itself slowly, through Joyce's familiar practice of incremental development. From the Telemachus episode through Hades, although the identificative features of the narrative change, the discursive patterns established in earlier works obtain. Thus, the reader finds within the frame of the descriptive development an indissoluble bond between the evolution of individual characterizations and the voice directing the narrative. As a consequence, those familiar with the Joyce canon will return, more or less unconsciously, to the habits acquired from readings of *Portrait*, and they will refer to the same paradigm governing the stylistics of this earlier prose to guide their analyses of the descriptive development of the first six chapters of *Ulysses*.

Almost as soon as the six opening chapters have established the impact of the consciousnesses of Stephen and of Bloom on the formation of the narrative voice, however, the influence of their individual natures on the contextual constitution of the novel begins to diminish. As noted in the previous chapter, changes in narrative strategies realign the emphasis given to various elements, and subsequent episodes draw attention to the fact that neither figure exercises hegemonic control over the shaping of the narrative. As in *Exiles*, alternative natures and different types of influences intrude in a number of chapters, and the reader must move back and forth between a range of new perspectives to give meaning to the variety of forms that evolves.

The process quickly becomes even more complex. Aspects of the nature of a particular character continue to blend with the persona of the narrator, but the pattern appears sporadically. In several chapters specific figures reassert influence over the narrative: At various times Bloom and Stephen return to the forefront of the discourse; the unnamed dun's descriptions direct our perceptions of the action of the Cyclops episode; and Molly's personality overwhelms us through her soliloquy in the final chapter. As a result, after Hades the nature of a particular individual never again exerts dominance over the reader's perception of the narrative with the thoroughness, conviction, and extension found in the initial six episodes of the novel.

This shift in the features of the narrative has a pronounced impact on our perception of the work, but it forms only a portion of the distinctive formal elements that condition our response to *Ulysses*. As noted in the previous chapter, from Aeolus onward the narrative voice adapts its tone and diction from chapter to chapter to accommodate numerous stylistic variations that assert a discrete but insistent influence on various aspects of the discourse. This added flexibility allows Joyce to expand the scope of the entire narrative. Elements of popular literature, first introduced in the composition of *Exiles*, take on greater significance, creating resonances and oppositions within the narrative, and additional, nonliterary forms further contribute a new allusiveness to the experiences of reading *Ulysses*.

As with each of Joyce's preceding works, these changes relate directly to reconstitution of the paradigm. I have touched upon it briefly in the preceding chapter in terms of its influence on characterization. Now I would like to give more sustained attention to the formal implications of its realignment. Specifically I intend to consider the protocols suggested by the redirection of the narrative strategy one-third of the way through the novel, for the assumptions validating its subsequent stylistic discursiveness stand as representative of the broader paradigmatic suppositions that direct a reader's response to the entire work.

One can begin to formulate a sense of the new creative boundaries from elements in Aeolus, a chapter unfolding as something both more and less than what it initially seems to be. Michael Groden, in his meticulous study of the compositional process of *Ulysses*, quite rightly sees the episode as announcing a reformation of narrative structure: "In many ways, the finished 'Aeolus' seems like a new beginning for *Ulysses*: it is the first episode after the opening six scenes linked by a common time scheme; it represents the first extended appearance of both Bloom and Stephen in a single episode; and Dublin and the other Dubliners become increasingly prominent." James Maddox, also commenting upon this reconstitution, goes beyond Groden's assertions to suggest the implications of such a reordering on the remainder of the work. "Up to this point the stream of consciousness of Stephen and Bloom has fragmented our sense of the reality of Dublin; henceforth, the novel will proceed toward a more pervasive kind of fragmentation, as each chapter seems to break apart from the whole and to take on a life of its own."[1] I agree with Groden, Maddox, and other commentators that the structure of Aeolus draws attention to a significant expansion in the texture of the narrative and that its rhetorical structure signals a radical reconfiguration of the path traced by influence in the discourse.[2] At the same time, I feel that neither an inclination toward concentration nor a gesture toward diffusion provides a pattern large enough to encompass all of the demands of subsequent narrative development. To my mind, a more effective interpretive strategy affirms that the features of this episode announce the beginning of the Postmodern novel.

A critical commonplace, alluded to by Maddox, holds that chapters like Aeolus which do not seem to fit into the plan of the whole novel serve as microcosms describing its complexity. I believe that such a view avoids the difficult question of reconciliation and condemns any text created under this assumption to a series of enclosed redundancies. A more flexible interpretation, and one that more coherently outlines the paradigms of the discourse, sees Aeolus as greatly expanding the range of indeterminacies while remaining within the boundaries of the social repertoire of the work.

Despite formal shifts, it maintains the thematic limits delineated by the fictional representation of Dublin on 16 June 1904. At the same time it overturns assumptions that a naturalistic reading will produce a text capable of accommodating the diversity of structures constituting the novel. Aeolus does not simply adumbrate the stylistic complexities of later chapters like Oxen of the Sun. It radically changes our expectations for the novel so that we cannot read episodes like Lestrygonians—no matter what associations it may suggest with Calypso, Lotus Eaters, or Hades—with the same narrowness that one could apply to earlier chapters.

This descriptive dilation within the episode confronts the reader with the first of the work's series of unreconciled stylistic variations, calling into question the narrative norms presumably established by the structure adhered to in the initial six chapters. Up to this point in the novel only the consciousness of an identifiable individual—Stephen or Bloom—has intruded upon the narrative voice to reform it under the influence of a free indirect discourse delineated by its own image. Now, with an emphasis on conventions of formal exposition, the narrative introduces a completely new tone. Not only does it operate outside the influence of any identifiable consciousness, it proceeds to reverse the pattern already established by which characters, to one degree or another, shape the diction of the narrative voice.

Demands of the Postmodern paradigm set protocols for direct as well as for indirect discourse. In Aeolus they reform the way various characters speak, bringing their diction into conformity with the dominant tone of the narrative: J. J. O'Molloy recreates the courtroom style of Seymour Bushe. Professor MacHugh, with practiced pedantry, mimics the oratorical tour de force of John F. Taylor's speech to the college historical society. Both Lenehan and Stephen, although they fail, attempt to assume the role of raconteur. And throughout the chapter, rhetorical figures reflect and refract the consciousnesses of various characters.[3] Aeolus takes the first step in placing formal technique over characterization in the determination of the structure of the discourse, but the pattern will reappear throughout the work—most notably in Nausikaa,

Oxen of the Sun, and Ithaca, though prominent in most of the subsequent chapters.

In addition to the reconstitution of expectations within the discourse proper, the narrative of *Ulysses* now begins to formulate a metadiscourse. Interpolated phrases, set in boldface type and separated from material in the body of the chapter, subdivide the episode and resist integration. While displaying affinities to the material they bracket, the headings that punctuate the chapter appear unheralded and evolve in defiance of any linear pattern of association.

As Michael Groden suggests in the passage quoted above, from the first pages of *Ulysses* the ambiance forming the paradigm of the novel has not been bounded by the mind or minds of a few characters. It is centered, as the first of Aeolus's interpolated phrases tells us,

IN THE HEART OF THE HIBERNIAN

METROPOLIS

(*U*, 7.1–2)

These opening lines begin the process of broadening our expectations by forcefully drawing attention to habits of reading that, without our awareness, have already imposed improper limitations on any potential text we could create: They confront us with the limitations and the ambiguities inherent when the perspective of a single character constitutes the basis of the reader's expectations regarding the structure of any text growing out of the narrative. Sixty-three such interpolations, suggesting while not strictly imitating news headlines, underscore the chapter's topos—the setting in a newspaper office—but they also insinuate a variability of perception that will increasingly dominate subsequent episodes. (The headings in Aeolus appear fairly late in the process of composition, at about the same time that Joyce expanded the lists of Cyclops and the questions of Ithaca. These changes reflect the culmination of his strategy for involving readers in the act of creating the text. A transcription of the headings appears in appendix C.)

From their first appearance, the interpolations present an immediate problem for forming a text, for they give no inherent indication of their purpose beyond their putative immediate function: serving as an idiosyncratic gloss of the material in the body of the episode. Sometimes ironic, sometimes straightforward, sometimes prophetic, sometimes foolish, they introduce a polyphonic commentary and a metafictional counterpoint to the descriptions and dialogue. Further, these headings remain peripheral to the action of the chapter. Each makes some degree of sense in relation to the immediate context in which it appears. When taken together, however, they do not reflect any obvious affinities for one another or for the discourse that they seem to counterpoint. Finally, no obvious formal technique links them to the rest of the episode. To derive a text that accommodates one's cumulative sense of the novel and that reconciles the diverse elements within Aeolus, the reader must first fit the newly emerging features into a broad conception of the narrative.

The bifurcation of the chapter and the apparent stylistic disassociations with previous episodes, however, do not signal the complete abandonment of the previous formal structure. Distinct descriptive segments maintain links to the original format by continuing the integration of the stream of consciousness commentary of Bloom and of Stephen into the narration to provide conjunctions with the dialogue.

> He stayed in his walk to watch a typesetter neatly distributing type. Reads it backwards first. Quickly he does it. Must require some practice that, mangiD kcirtaP. Poor papa with his hagadah book, reading backwards with his finger to me. (*U*, 7.203–7)
>
> *   *   *   *
>
> Mouth, south. Is the mouth south someway? Or the south a mouth? Must be some. South, pout, out, shout, drouth. Rhymes: two men dressed the same, looking the same, two by two. (*U*, 7.714–16)

At the same time, the narrative voice no longer submits exclusively to the conventional (mis)direction of free indirect discourse. Instead its familiar representative pattern alternates at regular intervals with a somewhat pedantic tone full of oratorical flourishes that resemble no consciousness that has appeared up to this point. Direct discourse is similarly tinged by this inclination. For example, in the first spoken phrase of the chapters—"Rathgar and Terenure!" (*U*, 7.6)—ecphonesis or exclamation introduces the first instance of the rhetorical overtone that will condition our perception of much of the chapter's dialogue.

Because this diegetic pattern obtrudes upon the anticipated rhythm of the discourse more overtly than any of the previous digressive dialogic gestures, the reader becomes more conscious of the task of integrating this material—the headings and the layers of rhetorical technique—into the work. On one level such vagaries in the discourse can be explained by recalling the playfulness that David Hayman has associated with a meta-narrator—the arranger. I would like, however, to suggest a slightly different approach to discerning a unifying force within the apparent formal antinomies of the episode, for I believe that Aeolus encourages one to form habits of reading and rereading that will exert an important influence on our perception of the remainder of the work.

I do not propose here simply to redefine Hayman's concept, for the phenomena that I am describing do not usurp the function of the narrative voice or even displace it temporarily. Instead, these stylistic allusions interact with the narrative persona, influencing it in much the same manner as do the consciousnesses of Stephen and of Bloom. Unlike Modernist writing, the Postmodernist discourse does not embrace the either/or configuration of competing voices but maintains the both/ and quality of integrated, polyphonic expression. The significant difference that consequently obtains lies in the disembodiment of the formal influences acting upon the narrative voice and in the concomitant impulsion for the reader to define the natures of those influences.

Hovering over the body of the chapter, the boldface headings oppose incorporation into a text conditioned primarily by the words beneath them. The sheer variety of the headings resists any impulse to see them as ancillary to the body of the discourse. This tension creates a direct and profound confrontation. The very process of reading asserts an implicit contract between artist, audience, and artifact, acknowledging an intellectual engagement with the work and affirming belief in the possibility of forming some text encompassing the vagaries of the evolving paradigm. When the conventional patterns of reading do not satisfy those expectations, one initiates another approach. (The phrase that appears on every matchbook—CLOSE COVER BEFORE STRIKING—makes no sense from a linear perspective, but it serves as a perfectly coherent admonition nonetheless because the reader translates the directions to a multilayered context.)

The metafictional nature of the headings of Aeolus leads the reader towards the creation of a metatext, based primarily though not exclusively on style and existing in tandem with a text for the body of the episode. The shift in forces dominating the discourse removes the need to reconcile the metatext with previous narratives, and it opens the possibility of discerning a meta-discourse more amenable to rapprochement with the headings and the discourse. They coexist without commingling, and yet their juxtaposition invites colocation in the reader's imagination. This condition of formal elements existing in associative delineation sets up new conditions for perceiving the work.

The key feature of Aeolus lies in its presentation of a both/and condition of perception. The formal disruption of its headings and the tonal digression of its discourse assert the episode's stylistic separation from its predecessors. Simultaneously, the narrative advances the action with scrupulous attention to the contextual parameters laid down in the six preceding chapters. The central concern for the formulation of any text remains operative—the incorporation of the diverse elements of this episode—but the presumption of the efficacy of linear, cause-and-effect logic as the best approach for resolving antinomies no longer obtains. One must read Aeolus with the expectations produced by previous chapters but without an exclusive commitment to the perspectives that they have encouraged.

Critics have generally taken the opposite view, however, emphasizing in the body of the chapter a form reminiscent of the earlier episodes and confronting the evolving narrating presence as a feature that must be brought into conformity with the rest of Aeolus.[4] The key feature of most readings of the chapter has been a replication of the common method used for rendering an interpretation of *Portrait*: the identification of the normative elements and the reconciliation of other aspects of the episode to the standard that these elements establish. In Aeolus as elsewhere in *Ulysses*, any such approach rests upon a strategy chosen for bringing the stylistic figures incorporated into the narration and any variations in the narrative persona into conformity with a particular perspective that has already been given primacy. As I have already argued, this method mistakenly emphasizes a formal homogeneity that the paradigm simply does not support. Rather than viewing the headlines and the rhetorical techniques as stylistic or contextual deviations that one must subsume into the discourse, a more satisfactory and less inhibited response extrapolates the impulse of polyvocality. With Aeolus and the subsequent chapters, the narrative offers not simply a variety of perspectives but a range of different discourses disunited on the printed page but conjoined in the imagination of the reader in conformity with the governing principles of the text that he or she has created. The paradigm demands that these meta-discourses receive consideration, but it resists inclinations to amalgamate them.

This is not as freewheeling as it may seem, however, for familiar formal elements exert a persistent structural consistency upon the unfolding discourses to provide familiar points of departure for any response. The drawback of previous interpretations has been a tendency to ignore formal consistencies while simultaneously leveling contextual disjunctions. Karen Lawrence, for example, sees the influence exerted over the third-person narrative by free indirect discourse markedly receding in Aeolus, because the shaping presences of Bloom and Stephen no longer condition the development of the narrative.[5] Lawrence's delineation of free indirect discourse, however, describes the technique in terms that do not take full advantage of the alternatives of the paradigm because they presume the existence of only a single mode of discourse.

Mimetic and diegetic forces function together in Aeolus, much as they do in earlier chapters, but now their distinctive features receive greater emphasis as the tone evolves under the influence of an abstract presence. This alignment does not represent a diminution in the application of free indirect discourse, for the principle of the temporary reconstitution of the narrative by an independent influence still obtains. In fact, by maintaining a sensitivity to the central features of free indirect discourse—the intermingling of diverse consciousnesses—one acquires a heightened awareness of the levels of discourse at work in the novel.

By the time one reaches Aeolus, free indirect discourse has already conditioned the reader to perceive the narrator as a persona distinct from other characters in the work yet periodically integrated with them as part of the narrative. Within this chapter, the narrative overcomes the significant limitation imposed on this type of stylistic variation: free indirect discourse's customary dependence upon a limited number of characters appearing in the work to shape variations in the discourse. Through a gesture incorporating the features of rhetorical disquisition into the narration, *Ulysses* no longer needs to draw upon the consciousness of a specific individual in the novel to convey the mutability of the narrative. At the same time, because the preceding six chapters have shown the durability of the narrative persona, even this radical shift does not displace its presence in our texts.

Lestrygonians and Scylla and Charybdis seem to reassert the form of the first six chapters as they alternate free indirect discourse, emanating from Bloom in Lestrygonians and from Stephen in Scylla and Charybdis, with indirect discourse. Neither episode, however, can return the reader to a prelapsarian/pre-Aeolian state. Our sojourn in the newspaper office, even more than the time spent on Sandymount strand in the third chapter, has made us acutely aware of the Protean nature of the narrative.

Lestrygonians opens with a paragraph that superficially appears to follow the pattern of depiction laid down in previous chapters: a narrative shaped and conditioned through free indirect discourse by the nature of a character. "Pineapple rock, lemon platt, butter scotch. A sugarsticky girl shovelling scoopfuls of creams for a christian brother. Some school treat. Bad for their tummies. Lozenge and comfit manufacturer to His Majesty the King. God. Save. Our. Sitting on his throne sucking red jujubes white" (*U*, 8.1–4). In the two opening sentences the narrative voice draws our attention to the first instances of images of food that will fill the chapter. The next sentence, a transition between indirect discourse and stream of consciousness, leads to the Bloomian fourth sentence expressing fussy concern for the welfare of children, and the paragraph concludes with the store's logo turning Bloom's mind to a satirical picture of Edward VII.

As the chapter unfolds, however, a pattern governing the shape of the discourse emerges showing that the format to which we have become accustomed has been reversed. Rather than the consciousness of Bloom entering and influencing the discourse, an independent thematic impulse (a vestigial manifestation of the metadiscourse) has peppered the diction of the narrative voice with culinary metaphors. The same impulse modifies the familiar characteristics of Bloom's speech. Images of food now dominate his thoughts and conversation, reasonably enough since it is lunchtime. But they do more than fill his thoughts; they take control of his language as phrase after phrase develops metaphors from food images: "proof of the pudding" (*U*, 8.42–43), "Pillar of salt" (*U*, 8.135), "Drop him like a hot potato" (*U*, 8.444–45), "Molly looks out of plum" (*U*, 8.618–19), "*Crème de la crème*" (*U*, 8.888). While the affinity for clichés is all Bloom, the preponderance of food imagery suggests outside sources. The opening lines announce Lestrygonians's concern for food, and the topic spills over its usual bounds (as rhetoric did in Aeolus) to take control of the characters. Even Nosey Flynn, the barfly in Davy Byrnes's moral pub, cannot resist: "He doesn't buy cream on the ads he picks up. You can make bacon on that" (*U*, 8.955–56). It is true that all the preceding chapters have been devoted to particular symbols, but in none prior to Aeolus has a symbol had such a pronounced effect upon characterization. My point is simple: after Aeolus, even when *Ulysses* appears to revert to earlier forms, one cannot proceed in the creation of a text by relying on assumptions derived from the form of the opening episodes. The pattern for shaping the discourses remains the same, but the expanded range of sources invites one to see a multiplicity previously not in evidence.

The narrative of Scylla and Charybdis similarly reflects the influence of another voice—now more precisely characterized than general rhetorical figures or gastronomic images—operating outside the consciousnesses of the familiar characters participating in the discourse. From the opening lines archaic metaphors and Elizabethan allusions invite the reader's attentiveness to an undertone of Renaissance drama and cultural history that form a commentary on the chapter:

> He came a step a sinkapace forward on neatsleather creaking and a step backward a sinkapace on the solemn floor.

* * * *

Twicecreakingly analysis he corantoed off. Bald, most zealous by the door he gave his large ear all to the attendant's words: heard them: and was gone. (*U*, 9.5–6 and 12–14)[6]

Allusions run chockablock through the discourse inviting each of us to recuperate what we will. The witty erudition further personalizes our texts, for it relies upon individual knowledge and ingenuity to determine its significance. In addition the structure of the chapter, integrating genres in another variation of the pattern introduced in Aeolus, moves from the frame of prose fiction into a variety of forms related to public performances: music (*U*, 9.500), drama (*U*, 9.893–34), and poetry (*U*, 9.1143–52). As we condition our texts, we have the options of eliding or of stressing the differences to suit our own creative inclinations.

In Wandering Rocks another distinctive formal change, the nineteen separate segments of the chapter, calls immediate attention to itself, as an elaboration of the consciousnesses shaping the narrative continues to expand the forces conditioning our response. The informing spirit of the discourse again foregrounds the city of Dublin. The montage-like effect of the segregated passages combines contrasting images of dispersion and intimacy. The consciousnesses of a welter of characters impinge upon the tenor of the voice describing the action: Father Conmee's, Blazes Boylan's, the blond girl's in Thornton's, Miss Dunne's, M'Coy's, Lenehan's, Bloom's, Mr. Kernan's, Stephen's, Jimmy Henry's, Master Patrick Aloysius Dignam's, and Gerty MacDowell's. At one point or another in the chapter, the nature of each of these individuals comes to the forefront to shape the evolution of the narrative in much the same manner as did those of Stephen and of Bloom in the initial episodes. As a result, what initially may appear as an opaque rendition of events across the city in fact stands as a subtle survey of the attitudes of its inhabitants and, by extension, of the polyphonic voices peopling the discourse.

Wandering Rocks carefully reaffirms both the presence of the original narrative persona and its evolving nature. The chapter alternates instances when the personalities of twelve individuals intrude upon the narrative with longer segments in which a version of a more traditional, more unified third-person narrative form obtains. This construction combines a retrospective gesture towards a familiar formal mode with an identification of a shift in the narrative status, proceeding according to a carefully orchestrated plan of accretion. The first of the chapter's nineteen segments repeats the pattern that marks the opening passages of the novel, blending free indirect discourse and stream of consciousness into the narrative. Thus it requires only a relatively minor adjustment on the part of the reader to shift from expectations conditioned by the consciousness of Stephen or of Bloom to perceptions shaped by the voice opening the chapter. "The superior, the very reverend John Conmee S. J. reset his smooth watch in his interior pocket as he came down the presbytery steps. Five to three. Just nice time to walk to Artane. What was that boy's name again? Dignam. Yes. *Vere dignum et iustum est.* Brother Swan was the person to see. Mr Cunningham's letter. Yes. Oblige him, if possible. Good practical catholic: useful at mission time" (*U*, 10.1–6).

This form continues for several paragraphs, just long enough to accustom the reader to it as an apparent reversion to a familiar form, before the narrative begins to introduce the first of a series of interpolations that will appear throughout the chapter undermining the temporal consistency of the episode. As Father Conmee is walking along Mountjoy Square, the description abruptly shifts to another figure in another part of the city.

> Mr Denis J Maginni, professor of dancing &c, in silk hat, slate frockcoat with silk facings, white kerchief tie, tight lavender trousers, canary gloves and pointed patent boots, walking with grave deportment most respectfully took the curbstone as he passed lady Maxwell at the corner of Dignam's court.
>
> Was that not Mrs M'Guinness?
>
> Mrs M'Guinness, stately, silverhaired, bowed to Father Conmee from the farther footpath along which she sailed. And Father Conmee smiled and saluted. How did she do? (*U*, 10.56–64)

Anyone encountering the passage for the first time will experience momentary confusion over the apparent conflation of Lady Maxwell and Mrs. M'Guinness the pawnbroker. Whether or not this fluctuation in descriptive clarity represents an intentional or an unintentional lapse on the part of the narrative voice stands as a moot point. What seems to me of real significance is that this and subsequent instances of unexplained descriptive shifts foreground perceptual ambiguities and remind us of the multilayered discourses conditioning the nature of any text that comes out of our reading.[7]

The introduction of any specific stylistic development does not in itself exclusively determine the innovative nature of the form. Diversification has at least as great an impact. By alternating segments governed by the mode that has become the convention of the opening chapters with passages evolving through a style ostensibly free of the intrusion of consciousnesses outside the nature of the narrative persona, the novel accommodates the overt episodic nature of the chapter as it signals a shift at the generic level in the work's pattern of discourse.

If the remaining sections of Wandering Rocks all followed the form of its opening segment, the stylistic change being introduced would run the risk of being subsumed, and one might lose the sense of the new perspective evolving out of the discourse. As it stands, especially in the final segment which gives a rapid account of the various views of and responses to the viceregal cavalcade, the form of Wandering Rocks becomes the objective correlative for the attitude of shifting perspective being inculcated into the consciousness of the reader.

The chapter departs from some of the most basic elements that characterize both the conventional linear development of a narrative and the pattern of discourse of foregrounding the consciousness of a single individual established earlier in the novel. In addition, the narrative strategy seems to assume a pose of active confrontation as it shifts perspective with the apparent intention of creating ambiguity. The overlapping of consciousnesses within the narrative of the chapter creates not simply competing voices but competing modes of discourse. It gives formal recognition to an important aspect of Wandering Rocks, for the depiction of the simultaneous activities of a range of characters stands as the informing trait of the chapter. Even more significant, however, is the implicit adversarial nature that evolves between the narrative voice and the reader.

In the passage quoted above and in numerous others throughout the chapter, the narrative voice makes associations that are more than simply unreliable; they are purposely misleading. Clive Hart has drawn attention to this aspect of the discourse by annotating a series of instances in which the narrator "renames things already referred to in other and sometimes more unusual terms."

> Carlisle bridge [*U*, 10.947] is the same as O'Connell bridge [*U*, 10.599]; Dan Lowry's musichall [*U*, 10.495] is the Empire musichall [*U*, 10.497] under an older name; the "council chamber of saint Mary's abbey" [*U*, 10.408] is "the old Chapterhouse of saint Mary's abbey" [*U*, 10.929].

Hart also notes passages in which archaic terms are substituted for more familiar ones.

> "Mud Island" [*U*, 10.114] is an old name for the dumping ground which has now become Fairview Park; "Dame gate" [*U*, 10.1217], long since gone, was in the old east wall of the city, about where the southern end of Parliament street is now.

And he has also identified instances in which the narrator applies the same label to distinctly different persons, places, or events.

> The reverend Nicholas Dudley, Curate in Charge of saint Agatha's Church north William street [*U*, 10.1111], has nothing to do with the Viceroy, the Earl of Dudley; Mr Bloom the dentist [*U*, 10.1115] does not know Mr Leopold Bloom; Dignam's court [*U*, 10.60] is in an area of the city far too wealthy to interest the Dignam family. Lambert and O'Molloy, who have just been talking in "Mary's abbey" (the building, [*U*, 10.408]), come forth "slowly into Mary's abbey" (the street [*U*, 10.433–34]).[8]

Through these vagaries, the narration offers facts which are both palpably true and confusing. It evokes a Dublin that had long faded into obscurity by 1904 but that has a claim on our imagination as valid as the Galleys of the Lochlanns imaged by Stephen in Proteus. This infers the cultural discourse running through the narrative, and in doing so emphasizes its both/and qualities. Wandering Rocks underscores a penchant for ambivalence present throughout the work, and it reminds the reader, once again, of the provisionality of any discourse as well as of any text derived from *Ulysses*.

In its formal construction, the Sirens chapter figuratively and literally picks up where Wandering Rocks has left off. It begins with a truncated description of Lydia Douce and Mina Kennedy looking out over the crossblind of the Ormond bar at the passing of the viceregal cavalcade—"Bronze by gold heard the hoofirons, steelyringing" (*U*, 11.01) —and its opening movement goes on to summarize, in shorthand form, the basic action of the chapter. Functioning in a manner similar to an operatic overture and using a typographical restructuring as radical as the bold-face headings of Aeolus, the passage offers images suggesting the action to follow while leaving ample room for later elaboration.[9] In this abbreviated format, the first sixty-three lines of Sirens, like the sixty-three headings of Aeolus, underscore the role of the reader, foregrounding as they do the gaps or indeterminacies that will appear in the body of the episode: The chapter's initial section introduces a metadiscourse through narrative elements divorced from the subsequent narrative but adumbrating more drastic changes to follow, presenting perspectives on perspectives and variations of expected forms.

In the body of the passage free indirect discourse continues the expansion of voice initiated in Wandering Rocks, integrating the thoughts of minor characters into the narrative.

> Miss Kennedy sauntered sadly from the bright light, twining a loose hair behind an ear. Sauntering sadly, gold no more, she twisted twined a

hair. Sadly she twined in sauntering gold hair behind a curving ear. (*U*, 11.81–83)

* * * *

Miss Douce's brave eyes, unregarded, turned from the crossblind, smitten by sunlight. Gone. Pensive (who knows?), smitten (the smiting light), she lowered the dropblind with a sliding cord. She drew down pensive (why did he go so quick when I?) about her bronze, over the bar where bald stood by sister gold, inexquisite contrast, contrast inexquisite nonexquisite, slow cool dim seagreen sliding depth of shadow, *eau de Nil.* (*U*, 11.460–65)

The relative emotional stasis of the opening scene at the Ormond Hotel, less fleeting and fragmentary than the attitudes presented in Wandering Rocks, underscores the barmaids' disappointments, and pain becomes a significant part of the social ambiance. In contrast, the sections in the preceding chapter relating to Miss Dunne, Blazes Boylan's typist, or to any of the other minor figures seem to have an episodic aura and a transitory impact. Sirens, however, does more than simply elaborate the narrative frame of Wandering Rocks.

With the chapter's unfolding, the aims of the discourse become more confused, for the infusions of other voices and of shifting points of view seem to have weakened the narrator's grasp of the repertoire. For example, the two barmaids discuss "that old fogey in Boyd's [chemist shop]" and speculate on what it might be like to be the wife of such a man. In a manner that recalls the shifts in Wandering Rocks, the narration either loses the thread of the conversation or surreptitiously shifts the focus of attention to conflate their reference to confuse it with an allusion to Bloom: "Married to Bloom, to greaseabloom" (*U*, 11.180).

Later an even more disruptive intrusion occurs, one that clarifies the creative options opened to readers by this shift in the discursive strategy of the narrative. In the midst of Bloom's mulling over the postscript of his letter to Martha Clifford, a passage appears recalling a segment of Stephen's thoughts in Scylla and Charybdis (*U*, 9.651–54).

Too poetical that about the sad. Music did that. Music hath charms. Shakespeare said. Quotations every day in the year. To be or not to be. Wisdom while you wait.

In Gerard's rosery of Fetter lane he walks, greyed-auburn. One life is all. One body. Do. But do.

Done anyhow. Postal order, stamp. Postoffice lower down. Walk now. Enough. Barney Kiernan's I promised to meet them. Dislike that job. House of mourning. Walk. Pat! Doesn't hear. Deaf beetle he is. (*U*, 11.904–11)

Any of three alternatives stands as the possible source of this interpolation: as part of Bloom's thoughts (adumbrating sections of Circe), or as the narrative voice choosing this moment to counterpoint Bloom by mimicking Stephen, or as some completely different and unanticipated voice. The fragment of discourse, disassociated from the usual contextual markers, demands the intervention of the reader to resolve (if only provisionally) the situation.

The chapter continues with free indirect discourse expanding the shading of the narration and with the reader becoming increasingly unsure of the limits of the narrative persona. Bloom's consciousness remains the force most frequently influencing the nature of the discourse within the chapter, but at the same time disruptions of the narrative pattern and assertions of parallactic impulses continue to insinuate doubt as to the efficacy of adopting a single point of view for the provisional creation of a text. Even portions of the discourse apparently evolving under the dialogic influence of Bloom prove unstable. While recounting Bloom's composition of a letter to Martha Clifford, for example, the narrative bifurcates. One voice manifests itself in the actual correspondence as the raffish Henry Flower while another appears as the businesslike author of the letter that Bloom pretends to Richie Goulding to be writing in answer to an ad for a job. "Bloom mur: best references. But Henry wrote: it will excite me. You know how. In haste. Henry. Greek ee. Better add postscript. What is he playing now? Improvising. Intermezzo. P.S. The rum tum tum. How will you pun? You punish me?" (*U*, 11.888–91).

The passage quoted above also provides an example of the most blatant counter-discourse presented thus far in the novel: the musical motif suggested by the opening sixty-three lines that continues throughout the chapter as an informing presence. As Groden notes "[t]he musical metaphor dominates Bloom's interior monologue: occasionally Joyce even alters the appearance of Bloom's thoughts on the page to fit the pattern: 'Her wavyavyeavyheavyeavyevyevy hair un comb: 'd.'"[10] In addition to re-forming conventional construction to replicate orthographically the distribution of notes on a sheet of music, the musical motif has permeated the rhythm of the narrative voice, so that at several points its syntax comes closer to what one would find in the lyrics of a popular song than in a prose description. "With patience Lenehan waited for Boylan with impatience, for jinglejaunty blazes boy" (*U*, 11.289–90). Most significant, however, is the intrusion almost from the chapter's opening of verses from operas and popular songs upon the narrative to form a counterpoint to the central discourse.[11]

Up to this point in the work, changes in narrative perspective have been pronounced but of short duration. In eight of the first eleven chapters, the narrative voice has, by dint of repetition, evolved into a persona with consistent, recognizable characteristics generally influenced by the consciousnesses of either Bloom or Stephen. In the three other episodes—Aeolus, Wandering Rocks, and Sirens—alternative forms shape the evolving discourse, but a nostalgic evocation of the natures of the two central characters may continue to inform the reader's general sense of the narrative because the personalities of Bloom and of Stephen have left such a strong impression on one's perception of the discourse.

As I suggested in the preceding chapter, in an appreciable number of subsequent episodes—Cyclops, Nausikaa, Oxen of the Sun, Circe, and Ithaca—alternative narrative patterns assert themselves. In these episodes the narrative voice develops outside the influence of the central characters in the work, and other voices intrude, operating free of the circumscription of the dominant narrative frame. In several instances the diegetic portions of select chapters derive their framework from stylistic forms closely associated with some familiar literary antecedent. As a consequence of this allusiveness, a variety of voices engage one's attention according to the protocol of a familiar form while bending that style to suit the needs of the work. Simultaneously, by shifting their format from chapter to chapter, the narrative disrupts the hegemony of a single discourse. Instead a form of narrative polyphony emerges as recurring voices assume the status of independent discourses within the work.

In the Cyclops chapter, which immediately follows the Sirens episode, the division of discourses becomes quite blatant. Following the pattern established in *Portrait*, Cyclops, through a variety of integrated genres, centers attention on the question of context by a stark bifurcation of the descriptive process. On one hand, a more or less conventional first-person narrator recounts the naturalistic action of the chapter. In counterpoint, a polyvocal persona creates a series of readings inspired by but divorced from events in Barney Kiernan's pub.

The chapter begins with the words of a new narrator, an unnamed dun whose cynical views on humanity give the entire episode a jaundiced perspective. Exemplifying the principle of parallax, the dun offers a sardonic reappraisal of many of the characters already familiar to readers and harsh views of those presented for the first time in this episode.[12]

Decent fellow Joe when he has it but sure like that he never has it. (*U*, 12.65–66)

* * * *

So we turned into Barney Kiernan's and there, sure enough, was the citizen up in the corner having a great confab with himself and that bloody mangy mongrel, Garryowen, and he waiting for what the sky would drop in the way of drink. (*U*, 12.118–21)

* * * *

And begob what was it only that bloody pantaloon Denis Breen in his bathslippers with two bloody big books tucked under his oxter and the wife hotfoot after him, unfortunate wretched woman, trotting like a poodle. (*U*, 12.252–55)

The extravagance of the dun's language is matched by the equally demonstrative, though much less cynical, tones of the periodic interpolations breaking into the scene in the pub. From the first interlude describing, in mock legal jargon, the efforts of Moses Herzog to collect the unpaid bill of Michael E. Geraghty—"[f]or nonperishable goods bought of Moses Herzog, of 13 Saint Kevin's parade in the city of Dublin, Wood quay ward, merchant, herinafter called the vendor" (*U*, 12.33–35)—to the final depiction of the apotheosis of Bloom in the manner of the prophet Elijah—"[w]hen, lo, there came about them all a great brightness and they beheld the chariot" (*U*, 12.1910–11)—these alternative narrative discourses reflect an impulse, similar to the dun's, toward a prodigal use of language. In contradistinction to the dun, however, each displays a total disregard for establishing a consistent link to any of the other interpolations or to events in the chapter.

On the surface, they act as humorous extrapolations, but their impact on the reader goes beyond immediate amusement at the novel's manipulation of voice and tone. Though analogous to the interpolations of Wandering Rocks or to the headings of Aeolus, their elaboration and emphasis on distortion exceed the limits of previous digressive segments. Any pose of objectivity that the narrative may have maintained for itself over the first eleven chapters falls away. The episode advances by extremes, and it remains the task of the reader, conscious of the intentional distortion of the descriptions, to mediate, not simply between different perspectives but between generic protocols as well.

This method in turn impels us toward a radical revision of our perception of the paradigm of *Ulysses*. Up to this point, formal shifts have led us to perpetual reformation of our own interpretive concept since the point of view of a single character or for that matter a single genre proves insufficient to reconcile the complex elements of the work. At the same time, the reader has instinctually been able to rely on the cause-

and-effect laws of naturalism to serve as a basis for undertaking reconciliations within the work. Now, the reader must strive ever for a dual comprehension to satisfy the sometimes conflicting demands imposed by repertoire and by formal suppositions. The Cyclops chapter irreversibly erodes one's sense of formal stability, as a variety of genres, each asserting its own aggregation of conventions, successively assumes control over portions of the narrative.

Classifying these incorporated genres as parodic elements underestimates their impact, and slips into the very binary thinking that the work has been attempting to overturn. They exist in relation to the basic discourse of the chapter, not as simple satirical extensions of events but as periodic reformations of thematic concerns. As one recognizes each of the genres being introduced, the residual recollection of the traits of that genre has an impact upon how one perceives its function in the work. Like the best satire, the interpolations invite the reader to review suppositions for interpreting the episode. These discourses, however, go beyond the didacticism of satire, for they foreground not prescriptive responses but descriptive alternatives.

In subsequent chapters the narrative evinces a more sophisticated application of mundane styles for artistic purposes. Worn-out forms connect with contextual development and so seem less overtly intrusive. In a sense the variable discourses of *Ulysses* rehabilitate clichéd or degraded forms—sentimental romance and pornography come immediately to mind—encouraging the reader to acknowledge that they still retain a certain evocative power.

In Nausikaa, for example, the narrative voice resumes its direction of the discourse, but it progresses under the diffusive influence of contrasting instances of free indirect discourse. The nature of Gerty MacDowell shapes the first half of the episode, and Bloom's insinuates itself into the second half. The form, however, does not represent a temporary halt to stylistic evolution. The consciousness of Gerty is itself filtered through the distorting prism of the patois of the romance novel, with its affected style serving as a veneer.[13]

> As for undies they were Gerty's chief care and who that knows the fluttering hopes and fears of sweet seventeen (though Gerty would never see seventeen again) can find it in his heart to blame her? She had four dinky sets with awfully pretty stitchery, three garments and nighties extra, and each set slotted with different ribbons, rosepink, pale blue, mauve and peagreen, and she aired them herself and blued them when they came home from the wash and ironed them and she had a brickbat to keep the iron on

> because she wouldn't trust those washerwomen as far as she'd see them
> scorching the things. (*U,* 13.171–79)

Although one might initially feel the impulse to dismiss the banal discursiveness that the discourse acquires from the nature of Gerty, the social repertoire of *Ulysses* places her vanities in a harsher context. In the Wandering Rocks episode, when Stephen encounters his sister Dilly on the streets of Dublin, we have seen graphically degraded conditions of the life of a lower-middle-class Dublin girl.

> A Stuart face of nonesuch Charles, lank locks falling at its sides. It
> glowed as she crouched feeding the fire with broken boots.
>
> *   *   *   *
>
> She is drowning. Agenbite. Save her. Agenbite. All against us. She will
> drown me with her, eyes and hair. Lank coils of seaweed hair around me,
> my heart, my soul. Saltgreen death. (*U,* 10.858–59; 875–77)

Gerty herself appears in Wandering Rocks, and there, through free indirect discourse, she shows concerns similar to those voiced in Nausikaa but lacking the distorting presence of the romance tone.

> Passing by Roger Greene's office and Dollard's big red printinghouse Gerty
> MacDowell, carrying the Catesby's cork lino letters for her father who was
> laid up, knew by the style it was the lord and lady lieutenant but she
> couldn't see what Her Excellency had on because the tram and Spring's
> big yellow furniture van had to stop in front of her on account of its being
> the lord lieutenant. (*U,* 10.1205–11)

These images offer the reader a more complex alternative for reconciling the clash of form and content with the language. In doing so we come to see that the narrative aims not at ridiculing Gerty; rather in a discourse counter to that of Wandering Rocks it attempts to show how she must set up literal defenses within her consciousness to alleviate the tedium and degradation of her life.

The variegated narrative framework of Nausikaa reinforces an ethos of form based on innovation and progression while simultaneously subverting the stylistic process through the dual gestures of parody and imitation. The structure of *Ulysses* continually contradicts the Aristotelian assumptions of a stratification of forms and of a linear evolution of stylistic endeavors as articulated in Stephen's aesthetic formulas in *Portrait* (*P,* 214–15). It asserts instead an idiosyncratic value for formal structure manifesting vitality within specific applications. Joyce himself, in discussing Oxen of the Sun (*Letters,* I.138–39), outlined its organization along the lines of embryonic development in the same paragraph that he described its allusive rendition of the development of English prose styles from the Ango-Saxon period to his own. One need not, however, subscribe to the implication that stylistically this represents a movement from primitive to more sophisticated forms, for above all, the material enforces a sense of literary malleability. It shows that styles need not be restricted to a particular chronological era, a specific philosophical bias, or a single level of discourse, while demonstrating the inherent subjectivity of all descriptive language.

Such an effort necessarily exposes the ambiguity inherent in the styles reflected by the various forms throughout the Oxen of the Sun episode. The chapter does not, however, seek to hold up to ridicule the traditional canon of English prose; it only attempts to prevent the form from falling into a static condition. Oxen does not merely parody the styles of Joyce's predecessors, nor does it simply act as a monument to the achievements of literary antecedents. Rather, it creates a tension between the reader's generic and contextual expectations to reinvigorate familiar and even antiquated forms. It gives them existence in a new setting while playing upon the reader's response to the residual impact of their original characteristics.

Of course, one cannot ignore the disruptive features of such an approach, for in general this serial presentation of diverse styles works against what one might assume to be the ostensive contextual development of the chapter in much the same manner as do the dialogic elements of preceding episodes. From the opening lines these forms demonstrate no immediate conjunction with the material presented:

> Deshil Holles Eamus. Deshil Holles Eamus. Deshil Holles Eamus.
> Send us bright one, light one, Horhorn, quickening and wombfruit. Send us bright one, light one, Horhorn, quickening and wombfruit. Send us bright one, light one, Horhorn, quickening and wombfruit.
> Hoopsa boyaboy hoopsa! Hoopsa boyaboy hoopsa! Hoopsa boyaboy hoopsa! (*U*, 14.1–6)

Instead, by filling the narrative with archaic language and by inverting the usual discursive depictions with anachronistic perspectives, they distort descriptions of the action and impede efforts to form an impression of the discourse based on a fixed point of view.

While such forms are undeniably disorienting, by this point readers no longer view disruption as an inherently negative trait. Rather it simply has become an aspect of the discourses contributing to the range of interpretive approaches open to the reader. Of necessity, however, before attempting to create any coherent text from the amalgamated styles of the episode, one must reconcile the narrative idiosyncrasies of this chapter with the expectations based on the previous episodes that still govern our perceptions. The jarring process of reconciliation that results underscores the way that the chapter overturns basic assumptions. In conventionally governed readings we create a text by following a method of either/or thinking. We select particular perspectives and in maintaining them close down other interpretive possibilities. Oxen of the Sun repeatedly challenges the assumptions implicit in this strategy by denying primacy to a single form. As it unfolds, it increases the number of styles that we must reconcile. Consequently it adds to the number of alternative readings that we must choose from or incorporate into increasingly provisional interpretations.

This movement between form and content, between mimesis and diegesis, invites the reader to participate in the process of creation to fashion a text reconciled to the vagaries of the book's elements from the shifting environment of the work. The process may seem to some a presumption upon artistic prerogative, but one finds a useful argument for following this impulse in comments by Wolfgang Iser on the stylistics in the Oxen of the Sun episode.

> [Joyce's] awareness of the danger that he will capture only the surface view of things makes him approach the object as it were from all linguistic sides, in order to avoid a perspective foreshortening of it. And so the long appositions are not set out as such, and dependent clauses are left unmarked, for divisions of this kind would involve premature definition of the object concerned. At the same time, however, the language makes wide use of specialized vocabulary and precise nuances of meaning, and this gives rise to the impression that the institution is to be described with utmost exactitude, although in fact it tends to become more and more blurred.[14]

Iser goes on to note that the structure of Oxen outlines the paradigm of the book. I would like to press that point a bit further, for it leads to an important distinction that one needs to make in reading *Ulysses*. As with Aeolus, it has become a critical commonplace to view Oxen as a microcosm of the entire novel, but Iser draws attention to a more specific association than has been previously recognized. By accustoming ourselves to the vagaries of Oxen, we give precedence in our consciousness to the standards that we have evolved in responding to the work. In effect, our way of reading this episode signals how we have chosen to read the whole book.

In this analysis of the impact of Oxen, however, Iser stops short of recognizing the full degree of freedom that Joyce's method affords. As I have noted in previous chapters, in *The Implied Reader* Iser remains committed to the concept of authorial determinacy, believing that the form of Oxen brings out "the inadequacy of style as regards the presentation of reality, by constant changes of style, for only by showing up the relativity of each form could [Joyce] expose the intangibility and expansibility of observable reality."[15] (In fairness to Iser, I do not believe these views accurately convey his present attitude, but his remarks reflect an approach that still characterizes the thinking of many other readers.)

To a degree Iser makes a very important commentary on the technique that follows, but I believe that he overemphasizes its function in presenting negative opinions on form that Joyce may or may not have held. Iser's response implies a reliance on a determination of intentionality, an impulse to indulge in either/or reasoning, that the structure of Oxen intentionally frustrates. I would like to reword that statement to describe Joyce's technique from a less confining Postmodern perspective and to advance an alternative to the fragmented view of styles that Iser offers: Just as in *Portrait* recurring segments mimic the character of Stephen Dedalus without preventing one from coming to grips with his nature, in *Ulysses* formal variation serves to open the work to a range of readings rather than to restrict it to a narrow band of alternatives.

Furthermore, although the shifting diction within the succession of styles may appear to suppress the recognizable features of the narrative persona, this construction, in fact, follows patterns already established in earlier episodes. Throughout the chapter free indirect discourse keeps in prominence elements of the consciousness of Bloom, Stephen, and other characters. These traces of earlier instances of the discourse supply the reader with a nexus between the narrative of preceding chapters and the discourses of Oxen of the Sun. This sense of consistent narrative presences lurking beneath the tonal polyphony impels us toward forming unities within the chapters. While Iser points up the important relationship between an author's "presentation" and the reader's role of "imagination," I feel that the range of action accorded to the reader is much broader than such a view implies. The parodic impulse does not undercut the credibility of various characters. It places greater demands upon readers to reconcile parodic elements of an individual's nature with other aspects.[16]

To a degree, Oxen of the Sun confirms the obvious: *Ulysses* does more than simply extend the formal experiments begun in *Portrait*. It exploits the impact of a variety of styles on the consciousness of the reader. As a consequence it does not reveal the limitations of particular styles; rather it highlights the multiplicity inherent in seemingly restrictive forms. This method shows the author's deep awareness of the literary connotations that any recognizable style brings with it no matter what the context in which it appears—another instance of the phenomenon that Derrida calls *sous rature*. The term from deconstructive criticism reminds us of the subjectivity that characterizes any discourse, but it also very nicely encapsulates the tension between the expectations and elaborations informing any encounter with a piece of literature. This residue of impressions mediates between the reader and the printed page, and it forces one to reconcile expectations derived from the recollection of the application of that particular style in other works with its function in the passage confronting the reader.

Even as the form of *Ulysses* continues to evolve beyond the styles suggested by Oxen of the Sun, the narrative structure still plays upon impressions derived from the concentration of integrated genres in this chapter. Consequently the reader approaches every subsequent episode already conditioned by the mutability of the discourse(s). Despite the extravagance of many of the literary and subliterary styles (functioning in a carnival mode similar to that described by Bakhtin), the familiar genres that they invoke allow one to discern the implied unities offsetting the superficial displacements. In Circe, for example, while the salacious tone of the chapter cannot be ignored, even those unfamiliar with the common conventions of Victorian pornography will agree with Judge Woolsey's opinion in the book's 1933 obscenity trial that much of the chapter reiterates the clichés of sensuality without evoking "the leer of the sensualist." One might, in fact, wish to assert that the emphasis falls not on the physical sensations but on the psychological needs motivating them, specifically the sadomasochistic impulses shaping a significant portion of Bloom's nature. The scenes in the chapter involving fantasies of Bloom and of Stephen underscore tendencies that have already appeared throughout the work. As a result of Circe's general aura of distortion, the narrative implicitly calls upon the reader to weight the impact of the discourse invoking pornographic images against competing discourses to determine what revaluation of character these scenes should produce.

On one level the dominant formal shift of this chapter harkens back to the structural counterpointing of earlier episodes—the headlines of Aeolus, the dramatic segment of Scylla and Charybdis, the overture of Sirens—yet the layout, evoking the dramatic form moving the narrative from a diegetic to a mimetic emphasis places a much greater burden for recuperation on the reader. Direct discourse dominates the action, and the descriptions of indirect discourse unfold without the shaping impact of an ulterior consciousness. As I noted in the previous chapter, this draws us into the role of the narrator, so that as part of the process of reading we provide implicit descriptive connections between various incidents in the chapter.

Prior concepts of discourse, however, give no clear prescriptive sense of how this process should unfold. Despite the situation's mimetic inclinations, the ambiance of fantasy—with fans and gas jets that talk, gothic appearances and disappearances, and psychodramatic shifts in setting and action—blurs distinctions in characterization and requires rigorous engagement with its indeterminacies to form a text. As Michael Groden notes, elements from the consciousness of one character often appear within the discourse of another.[17] Much of the action proceeds under topical motivation. A rough naturalistic empiricism can guide one through the basic events, but to derive a complete meaning for the vignettes contained in the chapter the reader must amalgamate the diverse narrative presences of the preceding chapters into an imaginative rendition of a persona of the multivocal narrator. At the same time, in making compatible the divergent fantasies of Bloom and Stephen, the reader assumes control over the narrative. In the very act of affirming the presence of a narrator as conjoiner of the discourse/meta-discourse dialectic, the reader refines the expectations for approaching the work adduced in Oxen. This overturns the sense of dispersion and diversity that informs one's initial impression of the chapter, replacing that attitude with a feeling of an overriding self-consciousness (both in the work and in the reader's text) directing and unifying the action.

Just as the dialogic revisions of Oxen condition the reader for Circe, so also do they shape our reactions to Eumaeus and to Ithaca. In effect, the chapters reiterate previous gestures and reinforce paradigmatic assumptions. A common response to Eumaeus holds that the chapter, in dealing with the exhaustion of Stephen and of Bloom, reveals the enervation that Joyce felt after laboring over Circe. In fact the language follows a carefully calculated allusive pattern. Tautology and inflated diction do not elide central concerns of the discourse. Rather they simultaneously underscore and undercut much of what the narrative voice says, providing from yet another perspective the both/and condition that has obtained since Aeolus.

The opening lines, for example, create a paradox through the oxymoronic description of Bloom behaving "in orthodox Samaritan fashion" (*U*, 16.3). Bloom, in fact, does act the part of the archetypal Good Samaritan, but, like the Samaritan of the Gospels whose faith separates him from the Jew to whom he gives comfort, Bloom's beliefs—religious, cultural, social—rest on values not shared by the majority of the characters in *Ulysses*. We have come to see him both as a model citizen and as an outcast alienated from his fellow Dubliners. The density of such constructions persists throughout the chapter to revivify apparently exhausted imagery. The narrator engages our attention with a voice in tune with the consciousness of Bloom (like the narrator of Calypso and other chapters) while a counter-discourse insinuates a sardonic commentary. As a result, the narrative does not resume the predictable binary relationship of *Portrait* because the hegemony of a particular subgenre no longer obtains. Competing voices are not subsumed but held in an equilibrium determined by the text evolving from the reader's imagination.

Ithaca introduces a new type of intimacy into our engagement with the work. The question-and-answer format calls upon us to delineate the protocols that we have identified as conditioning our response to the novel. It emphasizes once again the reader's power, cultivated in Circe, to complete meaning by creating coherent links with preceding styles. Its structure strips the narrative of its ability to enhance depictions through normal descriptive ascendancy, and it saps the power of characters to assert their influence through dialogic manipulation. Taken out of its broader narrative context, such a format would give one little sense of the dynamics of the novel. The reader, however, approaches Ithaca from the experience of the previous sixteen chapters. Consequently, its detached discourse presents a palimpsest by overlaying previous impressions with its cold articulation of the actions of Stephen and of Bloom. Furthermore, since its consciously self-effacing form limits its prescriptive impact, the structure enables the reader to elaborate upon its creative options. While indeterminacies abound in the episode, the contradictions so apparent in earlier chapters seem to disappear. Of necessity, the text created for Ithaca depends heavily on the reader's cumulative impressions of the novel, and in exercising this dependence the reader attempts to impose unity upon the chapter and confronts the unifying system that he or she has created to give coherence to the entire work.

As noted in the previous chapter, Penelope recapitulates for us the central experiences of *Ulysses*. Like all paraphrases, however, it extends rather than recreates initial impressions. One engages the final episode with a text that has been evolving since Telemachus, yet the act of reading does not so much validate the integrity of our suppositions as underscore the indeterminacy of the work. The ambiguity of Molly's final affirmation rejects closure and invites us to begin reading again, aware that the provisionality of subsequent texts will enhance rather than undercut the force of the aesthetic experience.

A summary of the views on reading that come out of this examination of the formal structure of *Ulysses* brings one back to the concerns articulated in the opening lines of this chapter. In a characteristically Postmodern fashion, the paradigm conditioning *Ulysses* only incidentally relies on thematic markers. Content offers important decoration, but the central concerns of provisional textual constitution rest upon a polymorphous appeal to style. They demand a perspective that delays the dialectic synthesis that we continually wish to make. As noted in the preceding chapter, one can apply dialectic principles in forming a text for one of Joyce's works, but the most effective application also presumes a deconstruction of the synthetic mode even as it forms. Deferral acts as a key feature, for completing the dialectic would lead to limitations rather than to an opening of apprehension. Kenneth Burke explains the ideal application of the process in the following way:

> In strict accordance with dialectical principles, we may expect that the laws we discover will "transcend" previous laws, in proportion as the new conditions differ from previous conditions. And *furthermore*, as a corrective on empiricism, we shall be reminded that *our instruments are but structure of terms, and hence must be expected to manifest the nature of terms*. That is, we must always be admonished to remember, not that an experiment flatly and simply reveals *reality*, but rather that it *reveals only such reality as is capable of being revealed by this particular terminology* [Burke's emphasis].[18]

Thus, dialectic resolution is always provisional. The fullest meaning comes from a deferral of resolution, maintaining both/and for as long as possible.

In a modified sense, Joyce produces Roland Barthes's *scriptible* work. One does not rewrite the work, but rather one completes it (in *Portrait*) or one chooses a path to elaborate (in *Ulysses*). The process in *Ulysses* follows Burke's sense of dialectics, but it always makes us aware of the ideal dialectic moment when boundaries are merging but before individuality has been erased.

X | The Commodius Recirculation of *Finnegans Wake*

The informing principles of this study of the narrative features of Joyce's canon have led me to pay close attention to associations with his literary antecedents, for I believe that Joyce's fiction, far from developing in isolation, encapsulates the major literary movements of the last one hundred years. Thus the incipient self-reflexivity of *Dubliners* reminds us of its ties to the impulses of Impressionism. *Portrait*, with all its disaffections, still maintains an ongoing faith in the central tenet of Modernism: the ability of the individual voice to impose order on whatever it encounters. The impulse towards retrospection abates in *Ulysses*, as the novel proclaims the emergence of Joyce's Postmodern sensibilities. Its multiple levels of discourse overturn the last vestiges of primacy. No view assumes a privileged position, and all perspectives remain incomplete. Relativism obtains not as a flaw but as a liberating condition, endowing a broad range of possible responses with interpretive validity.

This realignment of attitudes marks the furthest point of Joyce's narrational development, yet some readers still fail to feel its full impact. They emphasize the naturalistic elements within various discourses in *Ulysses*, and elide all other aspects of the narration into a linearly dominated reading. *Finnegans Wake*, of course, eschews any evocation of naturalism, and so it frustrates any tendency to apply cause-and-effect logic. Nonetheless, it offers no innovations not already found in *Ulysses*; it merely makes them more blatant. In this respect, it acts as a coda, restating the salient formal and contextual features of the paradigm directing Joyce's mature creative endeavors.

As I have tried to show throughout this study, one can find in Joyce's earliest writing not simply the inclinations but the techniques that came to function so prominently in the later pieces. Thus, despite its reputation for linguistic formidability, in many ways *Finnegans Wake* offers the most straightforward and literal rendition of the creative inclinations in all Joyce's works. It simplifies language, in the purest sense of such an action, by stripping away the devices traditionally employed by prose fiction to achieve misleading elisions and putative closures. I have already referred to Hugh Kenner's remark, now a critical commonplace, that the narrative discourse of *Ulysses* devotes a great deal of space to instructing us on how best to approach this book. I would like to extend that view to note that, as one reads it, *Finnegans Wake* reiterates strategies for reading that have grown out of our experiences with the rest of the canon.

Although many critics of Joyce's final work have offered commentaries on aspects of the reader's engagement, an essay by David Hayman devoted to its formal constitution provides particularly useful imagery for highlighting the contribution of the narrative structure to shaping the relationship that has evolved between Joyce and his readers. Hayman initiates his examination with a revaluation of Clive Hart's ideas on the structure of *Finnegans Wake*. Hayman suggests an extension of Hart's views that in its turn articulates a more elaborate scheme for identifying the work's stylistic and contextual framework.

> Hart's account of the "motif" demonstrates one aspect of Joyce's method (an aspect of what might be called the *Wake*'s micro-structure). But Joyce's practice suggests another approach which, rather than the individual motif, would focus the coherent clusterings of motif-like materials and might be called "nodalization." The key element here is the "prime node" or apex of the "nodal system," a passage where some act, activity, personal trait, allusion, theme, etc. surfaces for its clearest statement in the text, is made manifest, so to speak, and in the process brings together and crystallizes an otherwise scattered body of related material. This prime node is the generative center for lesser and generally less transparent passages devoted to its elaboration or expansion and strategically located in the text.[1]

While Hayman concentrates specifically on illuminating aspects of Joyce's process of creation, his concepts also provide useful guidelines for a greater consideration of the role of the reader now foregrounded by *Finnegans Wake*. If one extends them to include the rhetorical dimension of the work (a key factor in the conjunction of various formal and contextual figures), the terms that he has produced will clarify important stages in the process of deriving a text from the novel and will serve as a lexicon for a summary of the central concerns of this study.[2]

As in *Ulysses*, the most effective use of any approach to *Finnegans Wake* lies in maintaining a relative rather than a literal perspective. While both Hart and Hayman have made important critical contributions to our comprehension of *Finnegans Wake*, adherence too scrupulous to the vocabulary of their methods can inhibit exploration of some of the most significant areas of inquiry that they highlight. The specific danger lies in readers with less critical sophistication than either Hart or Hayman inferring from certain descriptive terms like prime node, apex, and generative center a series of dualisms and hierarchies—high/ low, surface/depth, margin/center—conditions in which one side of the dualism always benefits from an evaluative preference. This approach would replace provisional choice with certitude derived from a consistent, linear either/or view of the work, an impulse that the canon has denied since *Dubliners*. Instead, one must see nodalization as functioning in a manner similar to the literary and the extraliterary references of *Ulysses*. It overlays a particular passage with allusions from previous portions of the work without prescribing the response one should make to the conjunction.

A more effective apprehension of the pattern of incremental repetition that Hayman identifies draws attention to the narrative's diversified rhetorical strategies aimed at reforming conventional habits of interpretation brought to the work by many readers. Since Hayman's nodalizations occur throughout *Finnegans Wake*, one might find in any of a number of selections ample illustration of their impact upon habits of reading. I propose to focus on one that has paradigmatic significance—the debate between Paddrock and the archdruid Balkelly—applying the general directions that I have suggested for responding to Joyce's works to the specific features of its narrative discourse.

This approach explores the heuristic rather than the interpretive aspects of *Finnegans Wake*. In keeping with my aim to use the work as representative of the entire canon, I will not attempt to delineate the full scope of the complexities adduced by its self-conscious multiplicity of discourse. Rather, through the examination of this single episode, I intend to trace the elements in the narrative strategy that recapitulate Joyce's development as an artist and that summarize the options open to readers responding to his canon.

With this purpose in mind, before taking up that passage, I would like to survey some of the narrative's impressionistic statements relating to the act of reading—what Hayman would term elements of the "nodal system"—that appear scattered throughout the discourse of *Finnegans Wake*. These observations, and others like them, insistently advance adoption of the same techniques for perceiving prose fiction that have been put forward in all of Joyce's preceding works, and they invite the reader to combine them into a grammar of rhetoric offering itself as a guide for "the ideal reader suffering from the ideal insomnia" (*FW,* 120.13–14).

> Thus the unfacts, did we possess them, are too imprecisely few to warrant our certitude . . . (*FW,* 57.16–17)

* * * *

No, assuredly, they are not justified, those gloompourers who grouse that letters have never been quite their old selves again since that weird week-day in bleak Janiveer (yet how palmy date in a waste's oasis!) when to the shock of both, Biddy Doran looked at literature. (*FW,* 112.23–27)

* * * *

He is cured by faith who is sick of fate. The prouts who will invent a writing there ultimately is the poeta, still more learned, who discovered the raiding there originally. (*FW,* 482.30–33)

* * * *

For newmanmaun set a marge to the merge of unnotions. Innition wons agame. (*FW,* 614.17–18)

The tenor of these remarks may appear at first marred by contradiction and even in some instances by an aura of malevolence. As one becomes accustomed to the linguistic fluctuations of the book, however, the persistent reader will find in these gnomic flourishes hints of the paradigmatic assumptions supplying the "metheg in your mindness." In each instance multiple puns and allusions create layers of discourse, implicitly calling attention to the range of possible interpretations even as the content affirms the underlying difficulty of achieving certitude from any point of view.

While the structure of *Finnegans Wake* overtly resists conventional interpretive approaches, in many ways it sums up patterns of discourse repeated throughout the canon. Joyce's intrusive commentary on the act of reading foregrounds the problem of perception while it simultaneously attempts to mitigate the frustration that its form inevitably produces in readers accustomed to basing their responses to literature on the primacy of a single system of explication. This encourages an alternative to conventional habits of reading: one that abandons the tyranny of cause-and-effect logic ("the unfacts") and overturns the hegemony of "those gloompourers" who advocate the dominance of orthodox critical systems. In place of the traditional interaction, one must give oneself over to the work through an act of faith, depending not on any prescriptive system to release the pleasure of the text but on the polymorphic power of the book itself to push the border ("marge") of acceptance "to the merge of unnotions."

As I said at the opening of this chapter, the rhetorical framework of *Finnegans Wake* reiterates the efficacy of the techniques for reading that I have been applying to all of Joyce's canon. Through syntactic and

grammatic constructions that systematically disrupt single-minded interpretations, the diverse discourses remind readers to move away from
the pursuit of certitude through linear approaches and towards a dialectic acceptance of ambiguity. As they have throughout the canon,
either/or questions give way to both/and answers. Developing around
the "nodal system" of narration identified by Hayman, the language of
multilayered discourses presents a particular concept, image, or situation from a range of perspectives and produces equilibrium from the
tension of diverse perceptions held in suspension. This condition of balance, however, comes about only through the intervention of the reader
willing to give equal authority to a range of potential meanings. In a
harmonious response to the work, no single meaning will achieve primacy over other interpretations, and any reading cut off from all others
remains deficient in proportion to its degree of isolation. To counteract
the impulses of Enlightenment empiricism which still influence our response to experience, the discourse urges the acknowledgment and
even the pursuit of ambiguity as a means of opening one's consciousness to the mystery inherent in art. Ultimately, in *Finnegans Wake*, as in
the works which preceded it, the problem does not turn upon a resolution of contraries but upon a reconciliation with them.

This is precisely why Joyce could employ the particular creative vocabulary that constitutes the prose of *Finnegans Wake*. By the time he
began to write it he was determined to cultivate a full sense of the natural ambiguity of the aesthetic experience produced by a piece of art.
Consequently, one discerns time and again in *Finnegans Wake* a dialectic
questioning of attitudes relating to creation and perception, often bound
up with intertextual references to philosophical considerations of time
and space. These instances highlight the development of concepts central to Joyce's artistic views and repeat a process that has occurred
throughout his career.. By touching on just a few of these dialogic moments, one can trace significant points in the evolution of Joyce's stylistics.

In *A Portrait of the Artist as a Young Man*, for example, Stephen Dedalus, perhaps stimulated by a classmate's fatuous reference to Lessing
and the *Laocoon*, begins an explanation of his theory of art to the sul-
phurous Lynch by first distinguishing, along the lines laid down by Lessing, the means by which perceptions become impressions.[3]

> The first phase of apprehension is a bounding line drawn about the object
> to be apprehended. An esthetic image is presented to us either in space or
> in time. What is audible is presented in time, what is visible is presented

in space. But, temporal or spatial, the esthetic image is first luminously apprehended as selfbounded and selfcontained upon the immeasurable background of space or time which is not it. (*P,* 212)

Stephen's distinctions reflect to some degree impressionistic and artificial aspects of his own nature, but they nonetheless articulate the same concerns to which readers of *Portrait* must continue to return in search of some sort of provisional resolution of cruxes within the discourse.

In *Ulysses* one finds an increasingly assertive movement away from certitude and towards mutability. On Sandymount Strand in the Proteus episode, for example, Stephen struggles to overcome the limitations of his oversimplified view of the relation of the comprehension of a work of art in time and in space, and of necessity he begins to confront the inherent ambiguity of his conclusions. Lessing's ideas again appear as Stephen centers his aesthetic meditations on the competition for attention generated by synchronic and diachronic perceptions, but now Lessing's theories must struggle with temporizing views from Aristotle, Jakob Boehme, and Bishop Berkeley for Stephen's attention.[4]

> Ineluctable modality of the visible: at least that if no more, thought through my eyes. Signatures of all things I am here to read, seaspawn and seawrack, the nearing tide, that rusty boot. Snotgreen, bluesilver, rust: coloured signs. Limits of the diaphane. But he adds: in bodies. Then he was aware of them bodies before of them coloured. How? By knocking sconce against them, sure. Go easy. Bald he was and a millionaire, *maestro di color che sanno.* Limit of the diaphane in. Why in? Diaphane, adiaphane. If you can put your five fingers through it it is a gate, if not a door. Shut your eyes and see. (*U,* 3.01–09)

Late in the chapter Stephen returns to concepts of Berkeley with a more specific reference, introducing an incipient image of a rainbow in which colors conform to natural laws both of time and of space. "The good bishop of Cloyne [Berkeley] took the veil of the temple out of his shovel hat: veil of space with coloured emblems hatched on its field. Hold hard. Coloured on a flat: yes, that's right" (*U,* 3.416–18).[5] Stephen's momentary illumination does not fully resolve the questions of perception for himself or for the reader. Nonetheless, his allusion establishes the importance of the temporally and spatially evanescent rainbow that, as those familiar with *Finnegans Wake* realize, will become an important representation of Joyce's continuing investigation of the problem.

Although he never completely eliminates the competition for hegemony from his depictions of the two dimensions, in writing *Finnegans Wake* Joyce comes to present them in a way that encourages conjunction in the mind of the reader. In any given passage historical, cultural, and mythical allusions converge diachronically to underscore the perception of our civilization as developing through incremental progression. At the same time, through cyclical emphasis they synchronically level the primacy of any reference, making it congruent to familiar archetypal patterns. As images of time and space present contrasting though not mutually exclusive perceptions, readers move towards a reconciliation, though not a synthesis, of these positions by forming a stereoscopic vision of cumulative and simultaneous elements in *Finnegans Wake*.

The elements making up the debate over time and space occur in variant forms in a number of key passages (the meeting of the Mookse and the Gripes and the fable of the Ondt and the Gracehoper come immediately to mind), but the confrontation of Paddrock (St. Patrick) and the archdruid Balkelly (Berkeley) seems the clearest illustration of this process and the selection presenting Joyce's final statement on the question. In a letter to Frank Budgen written three months after the publication of *Finnegans Wake* Joyce drew attention to the implications of this passage, obliquely offering a guide to reading it. "Much more is intended in the colloquy between Berkeley the arch druid and his pidgin speech and Patrick the [?] and his Nippon English. It is also the defence and indictment of the book itself, B's theory of colours and Patrick's practical solution to the problem" (*Letters*, I.406). Despite the polarities apparent in the episode, one would be mistaken to assume that this letter advocates simply a linear response to an either/or question. I believe that "the defence and indictment of the book itself," and in fact of the entire canon, lie not in the opposition of one argument to the other but in the alternating emphasis throughout the passage on contrasting temporal and spatial methods of apprehension. This dialectic presentation of space and time demonstrates the paradigmatic advancement of the episode's contextual and stylistic framework, using diachronic and synchronic approaches to reach accommodation.

With its opening word—"Tunc," the title given to a famous and pivotal page in *The Book of Kells*—the paragraph associates the druid's ideas with a key nodal reference: It recalls the lengthy evocation of *The Book of Kells* in the Biddy Doran chapter (*FW,* 119.10–123.10) which includes a lingering description of the page itself (*FW,* 122.20–42), and it also establishes a link with the cryptic remark from the Studies chapter: "I've read you tunc's dimissage" (298.07). Finally, on the level of metadiscourse, the image from *The Book of Kells* acts as a commentary on the narrative strategies at work throughout *Finnegans Wake*. The muddy parchment background of the Tunc page, the circuitous intertwining of letters (*Tunc crucifixerant XRI cum eo duos latrones*: Then two robbers were crucified with him, [Matt. 27:38]) and illumination, and the traces of script which have bled through from the sheet's verso side do indeed make the message appear dim but not, for Joyce's purposes, indecipherable.

Allusion to the "Tunc" page also evokes a series of images that blur the pagan/Christian dichotomy between Balkelly and St. Patrick. As early as Campbell and Robinson's *Skeleton Key*, critics have remarked on the apparent contradictions within the page's illuminations, "strangely suggestive of pre-Christian and oriental symbols," and with this passage Joyce fully exploits such connotations.[6] Joyce has already introduced the concept of viewing the passage ambivalently by using the drawing at the end of the Studies chapter (*FW*, 308.26) to evoke the chi (X) of the tunc page while blurring the image of the two thieves with that of the *Dio Boia*.[7] The tunc's reference to the death of Jesus inverts the expected application of iconography, now associating the druid with the Judaeo-Christian tradition of the scapegoat/sacrifice and may obliquely allude to Balkelly's impending overthrow by Paddrock. The appearance, however, of "quoniam" early in the paragraph (*FW*, 611.10) mitigates the tone of defeat. The word appears on another illuminated page of *The Book of Kells* (Luke 1.1), and its brilliant decoration and position announcing a beginning again, the start of St. Luke's gospel, reminds one of the final triumph of the Resurrection.

While *The Book of Kells*, with its commingling of pagan and Christian aspects of Irish culture, emphasizes the complexity of Balkelly's nature, the word "Tunc" also underscores the central feature of his consciousness which will inform the debate: his association with time, which brings about his downfall but also suggests the process of his redemption. As his argument makes clear, the druid approaches knowledge by a procedure emphasizing diachronic perception. His method for understanding bases its authority on its assimilation of his cultural and intellectual heritage, and he claims that his ability to "absorbere" prior learning has enabled him to progress to the esoteric realms of the "numpa one puraduxed seer in seventh degree of wisdom of Entis-Onton" (*FW*, 611.21). To illustrate the efficacy of his system, the druid presents his theory of colors, a mixture of the views of Aristotle, Berkeley, and Kant with an adumbration of Freudian psychology. Unfortunately, the druid does not resist the impulse to level ambiguity. By sweeping away the "all too many much illusiones through photoprismic velamina of hueful panepiphanal world spectacurum of Lord Joss" (*FW*, 611.12–14), he articulates the enhanced understanding one enjoys through directing perception to the "true inwardness of reality, the Ding havd in idself id est" (*FW,* 611.21), but it comes about through oversimplification.

One critic who has carefully examined this passage, Pierre Vitoux, finds strong evidence of borrowings from Newton's *Opticks* and from his theory of light and colors. Vitoux also notes the impact of Berkeley's views on this passage, holding that "if we overlook the un-Berkeleyan emphasis on the 'illusory' character of perception, [the allusion] is not inconsistent with Berkeley's concept of 'signs on a veil.' "[8] Vitoux's approach, however, replicates the druid's error. To blend apparently conflicting perceptions into a single experience sacrifices the alternatives open through ambiguity to the pursuit of certitude. Vitoux's examination of the Paddrock and Balkelly episode seems to me quite ingenious, but the emphasis he places on establishing within the picture of Balkelly precise analogues to the concepts of Newton and of Bishop Berkeley works against the deliberate ambivalence of the passage. *Finnegans Wake* can accommodate the thinking of Newtonian/Berkeleyan viewpoints, but like the rest of Joyce's canon it will not give primacy to such a perspective.

The next portion of the passage underscores this point, as the impulse to ingest the wisdom of the past suffers the inevitable temporal consequence. While Balkelly is attempting to explain his ideas, the process of entropy sets in. As the druid speaks, progressively diminishing renderings of the phrase "hueful panepiphanal world" appear parenthetically. When Balkelly finally reaches the "sextuple gloria of light actually retained, untisintus, inside them" (*FW,* 611.23–24), he has ingested all but a trace of the accidents. The husk that remains after he has drawn off the substance, "(obs of epiwo)," suggests the desiccation of appropriative, solipsistic learning.

Despite the firmness of the druid's conviction, as the paragraph continues, the obvious flaws under which his system labors become increasingly apparent. Balkelly's example of the colors illustrates how acquisitiveness internalizes knowledge, how hoarding cuts off intellectual exchange. Growth for the druid comes only through expropriation, but because he gourmandizes without discrimination his method lacks consistency and stability. When Paddrock fails to follow the explanation, "no catch all that preachybook" (*FW,* 611.25), the druid again draws on his intellectual antecedents, rephrasing his theory in a conglomeration of Latinate and oriental-sounding phrases, "with other words verbigratiagrading from murmurulentous till stridulocelerious in a hunghoranghoangloly tsinglontseng" (*FW,* 611.27–29). To bolster his theory he attempts to demonstrate its application, but he cannot contain his nationalistic description of the greenness of King Leary. As he regurgitates his argument, one internalized color spills out over everything that he sees: "verdant readyrainroof . . . spit of superexuberabundancy plenty laurel leaves . . . like thyme choppy upon parsley, alongsidethat . . . olive lentil . . ." (*FW,* 612.03–10).

The debate shifts attention to the views of Paddrock, intellectually and temperamentally in diametrical opposition to those of the druid. Paddrock bases his response to Balkelly on a rudimentary but steadfast Christian faith. This belief is founded on an instantaneous moment of illumination and summarized spatially in the opening of his paragraph, "Punc." While the word lacks the cultural and religious overtones associated with the druid's temporal "Tunc," it draws force from Paddrock's synchronic approach to perception. His rigid devotion to a primitive form of Christianity stands as the immovable antithesis of Balkelly's progressive digestion of secularized philosophy.

Despite the fixity of Paddrock's faith, he does not remain static when confronted by the druid's contradictory approach to perception. Beginning aggressively by dismissing opposing views, Paddrock bends—"refrects": refracts, reflects—the argument of Balkelly back against him, articulating a sense of the world based on Paddrock's faith in the limitless and incomprehensible power of God. He dismisses the druid's linear, either/or view of the world—"you pore shiroskuro blackinwhitepaddynger" (*FW,* 612.18)—and Balkelly's attempts to gain understanding through *a posteriori* reasoning, which he labels "apatastrophied and paralogically periparolysed" (*FW,* 612.19–20), abbreviated, shrunken, and paralyzed.

Paddrock instead advocates a dogmatic ("dogmad") reliance on a garbled version of St. Augustine's doctrine of the Trinity, with the same sort of supreme confidence with which Balkelly presented his beliefs.[9] Turning from logic to iconography, Paddrock brushes aside as a pagan delusion the image of the rainbow (fundamentally evanescent in its character)—"Iro's Irismans ruinboon pot" (*FW,* 612.20)—introduced by the druid to illustrate his argument. Paddrock supplants it with another analogy to outline the central mystery of his faith, the Trinity, proposing the shamrock/handkerchief, "a handcaughtscheaf of synthetic shammyrag" (*FW,* 612.24–25), plucked out of the ground (and thus, removed from the cycle of nature, becoming putatively atemporal) and transformed into the sign of the cross as "the sound sense sympol in a weedwayedwold of the firethere the sun in his halo cast" (*FW,* 612.29–30). Unlike the time-bound druid who acquires understanding from the past over a period of time, Paddrock relies on faith, instead of on comprehension, to account for a mystery which operates outside chronological bounds.

As the passage closes, however, the elements within the discourse begin to shift emphasis away from the conflicting aspects of the views of the two men and towards a complementary, polychromatic view of elements. As Robert Boyle has observed, Paddrock derives his Triune invocation—"saving to Balenoarch (he kneeleths), to Great Balenoarch (he kneeleths down) to Greatest Great Balenoarch (he kneeleths down quitesomely)" (*FW,* 612.26–29)—from an inversion of "[a]n Italian word for 'rainbow,' 'arcobaleno.'"[10] In the manifestation of the Trinity through the citation of the same sign that he had just dismissed as Balkelly's "ruinboon," Paddrock's speech moves from denunciation and towards accommodation. The accession of all to this declaration— "[e]ven to uptoputty Bilkilly-Belkelly-Balkally" (*FW,* 612.38)—presents an analogous impulse in the druid. The passage's conclusion, with all bathed in twin reflection of the Pascal candle and the Celtic twilight of the "[g]ood safe firelamp" [God save Ireland] (*FW,* 613.01), points to a redemption of saint and sage without a resolution of their differences or an unequivocal admission of hegemony of one over the other. This finale has broad implications regarding the adjustments one continually makes in reading Joyce's canon.

St. Patrick's method of argument can overcome the logical inconsistencies that disrupt the druid's philosophy because of Paddrock's willingness to embrace the mystery of the Trinity without possessing the ability to understand it. In this way he avoids the obligation of accounting for any of the apparent contradictions often appearing in empirical approaches. This procedure, however, is not without its drawbacks. While freeing him from the possibility of error (at least within the boundaries of the system he has articulated), St. Patrick's approach blunts inquiry, and, in his garbled rendering of the mystery that he embraces, he conveys to others no clear sense of where he places his faith. Although the struggle ends with Paddrock's triumph by popular acclamation, the *deus ex machina* resolution of the conflict remains profoundly unsatisfying for the reader. Neither the theology of the saint nor the epistemology of the sage has produced completely satisfactory systems of perception, for "the unfacts . . . are too imprecisely few to warrant our certitude."

The multiple discourses of the passage incite feelings of dissatisfaction and insufficiency as the natural, initial responses, but they also suggest development beyond the cause-and-effect thinking informing those attitudes. Balkelly and Paddrock both assume the role of readers trying to comprehend, to the limit of their abilities, the world around them, and to articulate texts representative of their impressions. Their approaches illustrate the inability of the human mind to forge a single means of perception perfectly suited to all experiences, yet their efforts also present strategies for interpretation that we may accept, reject, or modify.

The debate between Paddrock and Balkelly offers benchmarks against which we can measure the efficacy of whatever method we adopt. The "nodal system" identified by Hart and by Hayman and the intricate decoration of *The Book of Kells* emphasize expansive, cyclical perception rather than linear, restrictive progression. Nonetheless, each method provides only limited illumination of the worlds encountered by the priest and by the druid and of the work of art that Joyce and the reader create. Like Balkelly, the reader must "set a marge to the merge of unnotions," drawing together what we encounter in the narrative into a conglomerate vision based on what we have previously absorbed. At the same time we must resist the impulse toward leveling lest, like the druid, we end with a monochromatic view. Paddrock, who has been "cured by faith," provides the encouragement necessary to make the leap toward the unknowable. His example makes clear that we must give ourselves over to the mysteries of the work, experiences evoking aesthetic satisfaction while resisting intellectual comprehension. Consequently, one must reach an accommodation with apparently contradictory conceptions, for Joyce encourages the reader to follow the example of King Leary, who "has help his crewn on the burkeley buy but he has holf his crown on the Eurasian Generalissimo" (*FW*, 610.11–13).

Riana O'Dwyer, examining Stefan Czarnowski's book *Le Culte des heros et ses conditions sociales: Saint Patrice, heros national de l'Irlande* (Paris: Alcan, 1919) as a source for *Finnegans Wake*, draws attention to an impulse toward integration in Czarnowski that seems to me to be analogous to the salient rhetorical features of the Paddrock/Balkelly passage. O'Dwyer notes that Czarnowski uses "the example of early Christian Ireland to study phenomena of hero veneration in general, and uses of Saint Patrick as a particular example of how a Christian saint was absorbed into the pre-Christian social framework."[11] Throughout the examination in *Finnegans Wake* of *The Book of Kells* (FW, 119.10–123.10) the narrative voice repeatedly suggests the general impulse of Christian and pre-Christian cultures to merge, "those superciliouslooking crisscrossed Greek ees awkwardlike perched there and here out of date like sick owls hawked back to Athens and the geegees too, jesuistically formed at first but afterwards genuflected aggrily toewards the occident" (*FW,* 120.18–22). These references prepare one for the more direct confrontation of the opposing societies in the Paddrock/Balkelly debate touched on in chapter three of Czarnowski's book. There he asserts that the struggle between St. Patrick and the Druids "ont l'aspect de batailles entre puissances opposées et également divines,"[12] hinting at further blurring of roles. While O'Dwyer's study emphasizes the close relationship between the figure of St. Patrick and that of HCE, broader associations also suggest themselves. In light of the proclivity of ancient Irish culture to "absorbere" the impact of St. Patrick's faith, his victory over the druid becomes less conclusive while the aim of the passage becomes clearer. The reader must initiate this process of amalgamation, not by leveling differences but by embracing them.

Finnegans Wake overtly fosters strategies for reading that have been asserting their efficacy with increasing insistence since Joyce's earliest prose fiction. No height, depth, integrity, or central references exist objectively or independently. All gain definition through paradigms that direct the reader in describable and always disputable ways. One cannot adjudicate between dualisms such as those presented in the confrontation of Paddrock and Balkelly because the narrative wants the reader to reflect on the futile, endless, and thus illuminating and liberating format of any dualism. The loosened languages of the multiple discourse— eclectic, idiosyncratic, dense, bizarre—show words refusing to be tamed or regulated by the semantic patterns that create such oppositions. At the same time these discourses depend heavily upon such semantic designs or restrictions to give them consequence for the reader. Thus the nodal phases of the discourse both assert and withdraw their own authority by giving heights that collapse, surfaces that recede without yielding any essence or depth. The nodes are not as solid, real, or comforting as we readers would like to hope. Rather, as Hayman suggests, they form points of concentration for provisional meanings, and thus, though more assertive in manner, they function in a role analogous to cruxes throughout Joyce's canon.

In presenting these contrasting figures, *Finnegans Wake* does not articulate the hopelessness of perceiving meaning. Instead it reminds us of all Joyce's paradigms that have encouraged us to reconcile extremes of apprehension, not in a synthetic way that erases the uniqueness of each position but in a manner that conjoins where possible and accepts with equanimity what cannot be fit into a system for understanding. It emphasizes the subjectivity of all views. "What can't be coded can be decorded if an ear aye sieze what no eye ere grieved for" (*FW,* 482.34– 36).

At the final formal session of the 1984 James Joyce Symposium in Frankfurt, Hans Walter Gabler, editor of the newly published Garland Press version of *Ulysses*, presented the first copy to Joyce's grandson, Stephen Joyce. Naturally enough the conference participants witnessing the event, including myself, felt suffused in an aura of anticipation and nostalgia (the hallmarks of highly subjective perceptions). Mr. Joyce, however, quickly dissipated these feelings, and replaced them with attitudes of uncomfortable ambivalence, for he began his speech accepting the volumes with remarks asserting that important manuscripts belonging to Paul Leon had not been considered in the preparation of the new edition. He then went on, with some bitterness, to condemn the publication of certain letters written by Joyce to Nora and never intended for public dissemination.[13] Unquestionably the incident in and of itself adds a certain dramatic pungency to recollections of the Frankfurt meeting. More importantly, I think it serves to illustrate, not merely with respect to *Ulysses* but in terms of the entire Joyce canon, the profound influence that the desire for certitude still exerts.

Stephen Joyce's apparent wish that the Garland edition reflect the most accurate version of *Ulysses* possible seems laudable, but events suggest that any copy text for it or for any of his grandfather's other works will always remain relative.[14] In relation to Joyce's other writings, the problems surrounding the publication of any edition of *Ulysses* seem to take on microcosmic qualities, for the printing history of Joyce's work from *Dubliners* onward is filled with instances detailing the difficulties that he faced in giving a physical existence, bound between boards, to the precise images he envisioned to illustrate his ideas. At various stages in the production of *Dubliners* and *A Portrait of the Artist as a Young Man*, publishers, printers, and public officials in England, Ireland, and the United States intervened because of material within the works which these groups considered objectionable. In the formation of *Ulysses*, Joyce confronted even more complex and frustrating impediments to the fabrication and the transmission of the work. Ongoing efforts at censorship, the transcription of portions of the manuscript by a number of different hands, Joyce's extensive revisions continuing through proofreading, and the limited comprehension of the demotic English of his work by the French foreman of the publishing house bringing out the work further enlarged the disparity between the version conceived by Joyce and the version in the printed form in the 1922 edition produced by Shakespeare and Company. All this certainly greatly reinforced Joyce's sense of the mutability of his words.

By the time he had completed work on *Ulysses*, I believe that Joyce had come to accept these production variegations as an inevitable consequence of the process of giving a text a physical form, and this perception in turn must have influenced the shape he gave to his final work. My contention from the beginning of this study has been that the same sort of resignation should govern our efforts to derive a text from the physical form of Joyce's work. Just as editions of *Dubliners, Portrait, Ulysses,* and *Finnegans Wake* stand at variance to one another, so also do the texts created from successive readings of each. The anarchy that we feel threatening our experience with a work when a perfect copy text does not exist parallels that which seems to surround alternative readings. Through his writing Joyce came to accept the anarchy of printing and to embrace the anarchy of reading, seeking only to enforce a paradigm within which variations of the work exist. His example urges us in our reading to discover as precisely as possible the limits of that paradigm and within those limits to exercise the greatest degree of imaginative freedom.

Appendixes

A. FREE INDIRECT DISCOURSE

Charles Bally first identified the process of free indirect discourse in a seminal study written in 1912,[1] and since then scholars have traced its application in the works of a range of writers of prose fiction extending back through the eighteenth century and variously designated by critics as *erlebte Rede*, *style indirect libre*, free indirect style, or free indirect discourse. Basically, the method can be defined as a device for integrating linguistic traits associated with the speech and the thinking of specific characters into segments of the narrative. It provides the midpoint between the unmediated forms of direct discourse and stream of consciousness at one extreme and the narrator-dominated indirect discourse at the other.[2]

Brian McHale, in an article that presents an important survey of the major directions of free indirect discourse criticism, has laid down broad guidelines for determining when a work is employing free indirect discourse.[3] I have paraphrased them below. To highlight the various functions of free indirect discourse I have added illustrative selections from *A Portrait of the Artist as a Young Man*, the work by Joyce containing the most overt and sustained examples of the technique.

Grammar—the application of strict rules of usage that identify free indirect discourse. Most of these rules aim at recognizing elliptical variants of direct discourse imbedded in the narrative.

> [Stephen] beat his breast with his fist humbly, secretly under cover of the wooden armrest. He would be at one with the others and with God. He would love his neighbour. He would love God Who had made and loved him. He would kneel and pray with others and be happy. God would look down on him and on them and would love them all. (143)

Intonation—the appearance of words within the narrative associated with a particular character.

> Uncle Charles smoked such a black twist that at last his nephew suggested to him to enjoy his morning smoke in a little outhouse at the end of the garden. (60)

215

Context—verbs of speech or thought directing the reader's attention to a particular character.

> Stuff it into you, his belly counselled him. (102)

Idiom or register—lexical or orthographic materials which are mimetic of a character's supposed utterance.

> Going home for the holidays! That would be lovely: the fellows had told him. Getting up on the cars in the early wintry morning outside the door of the castle. The cars were rolling on the gravel. Cheers for the rector!
>
> Hurray! Hurray! Hurray! (20)

B. A CHRONOLOGY OF THE INITIAL COMPOSITION AND REVISION OF THE STORIES OF *DUBLINERS* (ARRANGED IN ORDER OF COMPOSITION)

1. "The Sisters"—Composed July 1904 (*JJ*, 163–64); revised July 1906 (*Letters*, II.143)

2. "Eveline"—Composed c. August 1904 (*JJ*, 164); revised several times between date of composition and the appearance of the 1910 Maunsel page proofs, the precise dates of revisions are not available

3. "After the Race"—Composed October 1904 (*JJA*, IV.xxv); plans revisions August 1906 (*Letters*, II.151)

4. "Clay"—Composed under the title "Xmas Eve," October–November 1904 (*Letters*, II.67 and 69); revised as "Hallow Eve" January 1905 (*Letters*, II.77 and *JJ*, 189–90); rewritten as "Clay" September 1905 (*Letters*, II.109); revised November 1906 (*Letters*, II.186)

5. "The Boarding House"—Composed July 1905 (*Letters*, II.92 and 98, and *JJ*, 207); possibly revised May 1906 (*Letters*, I.61); revised again sometime before a version appeared in the late Maunsel page proofs of 1912

6. "Counterparts"—Composed July 1905 (*Letters*, II.98 and *JJ*, 207); revised July 1906 (*Letters*, II.144)

7. "A Painful Case"—Composed May 1905 (*JJ*, 207); revised August 1906 (*Letters*, II.151 and 153); revised October 1906 (*Letters*, II.182); revised August 1912 (*Letters*, II.314–15)

8. "Ivy Day in the Committee Room"—Composed by 1 September 1905 (*Letters*, II.105 and *JJ*, 207); revised July 1906 (*Letters*, II.144)

9. "An Encounter"—Composed September 1905 (*Letters*, II.108 and *JJ*, 207)

10. "A Mother"—Composed September 1905 (*Letters*, II.113 and *JJ*, 207)

11. "Araby"—Composed October 1905 (*Letters*, II.123 and *JJ*, 207)

12. "Grace"—Composed October 1905 (*Letters*, II.124 and *JJ*, 207); revised July 1906 (*Letters*, II.144); revised November 1906 (*Letters*, II.193)

13. "Two Gallants"—Composed January 1906 (*Letters*, II.129); revised July 1906 (*Letters*, II.144)

14. "A Little Cloud"—Composed April 1906 (*Letters*, I.61)

15. "The Dead"—Composed September 1907 (*JJ*, 264)

Peregrinations of the Manuscript

A. October 1905 proposed submission to Heinemann (*Letters*, II.97, 105, and 108–9)

B. 28 November 1905 sent ms. to Grant Richards (*Letters*, II.128 and 129)

C. 23 June 1906 Joyce acknowledges receipt of ms. from Grant Richards (*Letters*, I.63)

D. 9 July 1906 Joyce returns ms. to Grant Richards (*Letters*, II.143)

E. 26 October 1906 Grant Richards returns ms. to Joyce (*Letters*, II.185n)

F. 10 December 1906 sent ms. to John Long (*Letters*, II.203)

G. 28 February 1907 John Long returns the ms. (*Letters*, II.218–19)

H. November 1907–July 1908 Joyce sends ms. to various publishers (*JJ*, 267)

I. 19 August 1909 Joyce signs a contract with Maunsel & Co. to bring out *Dubliners* (*JJ*, 282)

J. 11 September 1912 after a breakdown in negotiations the printer for Maunsel & Co. destroys the sheets of *Dubliners* (*JJ*, 335)

K. 15 June 1914 Grant Richards publishes *Dubliners*

C. THE HEADINGS OF AEOLUS

The headings of the Aeolus chapter appear as follows:

IN THE HEART OF THE HIBERNIAN
METROPOLIS

THE WEARER OF THE CROWN

GENTLEMEN OF THE PRESS

WILLIAM BRAYDEN, ESQUIRE, OF OAKLANDS,
SANDYMOUNT

THE CROZIER AND THE PEN

WITH UNFEIGNED REGRET IT IS WE
ANNOUNCE THE DISSOLUTION OF A MOST
RESPECTED DUBLIN BURGESS

HOW A GREAT DAILY ORGAN IS TURNED OUT

WE SEE THE CANVASSER AT WORK

HOUSE OF KEY(E)S

ORTHOGRAPHICAL

NOTED CHURCHMAN AN OCCASIONAL
CONTRIBUTOR

A DAYFATHER

AND IT WAS THE FEAST OF PASSOVER

ONLY ONCE MORE THAT SOAP

ERIN, GREEN GEM OF THE SILVER SEA

SHORT BUT TO THE POINT

SAD

HIS NATIVE DORIC

WHAT WETHERUP SAID

MEMORABLE BATTLES RECALLED

O, HARP EOLIAN

SPOT THE WINNER

A COLLISION ENSUES

EXIT BLOOM

A STREET CORTEGE

THE CALUMET OF PEACE

THE GRANDEUR THAT WAS ROME

???

SHINDY IN WELLKNOWN RESTAURANT

LOST CAUSES
NOBLE MARQUESS MENTIONED

KYRIE ELEISON!

LENEHAN'S LIMERICK

OMNIUM GATHERUM

"YOU CAN DO IT!"

THE GREAT GALLAHER

A DISTANT VOICE

CLEVER, VERY

RHYMES AND REASONS

SUFFICIENT FOR THE DAY . . .

LINKS WITH BYGONE DAYS OF YORE

ITALIA, MAGISTRA ARTIUM

A POLISHED PERIOD

A MAN OF HIGH MORALE

IMPROMPTU

FROM THE FATHERS

OMINOUS—FOR HIM!

LET US HOPE

DEAR DIRTY DUBLIN

LIFE ON THE RAW

RETURN OF BLOOM

INTERVIEW WITH THE EDITOR

K.M.A.

K.M.R.I.A.

RAISING THE WIND

SOME COLUMN!—THAT'S WHAT WADDLER
ONE SAID

THOSE SLIGHTLY RAMBUNCTIOUS FEMALES

DAMES DONATE DUBLIN'S CITS
SPEEDPILLS VELOCITOUS AEROLITHS, BELIEF

SOPHIST WALLOPS HAUGHTY HELEN SQUARE
ON PROBOSCIS. SPARTANS GNASH MOLARS.
ITHACANS VOW PEN IS CHAMP.

HELLO THERE, CENTRAL!

WHAT?—AND LIKEWISE—WHERE?

VIRGILIAN, SAYS PEDAGOGUE. SOPHOMORE
PLUMPS FOR OLD MAN MOSES.

HORATIO IS CYNOSURE THIS FAIR JUNE DAY

DIMINISHED DIGITS PROVE TOO TITILLATING
FOR FRISKY FRUMPS. ANNE WIMBLES, FLO
WANGLES—YET CAN YOU BLAME THEM?

For detailed discussions of the insertion of the headings see Harry Levin's "Introduction" to the holograph facsimile of the *Ulysses* manuscript, A. Walton Litz's *The Art of James Joyce*, and Michael Groden's Ulysses *in Progress*.[1]

Notes

CHAPTER ONE

1. For a detailed discussion of Joyce's anti-Newtonian strategies, especially in their application in *Ulysses*, see Patrick A. McCarthy's "*Ulysses* and the Printed Page." In *Joyce's* Ulysses: *The Larger Perspective*, ed. Robert D. Newman and Weldon Thornton (Newark: University of Delaware Press, 1987), pp. 59–73.

2. See especially Iser's *The Implied Reader: Patterns of Communication in Prose Fiction from Bunyan to Beckett* (Baltimore and London: The Johns Hopkins University Press, 1974) and *The Act of Reading: A Theory of Aesthetic Response* (Baltimore and London: The Johns Hopkins University Press, 1978).

3. Neither the contemporary repertoire defined by Iser nor the hybrid, ideal reader of Stanley Fish can cope with the full range of possibilities inherent in an artistically pleasing world. Iser speaks of the repertoire of a work: the familiar literary territory of social and cultural norms and the literary tradition from which it emerges. He sees the repertoire conditioning both the process of composition and our response, but remains rather general in his assessment of how this occurs. Fish seems even more vague in his description of the ideal reader, and he cannot relinquish the hope of achieving a definitive reading. The "horizon of expectations" of Hans Robert Jauss comes closer to the approach that I advocate, but his sense of paradigm (a term that I will apply with a different emphasis) is too static. Overall, I feel that these critics are hampered by a commitment to an either/or dichotomy that privileges the creative efforts of the reader.

See Iser, *The Act of Reading*, pp. 53–85. Stanley Fish, *Is There a Text in This Class? The Authority of Interpretive Communities* (Cambridge: Harvard University Press, 1980). Hans Robert Jauss, *Toward an Aesthetic of Reception*, trans. Timothy Bahti (Minneapolis: University of Minnesota Press, 1982). Norman Holland's *5 Readers in Reading* (New Haven: Yale University Press, 1975) develops along similar theoretical lines.

4. See, for example, Hirsch's *Validity in Interpretation* (New Haven: Yale University Press, 1967).

5. Iser, *The Act of Reading*, p. 27.

6. In developing this approach I have drawn eclectically on theories ad-

vanced by Roland Barthes, Mikhail Bakhtin, and Kenneth Burke, and I have reacted to the methods of Jacques Derrida, Gérard Genette, and a number of others.

7. Cf. James S. Atherton's *The Books at the Wake: A Study of Literary Allusions in James Joyce's* Finnegans Wake (Carbondale and Edwardsville: Southern Illinois University Press, 1974). Since the publication of Atherton's masterly study, scholars have accepted the concept that neither pedestrian style nor overly familiar subject matter necessarily disadvantaged a work in Joyce's eyes.

8. See especially his *The Anxiety of Influence: A Theory of Poetry* (New York: Oxford University Press, 1973).

9. Hugh Kenner offered one of the earliest and most forceful justifications of *Exiles*. Kenner centers his analysis on an examination of Joyce's anxiety of influence—the struggle against Ibsen and the movement towards Modernism—but his views remain an important introduction to the play. See *Dublin's Joyce* (Boston: Beacon Press, 1962), pp. 69–94.

CHAPTER TWO

1. These are outlined in *Metahistory: The Historical Imagination in Nineteenth-Century Europe* (Baltimore: The Johns Hopkins University Press, 1973); and in his essays collected in *Tropics of Discourse: Essays in Cultural Criticism* (Baltimore: The Johns Hopkins University Press, 1978). White's work summarizes the salient features of the normative/relativist debate.

2. This material is collected in *The James Joyce Archive*, ed. Michael Groden (New York & London: Garland Publishing, Inc., 1978), cited in this study as *JJA*; and in *The Letters of James Joyce*, vol. I, ed. Stuart Gilbert (New York: Viking Press, 1957); reissued with corrections 1966. Vols. II and III ed. Richard Ellmann (New York: Viking Press, 1966), cited in this study as *Letters*.

3. Marvin Magalaner's *Time of Apprenticeship: The Fiction of Young James Joyce* (London, New York, Toronto: Abelard-Schuman, 1959), pp. 72–96 and in Marvin Magalaner's and Richard M. Kain's *Joyce: The Man, the Work, the Reputation* (New York: Collier Books, 1962), pp. 82–87. Robert Scholes's "Some Observations on the Text of *Dubliners*: 'The Dead,'" *Studies in Bibliography* 15 (1962): 191–206 and his "Further Observations on the Text of *Dubliners*," *Studies in Bibliography* 17 (1964): 107–22. Florence Walzl's " 'The Sisters': A Development," *James Joyce Quarterly* 10 (Summer 1973): 375–421.

4. For a summary of the composition of *Stephen Hero* see Hans Walter Gabler's "The Seven Lost Years of *A Portrait of the Artist as a Young Man*." In *Approaches to Joyce's Portrait: Ten Essays*, ed. Thomas F. Staley and Bernard Benstock (Pittsburgh: University of Pittsburgh Press, 1976), pp. 25–60.

5. "Further Observations on the Text of *Dubliners*," p. 11. In *Joyce's Voices* (Berkeley, Los Angeles, London: University of California Press, 1978), pp. 15–16, Hugh Kenner mentions this same technique, generally identified as free indirect discourse, when referring to the opening pages of "The Dead," labeling

it the Uncle Charles Principle. As noted in appendix A, the process itself is even more pervasive and variegated than one might assume from Kenner's remarks, although it comes to the foreground in *Portrait*. I will discuss this technique in greater detail in my chapter dealing with the narrative form of *Portrait*.

6. I have discussed the impact of books in his library on Joyce's work in *Inverted Volumes Improperly Arranged: James Joyce and His Trieste Library* (Ann Arbor: UMI Research Press, 1983).

7. Mary T. Reynolds's "Torn by Conflicting Doubts: Joyce and Renan," *Renascence* 35 (Winter 1983): 98 and 109–12.

8. *Denmark's Best Stories: An Introduction to Danish Fiction*, ed. Hanna Astrup Larsen (New York: W. W. Norton and Company, Inc., 1928), p. 120.

9. Ivan Turgenev, *A Lear of the Steppes*, trans. Constance Garnett (London: William Heinemann; New York: The Macmillan Company, 1906), p. 25.

10. Mikhail Lermontov, *A Hero of Our Time*, trans. Philip Longworth (London: New English Library, 1962), pp. 68–69.

11. Quoted in Marvin Magalaner's *Time of Apprenticeship: The Fiction of Young James Joyce* (London: Abelard-Schuman, 1959), p. 19.

12. Mikhail Bakhtin, *Problems of Dostoevsky's Poetics*, trans. R. W. Rostel (Ann Arbor: Ardis, 1973).

13. A clear record of Richards's account of the affair has been collected by Robert Scholes in his "Grant Richards to James Joyce," *Studies in Bibliography* 16 (1963): 145. This essay publishes all available letters from Richards to Joyce on the matter. For Joyce's summary of the affair, see *Letters*, II.176–78 and 178–80.

14. For Scholes's comments on the change, see "Further Observations on the Text of *Dubliners*," pp. 117–18.

15. Anne S. Highham has offered an illuminating examination of similar linguistic constructions that appear in Joyce's "Araby" in her essay "An Aspect of Style in 'Araby'," *Language and Style* 15 (Winter 1982): 15–22.

16. For details of how Joyce adapted the style of Ibsen to an early dramatic work of his own see Richard Ellmann's biography, *James Joyce*, new and revised edition (Oxford: Oxford University Press, 1982), pp. 78–80.

17. A number of scholarly articles have been written debating claims that de Maupassant influenced Joyce. In *Joyce: The Man, the Work, the Reputation*, pp. 70–71, Magalaner and Kain summarize the arguments and conclude that Joyce derived little from de Maupassant's writing. This study, however, appeared before the publication of the letters in which Joyce refers pointedly to de Maupassant, and it relies on a very narrow concept of influence.

For a description of the books by de Maupassant that Joyce owned see my *Annotated Catalogue of the James Joyce's Trieste Library* (Austin: The Humanities Research Center, The University of Texas, 1986). Additional passages from the letters show a sustained, if somewhat ambivalent, interest in de Maupassant. "I've read a few volumes of G de M lately for amusement and was amused by the same. Now I am on to Anatole France again. But if I want real esthetic satisfaction I must wait till the MS of *Dubliners* returns to me once more to roost" (*Letters*, II.210).

18. Guy de Maupassant, *The Odd Number: Thirteen Tales*, trans. Jonathan Sturges and with an introduction by Henry James (New York and London: Harper & Brothers Publishers, 1889), p. xv.

19. This same style, with its attention to detail using the briefest of descriptions to characterize individuals, may have influenced the changes that Joyce introduced into "Ivy Day in the Committee Room." Like "Counterparts," the story contained passages that Grant Richards found objectionable, and, again like "Counterparts," Joyce probably analyzed carefully the precise significance of its phrases before he revised it in June or July of 1906 (*Letters*, II.144). In greater proportion than any other story in *Dubliners*, dialogue advances the action of "Ivy Day in the Committee Room." Consequently, Joyce's changes focus on defining more precisely the characterization of individuals by underscoring through their language the different personalities of each. Joyce's changes comply with Grand Richards's request to delete the word "bloody" at several points, but they also include several more subtle enhancements of characters. The dialogue of Jack, the caretaker, for example, becomes more colloquial, using phrases like "a sup taken." Hynes, the Parnellite, refers to "King Eddie" rather than "King Edward." And throughout, Mr. Henchy's language takes on a more formal, less idiomatic tone, befitting his position in the story.

20. See my *Annotated Catalogue*, entries 544–51. The copy of *Dorian Gray* that survives in the library, however, has a copyright date of 1908, and so it is not the same edition referred to by Joyce in the August 1906 letter.

21. Oscar Wilde, *The Picture of Dorian Gray*, ed. Isobel Murray (London, New York, Toronto, Melbourne: Oxford University Press, 1981), pp. 149–52. All subsequent citations are from this edition.

CHAPTER THREE

1. Hans Walter Gabler has compiled a detailed discussion of the composition of *Stephen Hero*. In addition to "The Seven Lost Years of *A Portrait of the Artist as a Young Man*," pp. 25–60, see his essays "Towards a Critical Text of James Joyce's *A Portrait of the Artist as a Young Man*," *Studies in Bibliography* 27 (1974): 1–53; and "The Christmas Dinner Scene, Parnell's Death and the Genesis of *A Portrait of the Artist as a Young Man*," *James Joyce Quarterly* 13 (Fall): 27–38. For additional information see *The Workshop of Daedalus*, ed. Robert Scholes and Richard M. Kain (Evanston: Northwestern University Press, 1965).

2. Richard Ellmann, *James Joyce*, p. 147.

3. Gabler, "The Seven Lost Years," pp. 54–55. See also *Letters*, II.132.

4. Gabler, "The Seven Lost Years," pp. 55–56.

5. James J. Sosnowski has surveyed critical opinions regarding the ironic elements of *Portrait* in his essay "Reading Acts and Reading Warrants: Some Implications for Readers Responding to Joyce's Portrait of Stephen," *James Joyce*

Quarterly 16 (Fall 1978/Winter 1979): 43–63, but he does not take up the question of irony in *Stephen Hero*.

6. Roland Barthes, *S/Z*, trans. Richard Miller and with a preface by Richard Howard (New York: Hill and Wang, 1974), p. 105.

7. One of the earliest and certainly one of the most lucid descriptions of this trait appears in Hugh Kenner's *Dublin's Joyce*, pp. 120–21.

CHAPTER FOUR

1. Dorrit Cohn, in "Narrated Monologue: Definition of a Fictional Style," *Comparative Literature* 18 (Spring 1966), p. 107, sees evidence of free indirect discourse as early as the works of Jane Austen and goes on to trace its use in nineteenth-century fiction. See also Birthe Tandrup's "A Trap of Misreading: Free Indirect Discourse and the Critique of the Gothic in *Northanger Abbey*," in *The Romantic Heritage: A Collection of Critical Essays*, ed. Karsten Engelberg (Copenhagen: Publications of the Department of English, University of Copenhagen, 1983), pp. 81–91.

2. A full description of the books in Joyce's personal library, 1904–1920, including a discussion of the dates of acquisition of a number of the titles, appears in my *Annotated Catalogue*. A slightly different list appears in Richard Ellmann's *The Consciousness of Joyce* (New York: Oxford University Press, 1977), pp. 97–134.

3. Although *A Woman of Thirty* has a 1910 copyright date, it bears an inscription by Joyce to his wife dated 1916. See my *Annotated Catalogue*, entries 25–37, for a full bibliographic description of each volume.

4. Ellmann, *James Joyce*, p. 354n.

5. Ellmann, *James Joyce*, p. 354.

6. Roland Barthes, *S/Z*, p. 41. Roy Pascal has also commented on elements of free indirect discourse present in Balzac, although he is careful to point out that the efforts of Balzac remain limited in comparison to those of Flaubert. Roy Pascal, *The Dual Voice: Free Indirect Speech and Its Functioning in the Nineteenth-Century European Novel* (Manchester: Manchester University Press; Totowa, New Jersey: Rowmann and Littlefield, 1977), p. 67.

7. Honoré de Balzac, *The Country Doctor*, trans. Ellen Marriage and with a preface by George Saintsbury (London and New York: Macmillan and Co., 1896), p. 9. Whenever I have quoted from books owned by Joyce, I have used the same edition as the one that he owned.

8. Honoré de Balzac, *La Femme de trente ans* (Paris: Calmann-Lévy. Éditeurs, [1891]), p. 9.

9. For a full discussion of Joyce's methods of marking his books, see the introduction to my *Annotated Catalogue*, pp. 12–17.

10. Charles Jones, "Varieties of Speech Presentation in Conrad's *The Secret Agent*," *Lingua* 20 (1968): 165. See also George L. Dillon and Frederick Kirch-

hoff's "On the Form and Function of Free Indirect Style," *PTL* 1 (October 1976): 437.

11. Joseph Conrad, *The Secret Agent: A Simple Tale* (Leipzig: Bernhard Tauchnitz, 1907), p. 61.

12. Joseph Conrad, *A Set of Six* (Leipzig: Bernhard Tauchnitz, 1908), p. 36.

13. Joseph Conrad, *Tales of Unrest* (Leipzig: Bernhard Tauchnitz, 1898), pp. 160–61.

14. Emile Zola, *Nana*, II (Paris: Les Editions Parisiennes, n.d.), p. 42.

15. Emile Zola, *Nana*, II.106.

16. Emile Zola, *Nana*, II.116.

17. Stanislaus Joyce, *My Brother's Keeper*, ed. Richard Ellmann (New York: The Viking Press, 1958), p. 79.

18. Three of the books—*The Adventures of Oliver Twist, Barnaby Rudge*, and *David Copperfield*—belong to a series issued by Thomas Nelson and Sons between 1911 and 1916 commemorating the Dickens centenary. Another, *The Life and Adventures of Nicholas Nickleby*, was brought out in 1910 or 1911 by Chapman and Hall/Charles Scribner's Sons as part of another centenary edition of Dickens's works. The fifth Dickens book in the library, *Bleak House*, bears a copyright date of 1853. Prices marked in Austrian kronens inside the covers of *Barnaby Rudge* and of *David Copperfield* confirm that these books were acquired by Joyce in Trieste, and they suggest that he may have purchased the others there as well. For full details, see my *Annotated Catalogue*, entries 135–39.

19. James Joyce, *James Joyce in Padua*, ed. & trans. Louis Berrone (New York: Random House, 1977), pp. 34–35.

20. *James Joyce in Padua*, p. 37.

21. *James Joyce in Padua*, pp. 73–74.

22. Pascal, *The Dual Voice*, p. 68. Randolph Quirk in his *Charles Dickens and Appropriate Language* (Durham: University of Durham, 1959), pp. 9–10 and 23, also points out instances of free indirect discourse in *David Copperfield* and in other works by Dickens.

23. Pascal, *The Dual Voice*, p. 69.

24. W. J. M. Bronzwaer, *Tense in the Novel: An Investigation of Some Potentialities of Linguistic Criticism* (Groningen, The Netherlands: Wolters-Noordhoff Publishing, 1970), p. 57.

25. Charles Dickens, *David Copperfield* (London: Thomas Nelson and Sons, [1911–1916]), p. 66.

26. C. P. Curran, *James Joyce Remembered* (New York and London: Oxford University Press, 1968), p. 29.

27. For more detailed information, see my *Annotated Catalogue*, entries 168–70.

28. R. Butler, for one, has noted the parallels existing in the stylistic techniques of Flaubert and of Zola, but he has also analyzed their different applications of free indirect discourse. Butler's comments on the role of the narrator in the use of free indirect discourse in *Madame Bovary* point to strong analogues

between the writing of Flaubert and of Joyce. See his "Flaubert's Exploitation of the 'Style Indirect Libre': Ambiguities and Perspectives in *Madame Bovary,*" *Modern Language* 62 (December 1981): 190–96.

Several other critics have already commented on general parallels between the works of these two men and have touched on stylistic similarities. See, for example, Richard K. Cross's *Flaubert and Joyce: The Rite of Fiction* (Princeton: Princeton University Press, 1971); Hugh Kenner's *The Stoic Comedians: Flaubert, Joyce, and Beckett* (Berkeley, Los Angeles, London: University of California Press, 1974); and David Hayman's "*A Portrait of the Artist as a Young Man* and *L'Education Sentimentale*: The Structural Affinities," *Orbis Litteratum* 19 (1964): 161–75.

29. A full explication of the allusion appears in the Viking Critical Edition of *Portrait*, p. 537.

30. Pascal, *The Dual Voice*, p. 98. See also Cohn's "Narrated Monologue," p. 107, and Harry Levin's *The Gates of Horn: A Study of Five French Realists* (New York: Oxford University Press, 1963), p. 254.

31. Henry J. Weinberg, "Irony and 'Style Indirect Libre' in *Madame Bovary,*" *Canadian Review of Comparative Literature* 8 (Winter 1981): 1.

32. Gustave Flaubert, *Madame Bovary,* trans. Henry Blanchamp (London: Greening & Co; New York: Brentano's, [1905]), p. 38.

CHAPTER FIVE

1. Bernard Benstock touches on this inclination in his essay "Text, Sub-Text, Non-Text: Literary and Narrational In/Validities," *James Joyce Quarterly* 22 (Summer 1985): 355–65.

2. Fritz Senn sees even more ambiguity in the epigraph, deconstructing (although he does not use that word himself) the entire passage in his essay "The Challenge: '*ignotas animum*' (An Old-Fashioned Close Guessing at a Borrowed Structure)," *James Joyce Quarterly* 16 (Fall 1978/Winter 1979): 123–34.

3. Iser, *The Act of Reading*.

4. Gerard Genette, *Narrative Discourse: An Essay in Method*, trans. Jane E. Lewin (Ithaca, New York: Cornell University Press, 1980), pp. 189–99.

5. In the epiphany that forms the original version of this incident, reprinted in the Viking Critical Edition of *Portrait* on p. 268, the rhyme is clearly assigned to the young James Joyce. The shift from the clarity of the source in the epiphany to the ambiguity of reference in the discourse of *Portrait* reflects synecdochically the shift in rhetorical strategy over the composition of the entire novel.

6. For a summary of the basic assumptions of this approach, see K. E. Robinson's "The Stream of Consciousness Technique and the Structure of Joyce's *Portrait*," *James Joyce Quarterly* 9 (Fall 1971): 63–84.

7. Erwin R. Steinberg, "Author! Author!" *James Joyce Quarterly* 22 (Summer 1985): 422.

8. David Hayman, Ulysses: *The Mechanics of Meaning* (Englewood Cliffs, N.J.: Prentice-Hall, 1970), pp. 78–88.

9. Some critics have questioned whether irony can be used in conjunction with free indirect discourse. George L. Dillon and Frederick Kirchhoff elaborate on register in their "On the Form and Function of Free Indirect Style," *PTL* 1 (October 1976): 431–40. For a summary of their arguments and a rebuttal, see Henry H. Weinberg, "Irony and 'Style Indirect Libre' in *Madame Bovary.*"

10. Hugh Kenner, *Joyce's Voices*, p. 18.

11. John Paul Riquelme, *Teller and Tale in Joyce's Fiction: Oscillating Perspectives* (Baltimore and London: The Johns Hopkins University Press, 1983), p. 51.

12. Wayne C. Booth, *The Rhetoric of Fiction*, second edition (Chicago & London: The University of Chicago Press, 1983), p. 138.

13. Wayne C. Booth, *The Rhetoric of Fiction*, pp. 335–36. For a full response to Booth, see James Naremore's "Style as Meaning in *A Portrait of the Artist*," *James Joyce Quarterly* 4 (Summer 1967): 331–42. For a discussion of Booth's terms, see Seymour Chatman's "The Structure of Narrative Transmission" in *Style and Structure in Literature: Essays in the New Stylistics*, ed. Roger Fowler (Ithaca, N.Y.: Cornell University Press, 1975), pp. 213–57. Common habits of reading and of interpretation make the question of locating precisely the source or sources directing the narrative more than a linguistic quibble. Booth's *The Rhetoric of Fiction*, probably more than any other work of criticism, has drawn attention to the primacy of narrative influence in shaping a reader's response to the text. For Booth the position of the narrator serves as a guide for evaluating the development of the action, and the credibility of the narrator directs the reader towards a straightforward or an ironic interpretation of the work. The key to such an approach lies in the reader's ability to discern the way the author wishes the narrator to be perceived. Booth defines the situation from a binary perspective: "I have called a narrator *reliable* when he speaks for or acts in accordance with the norms of the work (which is to say, the implied author's norms), *unreliable* when he does not" (Booth's emphasis, pp. 158–59). The speedy assimilation of these terms into the critical lexicon testifies to their usefulness, but the assumptions upon which they rest, as Booth himself has noted (p. 409), have subsequently been modified as a result of the work of critics like Mikhail Bakhtin.

14. Roland Barthes, *Image, Music, Text*, essays selected and translated by Stephen Heath (New York: Hill and Wang, 1977), pp. 143 and 147.

15. For a full discussion of this matter, see Thrane's "Joyce's Sermon on Hell," *A James Joyce Miscellany*, third series, ed. Marvin Magalaner (Carbondale: Southern Illinois University Press, 1962), pp. 33–78.

16. Mikhail M. Bakhtin, *The Dialogic Imagination: Four Essays*, ed. Michael Holquist, trans. Caryl Emerson and Michael Holquist (Austin: University of Texas Press, 1981), pp. 262–63. Cf. also pp. 45–49 and 312–31. The "Glossary," p. 428, expands this concept: "Heteroglossia is as close a conceptualization as is possible of that locus where centripetal and centrifugal forces collide; as such, it is that which a systematic linguistics must always suppress."

17. Bakhtin, *The Dialogic Imagination*, p. 324.

18. Cf. "The Death of the Author" in Barthes's *Image, Music, Text*, pp. 142–48, and Michel Foucault's "What Is an Author" in *Textual Strategies: Perspectives in Post-Structuralist Criticism*, ed. Joseph V. Harari (Ithaca, New York: Cornell University Press, 1979), pp. 141–60.

19. In many ways Burke's ideas are at the center of what I am suggesting here. See especially his *A Grammar of Motives* (Berkeley and Los Angeles: University of California Press, 1969).

20. Michael McCanles's *Dialectical Criticism and Renaissance Literature* (Berkeley, Los Angeles, London: University of California Press, 1975), pp. 214–15. For examples, see Marshall Brown's " 'Errours Endlesse Traine': On Turning Points and the Dialectical Imagination," *PMLA* 99 (January 1984): 9–25; and Michael McCanles and Marshall Brown, "Forum," *PMLA* 99 (October 1984): 996–98.

21. Mikhail Bakhtin, *Problems of Dostoevsky's Poetics*, p. 40.

CHAPTER SIX

1. Frank Budgen, *James Joyce and the Making of* Ulysses (Bloomington: Indiana University Press, 1960), p. 105.

2. The following summary is derived from material drawn out of John MacNicholas's textual study. For a full chronology of the process of composition and publication see MacNicholas's *James Joyce's* Exiles: *A Textual Companion* (New York and London: Garland Publishing, Inc., 1979), pp. 27–49.

3. Based on physical differences in various sheets making up the fair copy version of the work, MacNicholas has convincingly argued that Joyce revised significant portions of the first act and one page of the second at least once between Joyce's inscription of the holograph (January–March 1915) and the appearance of the published work on 25 May 1918. *James Joyce's* Exiles, pp. 40–41. For additional comments on manuscripts related to *Exiles*, see Robert M. Adams's "The Manuscript of James Joyce's Play," *Yale University Library Gazette* 39 (July 1964): 30–41; his "Light on Joyce's *Exiles*? A New MS, a Curious Analogue, and Some Speculations," *Studies in Bibliography* 17 (1964): 83–105; and A. Walton Litz's introduction to the *Exiles* volume of the *James Joyce Archive*, ed. Michael Groden (New York & London: Garland Publishing, Inc., 1978).

4. MacNicholas, *James Joyce's* Exiles, pp. 41–42.

5. MacNicholas takes a different view. He argues that Joyce's excisions aimed at reducing the political undertone of the play, but he can offer only five relatively isolated examples to support his argument. *James Joyce's* Exiles, pp. 38–40.

6. Hugh Kenner, in *Dublin's Joyce*, pp. 72–94, most accurately details Joyce's struggle both to incorporate and to overcome the influence of Ibsen on *Exiles*. For additional information see Ellmann's *James Joyce*, pp. 73–77, "Ibsen's New Drama," *CW*, pp. 47–67, and B. J. Tysdahl's *Joyce and Ibsen: A Study in Literary Influence* (Oslo: Norwegian Universities Press; New York: Humanities Press, 1968).

7. For a more specific speculation on the composition dates of the fragments, see MacNicholas's *James Joyce's* Exiles, p. 32.

8. In *The Penetration of Exiles* (Colchester: A Wake Newslitter Press, 1984) Simon Evans has offered an idiosyncratic but provocative analysis of the metaphor of the wound expressed in this passage, especially in relating it to *Finnegans Wake*. While I do not subscribe to Evans's interpretation, his views offer a lucid example of range of interpretations possible within the fluctuating perspectives of the play.

9. This, of course, is similar to the polyvocality identified by Bakhtin in *The Problem of Dostoevsky's Poetics* and in his *The Dialogic Imagination*.

10. In his introduction to the Random House edition of the play, Patrick Colum, without elaborating upon their implications, makes similar observations regarding Bertha's nature (*E*, pp. 9–10).

11. In my opinion, one of the most incisive studies is Michael Mason's "Why Is Leopold Bloom a Cuckold?" *ELH* 44 (Spring 1977): 171–88. Mason's essay examines in detail the development of the topic of cuckolding from *Exiles* to *Ulysses*. Frank Budgen's remarks in "Further Recollections of James Joyce," *James Joyce and the Making of* Ulysses (Bloomington: Indiana University Press, 1960), pp. 314–15, give an indication of Joyce's view of the relation between the two works.

12. I am grateful to Phillip Herring for pointing out the correspondences between entries in Joyce's notes for *Exiles* and those that appear in his notes for *Ulysses*. For full details of the notes for *Ulysses*, see his *Joyce's* Ulysses *Notesheets in the British Museum* (Charlottesville: The University Press of Virginia, 1972).

13. In "Why Is Leopold Bloom a Cuckold" Mason sees the central issue in both *Exiles* and *Ulysses* as "the tolerance of acts against oneself" (p. 185). While this and the willingness to relinquish control are quite similar, the latter gives a greater breadth to one's view of the novel, and I feel that it should be given particular emphasis.

CHAPTER SEVEN

1. Michael Mason, in his "Why Is Leopold Bloom a Cuckold," p. 177, explains this passage as "an idiosyncratic mention of the first full edition of *Madame Bovary*." John MacNicholas, in *James Joyce's* Exiles, pp. 203–4, offers summaries of the plots of Marco Praga's *La Crisi* and of Giuseppe Giacosa's *Tristi Amori*.

2. The figure of Robert Hand offers a clear example of Joyce's efforts to inculcate a feeling of ambivalence. The portrayal of Hand mixes depictions of his forceful ability with instances making him out to be a bumbler and an object open to ridicule. The connection to Flaubert's picture of the degraded fancyman becomes particularly obvious when Robert, through coitus with a strange woman in a cab, replicates the first liaison between Emma and Leon.

3. Tony Tanner, *Adultery in the Novel: Contract and Transgression* (Baltimore and London: The Johns Hopkins University Press, 1979), p. 308.

4. De Kock's book bears an ink inscription, not in Joyce's hand, "Triest 15/5 1901" suggesting that he acquired it secondhand sometime before he began work on *Exiles*. For a full description of Joyce's copy see my *Annotated Catalogue*, entry 266.

5. Paul de Kock, *Le Cocu* (Gand [Ghent]: Imprimerie de Vanderhaeghe-Maya, 1839), III.45. All quotations from this edition. The translations following them are mine.

6. Further evidence indicating Joyce's preference for the newer, more sympathetic view of the cuckold comes from the Trieste library. Joyce did have a copy of Molière's works in his library, but he made no markings in this work. Nor did he comment on the plays in entries in his notes for *Exiles*. *Le Cocu*, on the other hand, was annotated and referred to in the notes, suggesting that the point of view of de Kock apparently more closely suited his intentions for *Exiles*.

7. Joyce, of course, read a number of works relating to adultery and sexual perversity. Richard Brown comments on a range of possible sources in his *James Joyce and Sexuality* (Cambridge: Cambridge University Press, 1985). See especially pp. 22–31 and pp. 86–87.

8. *The Woman Who Did* bears a copyright date of 1895, making it reasonable to assume that he might have acquired the work well before he began work on *Exiles*. (As early as 1903 Joyce had shown an interest in another work by Allen, the novel *Paris* [*Letters*, II.25].) For a full description of Joyce's copy see my *James Joyce's Trieste Library*, entry 5.

9. Frank Harris, *My Life and Loves*, vol. 3 (Paris: The Obelisk Press, 1945), p. 98.

10. Grant Allen, *The Woman Who Did* (Leipzig: Bernhard Tauchnitz, 1895), p. 165. All quotations from this edition.

11. Steven Marcus, *The Other Victorians: A Study of Sexuality and Pornography in Mid-Nineteenth-Century England* (New York: Basic Books, Inc., Publishers, 1966), pp. 266–86.

12. For a more precise identification of possible stylistic sources for this chapter see my *Inverted Volumes Improperly Arranged*, pp. 84–85.

13. Cf. Steven Marcus's *The Other Victorians*, pp. 252–65. Although the precise works which Joyce drew upon as models may be difficult to identify, the works of Leopold von Sacher-Masoch would have been a popular and therefore likely source. Two books by Sacher-Masoch, *Katharina II* and *Liebesgeschichten* were in Joyce's Trieste library. See entries 408 and 409 in my *Annotated Catalogue*.

14. Other sources, of course, informed many of the narrative scenes of *Ulysses*. See, for example, a discussion of Swiftian allusions in this passage in my "A Swift Reading of *Ulysses*," *Texas Studies in Literature and Language* 27 (Summer 1985): 178–90.

15. *U*, 4.385; 11.500; 11.986–87; 15.1023; 15.3045; and 18.969.

16. For a full discussion see Mary Power's "The Discovery of Ruby," *JJQ* 18 (Winter 1981): 115–21 and Bernard Benstock's response, "Reflections on *Ruby,*" *JJQ* 19 (Spring 1982): 339–41.

17. See for example my remarks on style in Cyclops, "A Swift Reading of *Ulysses,*" and on Sirens, "Wagner in the Ormond Bar," *Irish Renaissance Annual* (1983): 157–73. For an examination of Oxen of the Sun, see Robert Janusko's *The Sources and Structures of James Joyce's "Oxen"* (Ann Arbor: UMI Research Press, 1983). For a similar analysis of Ithaca see Richard E. Madtes's *The "Ithaca" Chapter of Joyce's* Ulysses (Ann Arbor: UMI Research Press, 1983). See also A. Walton Litz's discussion of Richmal Mangnall's *Historical and Miscellaneous Questions* as a source for the format of Ithaca in his "Ithaca," *James Joyce's* Ulysses: *Critical Essays,* ed. Clive Hart and David Hayman (Berkeley, Los Angeles, London: University of California Press, 1974), pp. 394–95.

CHAPTER EIGHT

1. The framework for a discussion of the issue of the place of the consciousness in the discourse has been laid down in a number of works, including Stanley Fish's *Is There a Text in this Class,* Wolfgang Iser's *The Act of Reading,* and Umberto Eco's *The Role of the Reader: Explorations in the Semiotics of Texts* (Bloomington: Indiana University Press, 1979). Fish calls specific attention to the question in his review essay of *The Act of Reading,* "Why No One's Afraid of Wolfgang Iser," *Diacritics* 11 (Spring 1981): 2–13. Iser responds to Fish in "Talk Like Whales," *Diacritics* 11 (Fall 1981): 82–87.

2. Even someone as unreliable as John Dowell, the narrator of Ford Madox Ford's *The Good Soldier,* commands attention. With Dowell the reader quickly becomes aware that his privileged position lacks legitimacy, but one must still overturn the natural inclination to convey authority to the voice telling the story.

3. Mikhail Bakhtin, *Problems of Dostoevsky's Poetics,* p. 5. See also his *The Dialogic Imagination.*

4. Bakhtin, *Problems of Dostoevsky's Poetics,* p. 14. Cf. also Roy Pascal's *The Dual Voice.*

5. Students of Homer will see the connection between this impulse and the formulaic epithet *polytropos* applied to Odysseus in the very first line of the *Odyssey* (and in numerous lines thereafter). In his edition of the poem, W. B. Stanford calls the term "ambiguous, either 'much travelled' or 'of many wiles, versatile.' . . . Translate 'the man of many moves' to preserve the ambiguity."

6. For a fuller discussion of this concept, albeit from a linear perspective, see Richard E. Palmer's *Hermeneutics: Interpretation Theory in Schleiermacher, Dilthey, Heidegger, and Gadamer* (Evanston: Northwestern University Press, 1969).

7. For a more detailed discussion of this trait see my "Redrawing the Artist as a Young Man" in *Joyce's* Ulysses: *The Larger Perspective* (Newark: University of Delaware Press, 1987), pp. 123–40.

8. Bakhtin's *Problems in Dostoevsky's Poetics,* pp. 38–39.

9. "Why No One's Afraid of Wolfgang Iser," pp. 2–3.

10. For a full discussion of musical allusions in the chapter see Zack Bowen's *Musical Allusions in the Works of James Joyce: Early Poetry through* Ulysses (Albany: State University of New York Press, 1974).

11. David Hayman, "Cyclops," *James Joyce's* Ulysses: *Critical Essays*, ed. Clive Hart and David Hayman (Berkeley: University of California Press, 1974), pp. 243–75. See also Herbert Schneidau's "One Eye and Two Levels: On Joyce's 'Cyclops'" and David Hayman's reply "Two Eyes at Two Levels: A Response to Herbert Schneidau on Joyce's 'Cyclops,'" both in *James Joyce Quarterly* 16 (Fall 1978/Winter 1979): 95–109.

12. Arthur Power, *Conversations with James Joyce*, ed. Clive Hart (New York: Barnes & Noble Books, 1974), p. 94.

CHAPTER NINE

1. Michael Groden, Ulysses *in Progress* (Princeton, N.J.: Princeton University Press, 1978), pp. 64–65. James H. Maddox, Jr., *Joyce's* Ulysses *and the Assault upon Character* (New Brunswick, N.J.: Rutgers University Press, 1978), p. 94.

2. A number of studies have examined the formal structure of *Ulysses*. Two of the most useful have already been referred to in relation to concerns similar to those raised in this chapter: Karen Lawrence's *The Odyssey of Style in* Ulysses, and John Paul Riquelme's *Teller and Tale in Joyce's Fiction*. In addition, an article by Monika Fludernik, "Narrative and Its Development in *Ulysses*," *Journal of Narrative Technique* 16 (Winter 1986): 15–40, extends the work of Riquelme to produce an extremely thoughtful delineation of the narrative process. My own analysis draws upon their studies, but necessarily diverges to posit a greater diversity in the narrative voice than has been previously acknowledged.

3. A listing of the various rhetorical figures employed in the chapter appears in Don Gifford's *Notes for Joyce: An Annotation of James Joyce's* Ulysses (New York: E. P. Dutton & Co., Inc., 1974), pp. 519–25.

4. Karen Lawrence, *The Odyssey of Style*, pp. 55–79, offers one of the clearest articulations of this view. As Wolfgang Iser notes in *The Implied Reader* with regard to Aeolus, "the reader must supply the missing links," p. 214.

5. Lawrence, *The Odyssey of Style*, p. 65. For alternative discussions of the integration of rhetorical forms into chapter's narration, in addition to Lawrence see the following: Stuart Gilbert, *James Joyce's* Ulysses: *A Study* (New York: Vintage Books, 1955); Don Gifford's *Notes for Joyce*; Hugh Kenner, *Ulysses* (London: Unwin, 1980); and M. J. C. Hodgart's "Aeolus," in *James Joyce's* Ulysses: *Critical Essays*, ed. Clive Hart and David Hayman (Berkeley, Los Angeles, London: University of California Press, 1974), pp. 115–30.

6. Gifford, p. 156, provides the following gloss, saying that the passage combines allusions to lines in two Shakespeare plays. In *Twelfth Night* Sir

Toby Belch advises Sir Andrew Aguecheek on the manners of a fop: "Why dost thou not go to church in a galliard and come home in a coranto? My very walk should be a jig; I would not so much as make water in a sink-a-pace" (I, iii, 136–39). A "coranto" is a running dance; and a "sink-a-pace" (after the French *cinque pace*) is a dance of five steps; a "galliard" is a very lively dance in triple time. In *Julius Caesar* a commoner (cobbler) who came to see Caesar enter Rome in triumph brags about his trade: "I am indeed, sir, a surgeon to old shoes; when they are in great danger, I recover them. As proper men as ever trod upon neat's leather have gone upon my handiwork." (I, i, 26–29)

7. Clive Hart has called these intrusions diachronic interpolations. He notes this instance and provides a detailed catalogue of all of the interpolations within the chapter as an appendix to his essay "Wandering Rocks" in *James Joyce's* Ulysses: *Critical Essays*, pp. 203–14.

8. Clive Hart, "Wandering Rocks," p. 195. See also Maddox, pp. 146–47.

9. For a more detailed discussion of this characteristic of the episode see my "Wagner in the Ormond Bar," pp. 157–73.

10. Groden, p. 39. In the Gabler edition the line reads as follows: "wavy-avyeavyheavyeavyevyevyhair" (*U*, 11.809).

11. See Zack Bowen's "The Bronzegold Sirensong: A Musical Analysis of the Sirens Episode in James Joyce's *Ulysses*," *Literary Monographs*, no. 1, ed. Eric Rothstein and Thomas K. Dunseath (Madison: University of Wisconsin Press, 1967), pp. 245–98; Groden, pp. 47–49; and John Gordon's "The Orphic *Ulysses*," *TSLL* 27 (Summer 1985): 191–208.

12. As noted in the previous chapter, the most detailed and insightful view of the dun's nature appears in David Hayman's "Cyclops" in *James Joyce's* Ulysses: *Critical Essays*, pp. 243–75. The essay also includes a catalogue of the insets appearing in the chapter.

13. For a discussion of the literary analogues of this form see my *Inverted Volumes Improperly Arranged*. For Joyce's description of the style see his *Letters*, I.135. See also Fritz Senn's "Nausikaa," *James Joyce's* Ulysses: *Critical Essays*, p. 305. Senn has noted the divergence of form within Gerty's portion of the chapter, and he has shown how recurring images suggest an association between the two parts. The fact remains, however, that the overriding concern of the chapter is the disjunction between the disparate voices of its two segments.

14. Iser, *The Implied Reader*, p. 186.

15. Iser, *The Implied Reader*, p. 192. Iser goes on to express mixed feelings about this variety of forms, asserting that "inevitably it must restrict the field of observation" (p. 201). Further in the same chapter Iser continues to question this approach:

And so one might assume that the chapters of the novel were organized, each as a sort of rebuttal to the others, with their respective *principium stilisationis*. The consequences of this principle of construction are very far-reaching. Joyce could parody the different styles in order to show the limitations of their capacity, but if he applied this technique to the whole novel, it would mean that in trying to present the events, etc., of June 16, 1904, he would have to parody himself continually. There are certainly traces of this in the text, but a constant self-parody would ultimately distract the reader from coming to grips with the events of June 16, 1904. And would this not in turn—like all parodies—lead primarily to a negative evaluation, as limited in its own way as the evaluations of the authors parodied? Such a form would itself constitute an "act of interpretation." (p. 203)

16. Iser, *The Implied Reader,* p. 204.
17. Groden, Ulysses *in Progress,* p. 55.
18. Kenneth Burke, *A Grammar of Motives,* p. 313.

CHAPTER TEN

1. Clive Hart, *Structure and Motif in* Finnegans Wake (Evanston: Northwestern University Press; London: Faber and Faber, 1962). David Hayman, "Nodality and the Infra-Structure of *Finnegans Wake,"* JJC 16 (Fall 1978/Winter 1979): 136.
2. In fn. 2, p. 149, Hayman himself indicates that he would exclude the rhetoric of the text from consideration in the system of nodes, but this reflects only the variance in our interests in applying his theories.
3. George Otte's "Time and Space (with the emphasis on the conjunction): Joyce's Response to Lewis," JJQ 22 (Spring 1985): 297–306, explores in detail the links in Joyce's works between time and space. William F. Dohman has also examined the Joyce-Lewis relationship in detail in his " 'Chilly Spaces': Wyndham Lewis as Ondt," JJQ 11 (Summer 1974): 368–86.
4. For specific identification of these allusions, see Weldon Thornton, *Allusions in* Ulysses: *A Line-by-Line Reference to Joyce's Complex Symbolism* (1968; New York: Touchstone, 1973), pp. 41–42. Don Gifford's *Notes for Joyce,* pp. 32–33.
5. Pierre Vitoux's "Aristotle, Berkeley, and Newman [Newton] in 'Proteus' and *Finnegans Wake,"* JJQ 18 (Winter 1981): 161–75, discusses Joyce's amalgamation of Berkeley's theories of perception with those of Aristotle. William T. Noon, S.J., in his *Joyce and Aquinas* (New Haven: Yale University Press; London: Oxford University Press, 1957), pp. 113–14, also takes up Berkeley's influence on Stephen's consciousness.
6. Joseph Campbell and Henry Morton Robinson, *A Skeleton Key to Finnegans Wake* (1944; New York: The Viking Press, 1973), p. 103.
7. For a discussion of this see Robert Boyle's *James Joyce's Pauline Vision: A Catholic Exposition* (Carbondale and Edwardsville: Southern Illinois University Press, 1978), p. 41.
8. Vitoux, pp. 170 and 170–74.
9. For a full discussion of Patrick's corruption of St. Augustine's teachings

and of Joyce's application of the doctrine of the Trinity see Robert Boyle's "Worshipper of the Word: James Joyce and the Trinity" in *A Starchamber Quiry: A James Joyce Centennial Volume, 1882–1982*, ed. E. L. Epstein (New York and London: Methuen, 1982), pp. 109–51.

10. Boyle, "Worshipper of the Word," p. 116.

11. Riana O'Dwyer, "Czarnowski and *Finnegans Wake*: A Study of the Cult of the Hero," *JJQ* 17 (Spring 1980): 282.

12. Quoted by O'Dwyer in "Czarnowski and *Finnegans Wake*," p. 283.

13. For a full description of this incident and of the entire Frankfurt conference, see Pieter Bekker. "The Ninth International James Joyce Symposium," *James Joyce Broadsheet* (June 1984): 1–2. James Joyce, *Finnegans Wake* (New York: The Viking Press, 1939).

14. See my essay "Why Does One Reread *Ulysses*?" in *Assessing the 1984 Ulysses*, ed. Clive Hart and George Sandelescu (Totowa, N.J.: Barnes & Noble, 1986), pp. 43–57.

APPENDIX A

1. Charles Bally, "Le Style indirect libre en français moderne," *Germanisch-Romanische Monatsschrift* 4 (1912). For the sake of clarity, I have adopted the term free indirect discourse to designate this method.

2. See also Seymour Chatman's "The Structure of Narrative Transmission," in *Style and Structure in Literature: Essays in the New Stylistics*, ed. Roger Fowler (Ithaca, N.Y.: Cornell University Press, 1975), p. 257; and Dorrit Cohn's "Narrated Monologue: Definition of a Fictional Style," *Comparative Literature* 18 (Spring 1966): 97–112.

3. Brian McHale, "Free Indirect Discourse: A Survey of Recent Accounts," *PTL* 3 (April 1978): 249–87.

APPENDIX C

1. *James Joyce Ulysses: A Facsimile of the Manuscript*. Harry Levin, introduction (New York: Octagon Books, 1975), pp. 1–11. A. Walton Litz's *The Art of James Joyce*, pp. 50–51, and Michael Groden's Ulysses *in Progress*, pp. 64–65 and 105–10.

Bibliography

PRIMARY SOURCES

Joyce, James. *The Critical Writings of James Joyce*. Ed. Ellsworth Mason and Richard Ellmann. New York: Viking Press, 1959.
———. Dubliners: *Text, Criticism, and Notes*. Ed. Robert Scholes and A. Walton Litz. New York: Viking Press, 1969.
———. *Exiles*. New York: Viking Press, 1951.
———. *Finnegans Wake*. New York: The Viking Press, 1939.
———. *The James Joyce Archive*. Ed. Michael Groden et al. New York & London: Garland Publishing, 1978.
———. *James Joyce in Padua*. Ed. and trans. Louis Berrone. New York: Random House, 1977.
———. *James Joyce* Ulysses: *A Facsimile of the Manuscript*. Intro. Harry Levin. New York: Octagon Books, 1975.
———. *Joyce's* Ulysses *Notesheets in the British Museum*. Ed. Phillip Herring. Charlottesville: The University Press of Virginia, 1972.
———. *Letters of James Joyce*. Vol. I ed. Stuart Gilbert. New York: Viking Press, 1957; reissued with corrections, 1966. Vols. II and III ed. Richard Ellmann. New York: Viking Press, 1966.
———. A Portrait of the Artist as a Young Man: *Text, Criticism and Notes*. Ed. Chester Anderson. New York: Viking Press, 1968.
———. *Stephen Hero*. Ed. John J. Slocum and Herbert Cahoon. New York: New Directions, 1944, 1963.
———. *Ulysses*. Ed. Hans Walter Gabler et al. New York and London: Garland Publishing, 1984, 1986.
———. *The Workshop of Daedalus*. Ed. Robert Scholes and Richard M. Kain. Evanston: Northwestern University Press, 1965.

SECONDARY SOURCES

Adams, Robert M. "Light on Joyce's *Exiles*? A New MS, a Curious Analogue, and Some Speculations." *Studies in Bibliography* 17 (1964): 83–105.

———. "The Manuscript of James Joyce's Play." *Yale University Library Gazette* 39 (July 1964): 30–41.

Allen, Grant. *The Woman Who Did.* Leipzig: Bernhard Tauchnitz, 1895.

Atherton, James S. *The Books at the Wake: A Study of Literary Allusions in James Joyce's* Finnegans Wake. Carbondale and Edwardsville: Southern Illinois University Press, 1974.

Bakhtin, Mikhail M. *The Dialogic Imagination: Four Essays.* Ed. Michael Holquist. Trans. Caryl Emerson and Michael Holquist. Austin: University of Texas Press, 1981.

———. *Problems of Dostoevsky's Poetics.* Trans. R. W. Rostel. Ann Arbor: Ardis, 1973.

Bally, Charles. "Le Style indirect libre en français moderne." *Germanisch-Romanische Monatsschrift* 4 (1912): 549–56.

Balzac, Honoré de. *The Country Doctor.* New York and London: Macmillan and Co., 1896.

———. *La Femme de trente ans.* Paris: Calmann-Lévy, Éditeurs, [1891].

Barthes, Roland. *Image, Music, Text.* Trans. Stephen Heath. New York: Hill and Wang, 1977.

———. *S/Z.* Trans. Richard Miller. Pref. Richard Howard. New York: Hill and Wang, 1974.

Bekker, Pieter. "The Ninth International James Joyce Symposium." *James Joyce Broadsheet* (June 1984): 1–2.

Benstock, Bernard. "Reflections on *Ruby.*" *James Joyce Quarterly* 19 (Spring 1982): 339–41.

———. "Text, Sub-Text, Non-Text: Literary and Narrational In/Validities." *James Joyce Quarterly* 22 (Summer 1985): 355–65.

Bloom, Harold. *The Anxiety of Influence: A Theory of Poetry.* London, New York: Oxford University Press, 1975.

Booth, Wayne C. *The Rhetoric of Fiction.* Second edition. Chicago: The University of Chicago Press, 1983.

Bowen, Zack. "The Bronzegold Sirensong: A Musical Analysis of the Sirens Episode in Joyce's *Ulysses.*" *Literary Monographs.* No. 1. Ed. Eric Rothstein and Thomas K. Dunseath. Madison: University of Wisconsin Press, 1967, pp. 245–98.

———. *Musical Allusions in the Works of James Joyce: Early Poetry through* Ulysses. Albany, N.Y.: State University of New York Press, 1974.

Boyle, Robert. *James Joyce's Pauline Vision: A Catholic Exposition.* Carbondale and Edwardsville: Southern Illinois University Press, 1978.

———. "Worshipper of the Word: James Joyce and the Trinity." In *A Starchamber Quiry: A James Joyce Centennial Volume, 1882–1982.* Ed. E. L. Epstein. New York and London: Methuen, 1982, pp. 109–51.

Bronzwaer, W. J. M. *Tense in the Novel: An Investigation of Some Potentialities of Linguistic Criticism.* Groningen, The Netherlands: Wolters-Noordhoff Publishing, 1970.

Brown, Marshall. '' 'Errours Endlesse Traine': On Turning Points and the Dialectical Imagination.'' *PMLA* 99 (January 1984): 9–25.

Brown, Richard. *James Joyce and Sexuality.* Cambridge, New York: Cambridge University Press, 1985.

Budgen, Frank. *James Joyce and the Making of* Ulysses. Bloomington: Indiana University Press, 1960.

Burke, Kenneth. *A Grammar of Motives.* Berkeley and Los Angeles: University of California, 1969.

Butler, R. ''Flaubert's Exploitations of the 'Style Indirect Libre': Ambiguities and Perspectives in *Madame Bovary.*'' *Modern Language* 62 (December 1981): 190–96.

Campbell, Joseph, and Henry Morton Robinson. *A Skeleton Key to* Finnegans Wake. 1944; rpt. New York: The Viking Press, 1973.

Chatman, Seymour. ''The Structure of Narrative Transmission.'' In *Style and Structure in Literature: Essays in the New Stylistics.* Ed. Roger Fowler. Ithaca, N.Y.: Cornell University Press, 1975, pp. 213–57.

Cohn, Dorrit. ''Narrated Monologue: Definition of a Fictional Style.'' *Comparative Literature* 18 (Spring 1966), p. 107.

Conrad, Joseph. *A Set of Six.* Leipzig: Bernhard Tauchnitz, 1908.

———. *The Secret Agent: A Simple Tale.* Leipzig: Bernhard Tauchnitz, 1907.

———. *Tales of Unrest.* Leipzig: Bernhard Tauchnitz, 1898.

Cross, Richard K. *Flaubert and Joyce: The Rite of Fiction.* Princeton, N.J.: Princeton University Press, 1971.

Curran, C. P. *James Joyce Remembered.* New York and London: Oxford University Press, 1968.

de Kock, Paul. *Le Cocu.* Gand [Ghent]: Imprimerie de Vanderhaeghe-Maya, 1839.

de Maupassant, Guy. *The Odd Number: Thirteen Tales.* Trans. Jonathan Sturges. Intro. Henry James. New York and London: Harper & Brothers Publishers, 1889.

Denmark's Best Stories: An Introduction to Danish Fiction. Ed. Hanna Astrup Larsen. New York: W. W. Norton and Company, Inc., 1928.

Derrida, Jacques. ''Differance.'' In *Speech and Phenomena and Other Essays on Husserl's Theory of Signs.* Trans. David B. Allison. Evanston: Northwestern University Press, 1973, pp. 129–60.

Dickens, Charles. *David Copperfield.* London: Thomas Nelson and Sons, [1911–1916].

Dillon, George L., and Frederick Kirchhoff. ''On the Form and Function of Free Indirect Style.'' *PTL: A Journal for Descriptive Poetics and Theory of Literature* 1 (October 1976): 431–40.

Dohman, William F. '' 'Chilly Spaces': Wyndham Lewis as Ondt.'' *James Joyce Quarterly* 11 (Summer 1974): 368–86.

Eco, Umberto. *The Role of the Reader: Explorations in the Semiotics of Texts.* Bloomington: Indiana University Press, 1979.

Ellmann, Richard. *The Consciousness of Joyce*. New York: Oxford University Press, 1977.

———. *James Joyce*. New and revised edition. Oxford: Oxford University Press, 1982.

Evans, Simon. *The Penetration of* Exiles. Colchester: A Wake Newslitter Press, 1984.

Fish, Stanley. *Is There a Text in this Class: The Authority of Interpretive Communities*. Cambridge: Harvard University Press, 1980.

———. "Why No One's Afraid of Wolfgang Iser." *Diacritics* 11 (Spring 1981): 2–13.

Flaubert, Gustave. *Madame Bovary*. Trans. Henry Blanchamp. London: Greening & Co.; New York: Brentano's, [1905].

Fludernik, Monika. "Narrative and Its Development in *Ulysses*." *The Journal of Narrative Technique* 16 (Winter 1986): 15–40.

Foucault, Michel. "What Is an Author?" In *Textual Strategies: Perspectives in Post-Structuralist Criticism*. Ed. Josue V. Harari. Ithaca, New York: Cornell University Press, 1979, pp. 141–60.

Gabler, Hans Walter. "The Seven Lost Years of *A Portrait of the Artist as a Young Man*." In *Approaches to Joyce's* Portrait: *Ten Essays*. Ed. Thomas F. Staley and Bernard Benstock. Pittsburgh, Pa.: University of Pittsburgh Press, 1976.

———. "Towards a Critical Text of James Joyce's *A Portrait of the Artist as a Young Man*." *Studies in Bibliography* 27 (1974): 1–53.

———. "The Christmas Dinner Scene, Parnell's Death and the Genesis of *A Portrait of the Artist as a Young Man*." *James Joyce Quarterly* 13 (Fall 1975): 27–38.

Genette, Gérard. *Narrative Discourse: An Essay in Method*. Trans. Jane E. Lewin. Ithaca, N.Y.: Cornell University Press, 1980.

Gifford, Don. *Notes for Joyce: An Annotation of James Joyce's* Ulysses. New York: E. P. Dutton & Co., Inc., 1974, pp. 519–25.

Gilbert, Stuart. *James Joyce's* Ulysses: *A Study*. New York: Vintage Books, 1955.

Gillespie, Michael Patrick. *A Catalogue of the Joyce Trieste Collection*. Austin: Humanities Research Center, The University of Texas, 1986.

———. *Inverted Volumes Improperly Arranged: James Joyce and His Trieste Library*. Ann Arbor: UMI Research Press, 1983.

———. "Re-drawing the Artist as a Young Man." In Ulysses: *The Larger Perspective*. Newark: University of Delaware Press, 1987, pp. 123–40.

———. "A Swift Reading of *Ulysses*." *TSLL* 27 (Summer 1985): 178–90.

———. "Wagner in the Ormond Bar." *Irish Renaissance Annual* 4 (1983): 157–73.

———. "Why Does One Reread *Ulysses*?" In *Assessing the 1984* Ulysses. Ed. Clive Hart and George Sandelescu. Totowa, N.J.: Barnes & Noble, 1986, pp. 43–57.

Gordon, John. "The Orphic *Ulysses*." *TSLL* 27 (Summer 1985): 191–208.

Groden, Michael. Ulysses *in Progress*. Princeton, N.J.: Princeton University Press, 1977.

Harris, Frank. *My Life and Loves*. Paris: The Obelisk Press, 1945.

Hart, Clive. *Structure and Motif in* Finnegans Wake. Evanston: Northwestern University Press; London: Faber and Faber, 1962.

———. "Wandering Rocks." In *James Joyce's* Ulysses: *Critical Essays*. Ed. Clive Hart and David Hayman. Berkeley: University of California Press, 1974, pp. 181–216.

Hayman, David. "*A Portrait of the Artist as a Young Man* and *L'Education Sentimentale*: The Structural Affinities." *Orbis Litteratum* 19 (1964): 161–75.

———. "Cyclops." *James Joyce's* Ulysses: *Critical Essays*. Ed. Clive Hart and David Hayman. Berkeley: University of California Press, 1974, pp. 243–75.

———. "Nodality and the Infra-Structure of *Finnegans Wake*." *James Joyce Quarterly* 16 (Fall 1978/Winter 1979): 135–50.

———. "Two Eyes at Two Levels: A Response to Herbert Schneidau on Joyce's 'Cyclops.'" *James Joyce Quarterly* 16 (Fall 1978/Winter 1979): 105–9.

———. Ulysses: *The Mechanics of Meaning*. Madison: The University of Wisconsin Press, 1982.

Highham, Anne S. "An Aspect of Style in 'Araby.'" *Language and Style* 15 (Winter 1982): 15–22.

Hirsch, E. D. *Validity in Interpretation*. New Haven: Yale University Press, 1967.

Hodgart, M. J. C. "Aeolus." In *James Joyce's* Ulysses: *Critical Essays*. Ed. Clive Hart and David Hayman. Berkeley, Los Angeles, London: University of California Press, 1974, pp. 115–30.

Holland, Norman N. *5 Readers Reading*. New Haven, Conn.: Yale University Press, 1975.

Iser, Wolfgang. *The Implied Reader: Patterns of Communication in Prose Fiction from Bunyan to Beckett*. Baltimore and London: The Johns Hopkins University Press, 1974.

———. *The Act of Reading: A Theory of Aesthetic Response*. Baltimore and London: The Johns Hopkins University Press, 1978.

———. "Talk Like Whales." *Diacritics* 11 (Fall 1981): 82–87.

Janusko, Robert. *The Sources and Structures of James Joyce's "Oxen."* Ann Arbor: UMI Research Press, 1983.

Jauss, Hans Robert. *Towards an Aesthetic of Reception*. Trans. Timothy Bahti. Minneapolis: University of Minnesota Press, 1982.

Jones, Charles. "Varieties of Speech Presentation in Conrad's *The Secret Agent*." *Lingua* 20 (1968): 162–76.

Joyce, Stanislaus. *My Brother's Keeper*. Ed. Richard Ellmann. New York: The Viking Press, 1958.

Kenner, Hugh. *Dublin's Joyce*. Boston: Beacon Press, 1962.

———. *Joyce's Voices*. Berkeley, Los Angeles, London: University of California Press, 1978.

———. *The Stoic Comedians: Flaubert, Joyce and Beckett*. Berkeley, Los Angeles, London: University of California Press, 1974.

———. *Ulysses*. London: G. Allen & Unwin, 1980.

Lawrence, Karen. *The Odyssey of Style in* Ulysses. Princeton, N.J.: Princeton University Press, 1981.

Lermontov, Mikhail. *A Hero of Our Time.* Trans. Philip Longworth. London: New English Library, 1962.

Levin, Harry. *The Gates of Horn: A Study of Five French Realists.* New York: Oxford University Press, 1963.

Litz, A. Walton. *The Art of James Joyce: Method and Design in* Ulysses *and* Finnegans Wake. New York: Oxford University Press, 1964.

————. "Ithaca." In *James Joyce's* Ulysses: *Critical Essays.* Ed. Clive Hart and David Hayman. Berkeley, Los Angeles, London: University of California Press, 1974, pp. 394–95.

MacNicholas, John. *James Joyce's* Exiles: *A Textual Companion.* New York and London: Garland Publishing, Inc., 1979.

Maddox, James H., Jr. *Joyce's* Ulysses *and the Assault upon Character.* New Brunswick, N.J.: Rutgers University Press, 1978.

Madtes, Richard E. *The "Ithaca" Chapter of Joyce's* Ulysses. Ann Arbor: UMI Research Press, 1983.

Magalaner, Marvin. *Time of Apprenticeship: The Fiction of Young James Joyce.* London, New York, Toronto: Abelard-Schuman, 1959.

Magalaner, Marvin, and Richard M. Kain. *Joyce: The Man, the Work, the Reputation.* New York, N.Y.: Collier Books, 1962, pp. 82–87.

Marcus, Stephen. *The Other Victorians: A Study of Sexuality and Pornography in Mid-Nineteenth-Century England.* New York: Basic Books, Inc., Publishers, 1966.

Mason, Michael. "Why Is Leopold Bloom a Cuckold." *Journal of English Literary History* 44 (Spring 1977): 171–88.

McCanles, Michael. *Dialectical Criticism and Renaissance Literature.* Berkeley, Los Angeles, London: University of California Press, 1975.

McCanles, Michael, and Marshall Brown. "Forum." *Publications of the Modern Language Association of America* 99 (October 1984): 996–98.

McCarthy, Patrick A. "*Ulysses* and the Printed Page." In *Joyce's* Ulysses: *The Larger Perspective.* Ed. Robert D. Newman and Weldon Thornton. Newark: University of Delaware Press, 1978, pp. 59–73.

McHale, Brian. "Free Indirect Discourse: A Survey of Recent Accounts." *PTL: A Journal for Descriptive Poetics and Theory of Literature* 3 (April 1978): 249–87.

Naremore, James. "Style as Meaning in *A Portrait of the Artist.*" *James Joyce Quarterly* 4 (Summer 1967): 331–42.

Noon, William T. *Joyce and Aquinas.* New Haven: Yale University Press; London: Oxford University Press, 1957.

O'Dwyer, Riana. "Czarnowski and *Finnegans Wake*: A Study of the Cult of the Hero." *James Joyce Quarterly* 17 (Spring 1980): 281–91.

Otte, George. "Time and Space (With the Emphasis on the Conjunction): Joyce's Response to Lewis." *James Joyce Quarterly* 22 (Spring 1985): 297–306.

Palmer, Richard E. *Hermeneutics: Interpretation Theory in Schleiermacher, Dilthey, Heidegger, and Gadamer.* Evanston: Northwestern University Press, 1969.

Parandowski, Jan. "Meeting with Joyce." In *Portraits of the Artist in Exile: Recollections of James Joyce by Europeans.* Ed. Willard Potts. Seattle and London: University of Washington Press, 1979, pp. 159–60.

Pascal, Roy. *The Dual Voice: Free Indirect Speech and Its Functioning in the Nineteenth-Century European Novel.* Manchester: Manchester University Press; Totowa, N.J.: Rowmann and Littlefield, 1977.

Power, Arthur. *Conversations with James Joyce.* Ed. Clive Hart. New York: Barnes & Noble Books, 1974.

Power, Mary. "The Discovery of Ruby." *James Joyce Quarterly* 18 (Winter 1981): 115–21.

Quirk, Randolph. *Charles Dickens and Appropriate Language.* Durham: University of Durham, 1959.

Reynolds, Mary T. "Torn by Conflicting Doubts: Joyce and Renan." *Renascence* 35 (Winter 1983), pp. 96–118.

Riquelme, John Paul. *Teller and Tale in Joyce's Fiction: Oscillating Perspectives.* Baltimore and London: The Johns Hopkins University Press, 1983.

Robinson, K. E. "The Stream of Consciousness Technique and the Structure of Joyce's *Portrait.*" *James Joyce Quarterly* 9 (Fall 1971): 63–84.

Schneidau, Herbert. "One Eye and Two Levels: On Joyce's 'Cyclops.'" *James Joyce Quarterly* 16 (Fall 1978/Winter 1979): 95–103.

Scholes, Robert. "Some Observations on the Text of *Dubliners*: 'The Dead.'" *Studies in Bibliography* 15 (1962): 191–206.

———. "Grant Richards to James Joyce." *Studies in Bibliography* 16 (1963): 139–60.

———. "Further Observations on the Text of *Dubliners.*" *Studies in Bibliography* 17 (1964): 107–22.

Senn, Fritz. "The Challenge: '*ignotas animum*' (An Old-Fashioned Close Guessing at a Borrowed Structure)." *James Joyce Quarterly* 16 (Fall 1978/Winter 1979): 123–34.

———. "Nausikaa." In *James Joyce's Ulysses: Critical Essays.* Ed. Clive Hart and David Hayman. Berkeley: University of California Press, 1974, pp. 277–311.

Sosnowski, James J. "Reading Acts and Reading Warrants: Some Implications for Readers Responding to Joyce's Portrait of Stephen." *James Joyce Quarterly* 16 (Fall 1978/Winter 1979): 43–63.

Steinberg, Erwin R. "Author! Author!" *James Joyce Quarterly* 22 (Summer 1985): 419–24.

Tandrup, Birthe. "A Trap of Misreading: Free Indirect Style and the Critique of the Gothic in *Northanger Abbey.*" In *The Romantic Heritage: A Collection of Critical Essays.* Ed. Karsten Engelberg. Copenhagen: Publications of the Department of English, University of Copenhagen, 1983, pp. 81–91.

Tanner, Tony. *Adultery in the Novel: Contract and Transgression.* Baltimore and London: The Johns Hopkins University Press, 1979.

Thornton, Weldon. *Allusions in* Ulysses: *A Line-by-Line Reference to Joyce's Complex Symbolism.* 1968, rpt.; New York: Touchstone, 1973.

Thrane, James R. "Joyce's Sermon on Hell." *A James Joyce Miscellany.* Third Series. Ed. Marvin Magalaner. Carbondale: Southern Illinois University Press, 1962, pp. 33–78.

Turgenev, Ivan. *A Lear of the Steppes.* Trans. Constance Garnett. London: William Heinemann. New York: The Macmillan Company, 1906.

Tysdahl, B. J. *Joyce and Ibsen: A Study in Literary Influence.* Oslo: Norwegian Universities Press; New York: Humanities Press, 1968.

Vitoux, Pierre. "Aristotle, Berkeley, and Newman [Newton] in 'Proteus' and *Finnegans Wake,*" *James Joyce Quarterly* 18 (Winter 1981): 161–75.

Walzl, Florence. "Joyce's 'The Sisters': A Development." *James Joyce Quarterly* 10 (Summer 1973): 375–421.

Weinberg, Henry H. "Irony and 'Style Indirect Libre' in *Madame Bovary.*" *Canadian Review of Comparative Literature* 8 (Winter 1981): 1–9.

White, Hayden. *Metahistory: The Historical Imagination in Nineteenth-Century Europe.* Baltimore: The Johns Hopkins University Press, 1973.

———. *Tropics of Discourse: Essays in Cultural Criticism.* Baltimore: The Johns Hopkins University Press, 1978.

Wilde, Oscar. *The Picture of Dorian Gray.* Ed. Isobel Murray. London, New York, Toronto: Oxford University Press, 1981.

Zola, Emile. *Nana.* III. Paris: Les Editions Parisiennes, n.d.

Index

The works of authors other than Joyce appear under the entry for the individual author. Joyce's works appear in alphabetical order in the index. The individual stories of *Dubliners* appear under the entry *Dubliners*. The chapter names for *Ulysses* appear under the entry *Ulysses*.